ALTERNATIVE ULSTERS

Mark Carruthers

LIB
ERT
IES
NORTH

First published in 2013 by
Liberties Press
140 Terenure Road North | Terenure | Dublin 6W
Tel: +353 (1) 405 5703
www.libertiespress.com | info@libertiespress.com

Trade enquiries to Gill & Macmillan Distribution
Hume Avenue | Park West | Dublin 12
T: +353 (1) 500 9534 | F: +353 (1) 500 9595 | E: sales@gillmacmillan.ie

Distributed in the United States by
IPM | 22841 | Quicksilver Dr | Dulles | Virginia 20166

Distributed in the UK by
Turnaround Publisher Services
Unit 3 | Olympia Trading Estate | Coburg Road | London N22 6TZ
T: +44 (0) 20 8829 3000 | E: orders@turnaround-uk.com

ISBN: 978 - 1 - 907593956
2 4 6 8 10 9 7 5 3 1

A CIP record for this title is available from the British Library.

Cover design and internal design by Fergal Condon
Printed by Hussar Books

The publishers gratefully acknowledge financial assistance from
the Arts Council of Northern Ireland

For my parents, Billy and Mabel,
who encouraged me from my earliest days
to ask questions

AN ULSTERMAN

This is my country. If my people came
from England here four centuries ago,
the only trace that's left is in my name.
Kilmore, Armagh, no other sod can show
the weathered stone of our first burying.
Born in Belfast, which drew the landless in,
that river-straddling, hill-rimmed town, I cling
to the inflexions of my origin.

Though creed-crazed zealots and the ignorant crowd,
long-nurtured, never checked, in ways of hate,
have made our streets a byword of offence,
this is my country, never disavowed.
When it is fouled, shall I not remonstrate?
My heritage is not their violence.

John Hewitt

CONTENTS

Acknowledgements 6

Photographic Acknowledgements 8

Introduction 9

Gerry Adams 15

Lord Ashdown 27

Professor Sir George Bain 37

Lord Bannside 45

Baroness Blood 57

Sir Kenneth Branagh 67

Joe Brolly 77

Simon Callow 85

William Crawley 95

Professor Gerald Dawe 107

Barry Douglas 115

Adrian Dunbar 121

Seamus Heaney 129

Ciarán Hinds 143

Jennifer Johnston 149

Marie Jones 159

Brian Kennedy 167

Gary Lightbody 179

Anna Lo 187

Michael Longley 195

Mary McAleese 205

Bernadette McAliskey 217

Eamonn McCann 229

Jackie McDonald 239

Martin McGinley 251

Martin McGuinness 257

Denis Murray 271

Liam Neeson 277

James Nesbitt 287

Frank Ormsby 299

Glenn Patterson 309

Dame Mary Peters 317

Paul Rankin 325

Stephen Rea 331

Peter Robinson 341

Peter Taylor 353

ACKNOWLEDGEMENTS

The efforts of a great many people have gone into the making of this publication. Clearly, without the enthusiastic co-operation of my interviewees there would be no book. Without exception they have delivered what I asked of them, embracing my challenge to reflect thoughtfully on their experiences of identity. Some of the contributors are close friends, some are acquaintances and several I had little or no contact with before this project, but without exception they impressed me with their willingness to grapple with the complex issues that identity poses in this contested part of the world. I thank all the contributors for taking part in the journey – and I hope they are as happy as I am with how our conversations appear in print.

Gathering together a stable of such distinguished interviewees was never going to be easy and I must thank those who helped me to assemble my wish list. Susie Tyrell, Tamar Thomas, Joana Cannon, Jimmy Nesbitt, John Robinson, Vincent Parker, Richard McAuley, Ian Paisley, Martin O'Brien, Grainne Mooney and Stuart Bailie all played a part in helping me to secure the co-operation of particular individuals and I am grateful for their support.

My agents Paul and Susan Feldstein were enthusiastic persuaders for the project from its earliest days and their support and encouragement is gratefully acknowledged. Sean O'Keeffe and his team at Liberties Press have been supportive throughout. Alan Murray, in particular, played a crucial role in transcribing the interviews into editable copy and he did so with consistent speed and accuracy. Alice Dawson, Clara Phelan, Therese Murray, Fergal Condon and Megan Marshal also deserve special mention.

The Arts Council of Northern Ireland was quick to offer support for the project under its Support for the Individual Artist Programme and I want to thank, in particular, Damian Smyth and Roisin McDonough. Several of the Belfast interviews took place in my home, but the Lyric Theatre was also the location for some of the conversations and my thanks go to the team there for their hospitality.

Colin Davidson and I have been working together for some time on another project and this publication has benefited enormously from that collaboration. Colin's remarkable portraits of eleven of the interviewees add greatly to the quality of the book and I'm delighted that he so enthusiastically agreed to them being used.

Several friends and colleagues provided assistance and advice with various drafts for which I am very grateful, among them Jacqueline McIntyre, Damien Magee, Mark Devenport, Seamus Kelters and Neil Martin. My son Andrew was the first to read the draft edits of each interview and he was unswervingly supportive and insightful in the advice he offered, and I am enormously in his debt. My good friends Stephen Douds and Stephen Walker have been unshakably encouraging throughout and their perceptive feedback has been hugely helpful.

Finally a word of thanks to Alison, Andrew, James and Kirsty. They have had to live with the ups and downs of the project for longer than any of us anticipated. I couldn't have managed it without their ever-present love, support and good humour – and I promise we can stop talking about identity all the time at home now.

Mark Carruthers
Belfast
12th July 2013

PHOTOGRAPHIC ACKNOWLEDGEMENTS

The publishers have made every effort to contact copyright holders. If any material has been used without permission, please contact the publishers.

Gerry Adams - *An Phoblacht*
George Bain - Bobbie Hanvey
May Blood - Harrison Photography
Joe Brolly - Ray McManus
Gerald Dawe - Bobbie Hanvey
Jennifer Johnston - Caroline Forbes
Mary McAleese - Tony Higgins
Eamonn McCann - Harrison Photography
Jackie McDonald - Pacemaker Press Photography
Martin McGinley - Jim McCafferty
Martin McGuinness - Harrison Photography
Denis Murray - Peter Cooper
Liam Neeson - Nigel Parry
Frank Ormsby - Jonathan Seath
Ian Paisley - Harrison Photography
Glenn Patterson - Harrison Photography
Mary Peters - Harrison Photography
Stephen Rea - Michael Donald
Peter Robinson - Harrison Photography

Original Portraits by Colin Davidson

An Ulsterman by John Hewitt is from *The Collected Poems of John Hewitt*, ed. Frank Ormsby (Blackstaff Press, 1991) reproduced by permission of Blackstaff Press on behalf of the Estate of John Hewitt.

Ulster teems with apparent contradictions. It is Irish and it is British. Its inhabitants look to Dublin and they look to London. People speak English, Irish and maybe even Ulster-Scots. They are Protestant and they are Catholic. There is no dispute that a great deal divides these people, but arguably it is their Ulster inheritance that unites them.

There is one geographical Ulster of course, which stretches from the northernmost tip of Malin Head in County Donegal, through the heartlands of Mid-Ulster and County Antrim, right down to Virginia in County Cavan, which is a mere fifty miles from the centre of Dublin. But within that majestic sweep there are countless Ulsters, each of them with a multitude of experiences, perspectives and prejudices. And, as this ancient Irish province eases itself into the twenty-first century, its population of almost two million now includes a smattering of Portuguese and Polish speakers. They live and work alongside fellow citizens who are Muslims, Hindus and Bahá'ís, demonstrating that Ulster is no longer a place of just two faith communities.

This collection of conversations is an attempt to take the notional temperature of a place where identity tends to inform a great deal of the day-to-day civic debate. Much public comment has been made in recent years, for example, about an apparent growth in acceptance of the term Northern Irish in certain quarters where that has not traditionally been so, though it is easy to over-simplify the point. The commentator Malachi O'Doherty summed up his own position in a *Belfast Telegraph* article in February 2013:

> When I tick a box that says I am Northern Irish, I am saying that my strongest identification is with this region and its people and that I want political stability here in a Northern Ireland that is connected to Ireland, Britain and Europe. I am saying that I see a decent prospect of that being achievable and that I put my political hopes in that future . . . As somebody who designates as Northern Irish, I am saying that where two large communal camps here obsess about identity over practical politics, I prefer politics to work and cancompromise further on identity to achieve that.

The poet John Hewitt is widely acknowledged as someone who did much to advance the idea of regional identity. His idea of a hierarchy of values, touched on by Malachi O'Doherty, became something of a recurring theme throughout this project. In 1974 in an *Irish Times* symposium, 'The Clash of Identities', Hewitt set out his stall:

> I'm an Ulsterman, of planter stock. I was born in the island of Ireland, so secondarily I'm an Irishman. I was born in the British archipelago and English is my native tongue, so I'm British. The British archipelago consists of offshore islands to the continent of Europe, so I'm European.

That ladder of identity appears to remain an attractive idea to many people today. What's interesting, though, is the way in which people have their own ideas about how to order the rungs. Identity is an intensely personal notion and it's something which people in this part of the world think about deeply. My challenge was to persuade three dozen public figures to discuss the subject on a very public platform.

What comes across very strongly in many of the conversations is that identity is not a fixed idea. Many interviewees talk about how their notion of it has changed over the years. Many also talk about how their identity still changes depending on where they are and who they happen to be with.

There are revealing admissions and anecdotes throughout the book – Peter Robinson and Ian Paisley confront their Irishness, Eamonn McCann admits he now relishes thinking of himself as Northern Irish, and Stephen Rea suggests that, despite his Irishness, he is, in essence, an English actor. Equally revealing is Brian Kennedy's reflection on taking part in the Queen's Diamond Jubilee celebrations at Stormont and Jackie McDonald's thoughts on his unexpected friendship with the former Irish President, Mary McAleese, and her husband, Martin.

Despite those demonstrations of flexibility, though, there is some evidence that for many people there is a bottom line; what was intriguing was to try to pin that down. So, how far would certain individuals have gone to defend their notion of Ulster? How far, on the other hand, would others have gone to pursue their notion of Irishness? There is a sharp irony, when you think about it, in loyalists being prepared to fight to keep Ulster British, while republicans have been prepared to do the same thing to secure Ulster's place in a United Ireland.

There are also reflections on this place and its people from long-time observers who are not themselves Ulster-born. Mary Peters embraces her adopted homeland warmly, Jennifer Johnston takes a dim view of political progress in the North, Peter Taylor casts an expert journalistic eye over the loyalist and republican communities he knows so well, and Simon Callow recalls his early days of political activism as a student at Queen's University.

On a personal level, I hold no firm view on the notion of Ulster identity, but I do think it provides a useful entry point into a deeper examination of the wider subject. Hence, each conversation in this book begins with some consideration of Ulster and what it means to the interviewee, but after that, each discussion charts its own course through the experiences and reflections of the individual. Furthermore, it strikes me as a timely opportunity to test the temperature of the water, not least since devolution in Northern Ireland is beginning to bed down and, across the island, commemorations continue as part of the Decade of Centenaries.

The fact that each interview in the book was, without exception, a sit-down, one-to-one conversation guaranteed a much deeper level of engagement than would otherwise have been the case. All of the interviewees were quick to overcome any reservations they might have had about baring their souls on the subject. Without exception they have been candid in the thoughts they have shared with me, whether we were enjoying lunch or coffee together in Belfast, Derry, Dublin, London, or even Rome or New York.

Drawing up my final list of interviewees was, not surprisingly, a huge challenge. My long list was comfortably in excess of 120 names. The final list of thirty-six was settled on after careful thought and discussion with my publisher and with several close colleagues and friends. It turned out to be something of an organic process, but I did want to try to ensure that the final collection of contributors represents as broad a range of opinions and experiences as possible. I make no claim that this list of interviewees is in any way definitive, but it does, I believe, represent a substantial and diverse cross-section of views. It is the case that many of those I have spoken to for the book are well-known, but this is not simply a compilation of celebrity conversations. The contributors are, without exception, public figures with interesting and challenging things to say on a subject which demonstrably matters to them. I hope that some of the views they volunteer will run counter to what the reader might be expecting.

Only a very few individuals declined to take part in the project and some of that was down to their availability as much as any kind of reticence about discussing such a potentially controversial subject in print. Those who did agree to participate, however, did so with tremendous commitment and enthusiasm.

No two conversations in this book are the same, but each one starts with the same question: **what does Ulster mean to you?**

GERRY ADAMS

A leading figure in Irish republican politics since the late 1960s, Gerry Adams was born in Belfast in 1948. He was interned in March 1972 but was released several months later to take part in abortive secret talks with the British government. He has consistently claimed he was never a member of the IRA, though this is disputed by several leading historians and commentators who maintain that he was part of the group's leadership since the 1970s. He has been the President of Sinn Féin since 1983 and served two periods as an abstentionist MP for West Belfast – 1983 to 1993 and 1997 to 2011. He was elected to Dáil Éireann as a TD for County Louth in 2011. An influential figure in the Northern Ireland peace process, he survived an assassination attempt by UFF gunmen in Belfast in 1984.

We meet in his office in Leinster House, the home of the Irish Parliament, in Dublin.

Gerry Adams:

I wouldn't say I was an Ulsterman. I would say I was Irish first of all, and if I was asked where I was from, I would probably say I was from Antrim. I still like the line in the song that says, 'An Ulsterman I'm proud to be'. I like that notional thing and clearly in rugby, or in any other competition where Ulster was playing, I would support Ulster. I would have a sense of the mythology of Ulster and I would see it as a province of Ireland, as opposed to a six-county province of England. I suppose if I was trying to figure out how I would see Ulster, it would be mostly in terms of the Ulster Championship in football. I love all the mythology and the folk history and the fables, but I don't have a very acute sense of being from Ulster.

Mark Carruthers:

Have you ever considered the idea that what unites people from very different political backgrounds here is their common Ulster heritage?
I think that's very true. Even when I'm talking to you I'm saying to myself,

'when I say that I don't see myself as an Ulsterman, is that strictly accurate?' I'm quite comfortable in who I am, so I haven't probably felt the need to hang my hook upon any particular description, but I agree with you entirely that what we have in common is that we're from the same place. We share the same sense of being; of town, of parish and of city.

Do you think if you have a slight aversion to the notion of Ulster, it might be because it's a term that has been so closely associated in recent decades with loyalism?

No, to be honest, I don't have any hang ups at all about Ulster. I have a greater hang up about Northern Ireland; it's still a term that doesn't resonate with me, even all these years later. I had a very interesting conversation with a three year old grandchild recently and I was trying to figure out how this came about. She said to me, 'Am I Irish?' I said, 'Of course you're Irish'. She says, 'Am I not English?' I said 'No, you're Irish'. And she says, 'Am I not just Irish when we go to Donegal?' Now, I was trying to figure out how a three year old child would be coming to have a conversation about identity. Obviously they speak Irish at home and she's doing Irish at her nursery school, so she'd be acutely aware that there's other people speaking English. I thought it was really quite amazing.

When do you think you first became aware of your sense of identity?

I grew up in the Falls Road and I had, I think, a very acute sense of comfort in who I was through where I was from, without being necessarily able to define it in any particular way. I also went to the Christian Brothers' school and they taught us hurling there. When I went to St Mary's Grammar School I also met guys who weren't from a working-class background, who were the sons of doctors, lawyers and architects. I dropped out of school and I went to work in a very traditional pub called The Ark, on the Old Lodge Road. Its customers were mostly working-class Protestant people who were the salt of the earth. I remember being there in 1966 during the 50th anniversary of the Easter Rising and they slagged me because I was seen in a photograph at the Easter parade. I do remember that they had great sing-songs and I've always been very fond of music, so I was in a fairly unique situation of knowing all these Orange ballads because I was just interested in folk music and root music. So, when we would be out socialising and going to what we called a *scoraíocht*, which was just a house party, as a joke at the end of it we would have sung *The Sash* or *Bold Orange Heroes of Comber*, just for the craic. Ironically enough, I ended up leaving The Ark, which was owned by Catholics, because they wouldn't pay me the union rate for working on the Twelfth of July!

So you were exposed to all of that but you still knew that you were different?

I was brought up in a house where there was a sense of national consciousness and of Irishness - but there wasn't a lot of politics, as we would understand politics today. Both sides of my family were politically active going right back to my grandparents. In fact, my first education came from a man called Jimmy Graham, who was a member of the Communist Party. When I went to work in The Duke of York [in which the Communist Party of Ireland met], Jimmy Graham, Jimmy Stewart, Edwina Stewart and Betty Sinclair were all CP members and there was a whole gang of shipyard men. It was Jimmy Graham who gave me my first copy of the writings of James Connolly [the Irish republican and socialist who was one of the leaders of the 1916 Easter Rising] and it was only then, when I started to read it, that I started to get some sense of what republicanism was about. I started to realise then, that there were acute political differences between me and people who I was very friendly with. The Duke of York was actually a huge education for me; it was a really wonderful establishment. The News Letter people were there, Sam Hanna Bell [the writer] drank in the place, the Labour Party's office was in Waring Street so you had them drinking in the place. The shipyard guys were in the main bar with the CP guys and they would sing working songs. Then, in what was called the lounge, they would have traditional music. That was my first contact with people who were essentially Protestant but who would have come to Dublin, who would have supported Ireland in the rugby or who would have gone to Donegal and had a slightly different take on things.

It was around this time that you joined the civil rights movement and you also became drawn into Sinn Féin politics in the late '60s as well. What was the tipping point that turned you from being a bystander into becoming politically involved?

The first awakening in a real sense was the Divis Street riots in 1964. I was still at school and I was staying with my granny at the time in the Falls. You know the story – it was an election and Ian Paisley was threatening to come and take the tricolour out of the window. So I went and got a copy of the Special Powers Act and read it and was quite fascinated by it. What influenced me? Two things – one: reading what I have just described, starting to get a wee bit of a context of why we were living in houses which had an outside toilet and a cold water tap. I was now meeting with people who were living in decent houses and who were professional people. They were people who might not have been very wealthy but who were white collar workers – and you started to get some sense of class politics and some sense of the social dimension to all of this. But also I was influenced by what was happening internationally. This was anti-Vietnam war time, so I went to those protests. It was the anti-apartheid movement, so I went to those protests. It was Bob Dylan, it was the Rolling Stones, it was the Beatles, it was the student protests across Europe and it was the American civil rights movement. By now I'm politically active and I'm working with kindred spirits.

What drew you specifically to physical force republicanism, though, when you could have gone down the road of constitutional nationalism or Labour politics?

What made me come around to support physical force republicanism, I suppose, was the developing way that the civil rights demonstrations were being dealt with. Then there was the militarisation in 1969. In my own home place of Ballymurphy, which would probably be one of the strongest Sinn Féin heartlands now, it was just a small handful of republican families then. A lot of the people were British ex-service – but the troops did what troops do, which isn't even their fault. That's what they were trained to do and they were an occupying force and this was the place in which I lived.

They took over the local church hall, they took over local schools, they took over football pitches and, within a month, they were beating people in the streets and making lewd remarks about womenfolk. At this point, I'm sort of well-versed in all of the teachings of those who would espouse physical force – Pádraic Pearse [Pádraig Pearse, one of the leaders of the 1916 Easter Rising] or Connolly or Fintan Lalor [the influential nineteenth-century Irish revolutionary and writer] – but I don't think anybody had a big plan and I think republican activism was fairly divided on these issues. There was a big split in 1969 but I think once politicians – and I'm talking here about the establishment – once they hand the problem over to the generals, then that's the death of diplomacy, that's the death of dialogue. I think that's always a mistake that's made in these situations.

So you're saying that's what the British politicians did and then that forced you to take the steps you took?

Don't get me wrong, I have my own responsibilities; I wasn't forced. I could have decided not to be involved. I could have decided to take some other course. Obviously I was a physical force supporter, but I was never taken to it as anything other than a means to an end, you know. I thought you could still argue a legitimate response to the political conditions in which we lived, and I would argue very strongly that the way you change these circumstances is by changing the political conditions. You can't blame the people – it's the political conditions in which the people live that lead them to take whatever decisions they take.

Your colleague Martin McGuinness has talked publicly about his involvement with the IRA and yet you continue to claim that you were not a member of the organisation. Why do you still say that, in spite of the fact that a lot of people who have studied the period and written about it are convinced that you were?

Well, that's my position. I've never tried to distance myself from the IRA. I think the IRA was a legitimate response to what was happening at the time. I'd be critical of some of its actions, of course, but I think in terms of the militarisation of the situation and given the history of the island and given the physical force tendency within republicanism, there was almost bound to be that sort of a response. But, I mean, my position is quite clear and people can make up their own mind about the validity of it.

But can you see how people struggle to accept that because you were interned, for example, in 1972 and the IRA insisted that you be released to take part in the Cheyne Walk talks with the government?
I quite honestly don't think that people care.

Well, some people do care.
Yeah but the vast majority of people will say, 'Ok, so he wasn't in the IRA'. Or people will say, 'Well, I don't believe that but, you know, he's saying what he's saying for whatever reason he's saying it', and they go on about their business.

Maybe that's true, but what some people might wonder is why you can't do what Martin McGuinness has done and say, 'Look, I was involved at the time. I would be lying if I said I regretted what I did, but we've all moved on'. You could say that as well, couldn't you?
Well, Martin and I have different positions on this and if I was to have the power to choose a different life journey, I wouldn't choose a different life journey.

You wouldn't do anything differently?
No, that's not what I'm saying. I wouldn't choose a different life journey. But I do regret many of the things that happened, you know.

Do you regret any of the things that you were responsible for, any of the decisions you took?
Well, I like to think of myself as a thinking human being. You'd have to hold it up to scrutiny and say, 'Would I do things differently?' Yes, as a visitor to these shores said, 'there were things that were done that would have been better not done' – that's what *Éilís a Dó* said when she came, that's what Queen Elizabeth said. I'm paraphrasing what she said. So, of course, I do think it is absolutely regrettable that there was a war. The more you think about it, it's absolutely regrettable that so many people were killed, injured or traumatised. And then, at the same time, when you think back into your own place, there were all these very fine young men and women, and those

who were not so young, who were absolutely courageous in terms of the stand they took and the stand their families took, whether it was visiting prisons or years of demonisation, of poverty and of real harassment.

I suppose what some people might say is that there didn't have to be a war.

Well, let me answer that in two ways. It's very easy to be blasé and to say something that doesn't take into account the actual awful suffering that people have endured as a result of the war. So I don't want to in any way make little of any of that. I'm just trying to say that while I regret the fact that there was a war, at the same time I have nothing but admiration for some of those fine people who took a stand and who reared their families and remained dignified and who never lost their humanity. Now, I know some people did lose their humanity, but I think that the people who came through all of that and who wanted to make peace, wanted somebody to break the cycle – and I think we succeeded in doing that. But yes, I can't contradict anything that you have said. Yes, republicans inflicted [things] not just on English soldiers or those who were part of what would be seen as the British war effort, but [also on] innocent civilians; people who were just going about their ordinary business. That's a matter of huge regret, of course it is.

Interestingly, both Peter Robinson and Ian Paisley, in their interviews for this book, say they don't think they could have done what they did if they hadn't been dealing with Martin McGuinness. There is a sense that they warmed to him in a way that they didn't warm to you. Do you regret that in any way?

Well, first of all, Martin is very sociable, very affable, very outgoing. I didn't know his father, but I knew his mother very well and I think he takes a lot of that from her. But look, Martin has brought his own very particular talents and I think he has been an example to all of us; but the unionists would have done business with whoever they would have had to do business with, whenever it came to it. Because of Martin's particular personality, I think it was perhaps easier. I watched the relationship between him and Ian Paisley because Martin was always respectful for an older man. You could see that even in terms of some of the body language between them. There was almost a deference, while at the same time Ian Paisley might have been referring to him, his deputy, in a slightly ironic way. Martin took that with a certain degree of grace but I was involved in all of the negotiations and that's what decided the dispensation that we worked out. It fell on me, as leader of the party, to choose whoever we were going to nominate, and I very consciously nominated Martin because I thought he was the best man for the job, and I think that's proven to be the case. He's grown into the job.

Do you think you would have found it difficult to have had that warm relationship with Ian Paisley? Would you have found it difficult to be deferential?

No, I actually came to like Ian Paisley very much. I formed two opinions. I formed an opinion that it was going to be extremely difficult to sustain a peace process with David Trimble [the former UUP First Minister]. No harm to David, but he couldn't deliver his own people. Time [and again] David would have come to an agreement with us and then would have gone off and couldn't bring his own party with him. So, in the course of that I said to our people, 'I think we're going to have to do a deal with the DUP'. There was a time when we would bump into the DUP and they would blank us and they would say something disparaging about us to whoever was in their company, and then there was a sense that some of them were actually listening to what we were saying. I remember very well that I was in Dublin one Friday night and Tony Blair phoned me and said to me that Ian Paisley had come to him and said he was prepared to do a deal but he couldn't do it now. I said to him, 'Tell him that isn't good enough and tell him to come and see us'. I remember Blair coming back the next day and saying, 'Paisley's prepared to talk'. He was always good humoured, always respectful and wise. I remember him saying to me at Stormont, 'What we need to do is come into a room like this, close the door, talk about the problem and solve the problem because that's what the people want'. I went to an event in honour of Ian Paisley in Hillsborough and when I was leaving, Mrs. Paisley – Eileen – was sitting on her own and I said, 'Do you mind if I join you?' We talked for an hour about growing vegetables, about grandchildren, about faith and about dogs. My wife was sick not long after that and she sent her over a lovely little note.

What do you think the Gerry Adams of thirty years ago would think if he heard the Gerry Adams of today recounting stories about sitting talking to Ian and Eileen Paisley?

Well, I formed a kind of hard-headed view that Ian Paisley had never been challenged and that there was a bit of a showman about him. Nobody had actually said, 'Come on, let's try and sort this', and maybe there's a tide in the affairs of men that you can't plan and you can't plot and you can't legislate for. But as it came to it, Ian Paisley became absolutely indispensable in moving the entire process forward. Would a teenage or a twenty year old Gerry Adams have looked with astonishment at the journey we've all been on? I suppose the younger Gerry Adams would say, 'What exactly is this guy doing at this point?' I have always, despite some of the awful things that have happened, had a sense that this has always been about politics and that politics essentially has to be about empowering people. So even though I supported the IRA, supported armed struggle and so on, I never saw that as being republicanism, you know. It was a tactic. Republicanism is about people's rights, it's about a society in which people are sovereign and it's about people having entitlements. It's about harmony between orange and green on this island. It's about tackling sectarianism. It's about all of those things.

But you still have to shoulder the fact that while republicanism might well be about all those things, it was a very painful 'tactic' for a lot of people here for a very long time.

Yeah and I don't want to repeat myself. I acknowledge that. I've been imprisoned on a few occasions, I've been beaten in prison, I've been beaten in interrogation centres and I've been shot. I've met more victims of the IRA and families of victims of the IRA than perhaps anybody else. That's, I think, part of my responsibility. When people want to deal with these issues and want to try and get closure and want to try and get beyond the trauma of what happened to them in the middle of the conflict, I think that people like me have a responsibility to help them.

Is that responsibility a burden on your shoulders? Does it weigh heavily?

Yes, it can. But whatever we have been able to do on those issues, the grace with which many of those people respond makes it worth it. Now, there are some people obviously who – and it's quite understandable – hate republicans; hate me, hate Martin McGuinness, hate other people because of what they have gone through. But there are other people who have suffered grievously, who are very strong supporters of the peace process and who are very strong supporters of Sinn Féin. There's a complexity about victims. A lot of victims come from republican families. Victims of the IRA come from republican families and it's uplifting to see how people can remain strongly republican or remain committed to the notion of a peace process and support those like myself, even though the IRA might have robbed them of a mother or a father or a brother or a sister. It's indicative of just how redemptive the human spirit can be. These are just decent people who have decided that they are going to forgive what happened and get on with their lives – and you'll never read about it or see it, but they are the people who relieve the burden that some of us might have.

Do you think your sense of identity has been altered by being a TD for Louth and being based in Dublin? Has that cast a new light on your identity in any sense?

Well, it's different, you know. We're in Leinster House and it's a very dysfunctional parliament and it's quite partitionist. I go into the Dáil chamber and on the balcony there's a bust of James Connolly and all the founders or leaders of republicanism. As you go into the big reception in the old part of the building, you'll see both sides of the Civil War – I think Cathal Brugha is up on one side and Michael Collins is on the other side. When we first went up into Stormont, I felt the way I imagined those anti-apartheid activists must have felt when they went into the parliament in South Africa, because we weren't really welcome. And then wee funny things happened, like our folks [at Stormont] organised a Christmas party and they brought in a bit of Irish music and a few drinks, and they invited everybody from the domestic staff, to the cleaners to the security staff and the people who enjoyed it most were the wee working-class, loyalist people who stayed at the session and had a bit of craic. Then a guy came over to me – one of the security guys – and he said to me, 'You know, I was in the British Army when you were arrested, when you got the crap beaten out of you, and I'm sorry'. And when I left, he put out his hand and we shook hands. So, there's a sense in the North of it being a work in progress.

LORD ASHDOWN

Born in New Delhi in 1941, Paddy Ashdown spent his formative years near Donaghadee in Northern Ireland, where his father owned a farm. He attended two local schools until, at the age of eleven, his education took him to England. He served in the Royal Marines – during which time he saw service in the Far East and on the streets of Belfast – before working for a time in Switzerland for the Secret Intelligence Service. In 1983 he became a Liberal MP and led the Liberal Democrats from 1988 to 1999. He entered the House of Lords in 2001 and served as the international High Representative for Bosnia and Herzegovina from 2002 to 2006. In April 2007 he was appointed to head a strategic review of parading in Northern Ireland.

We meet for breakfast in Belfast.

Paddy Ashdown:

I think Ulster means for me: my childhood, my antecedents, my blood, my mother in particular, who was an Ulsterwoman, and my grandfather. It's something more, I think, to do with heritage and tribe than anything else.

Mark Carruthers:

And is it something which, having lived away from this place for so long, still has some meaning for you?

Yes, it does. It has importance. I suppose that's the same as meaning. You know, it's part of my identity and a part which I both recognise and feel proud of. I suppose if you listen to me speaking you'll realise that most people don't take me for an Ulsterman, although I can put it on when I need to. My parents sent me to school over the water, as we used to say, and that rubbed out the Irish accent and I'm sad about that actually. I really am sad about it, because it takes away a bit of your identity. In that sense, I suppose I am, in part, an Englishman, although there isn't much English in my blood. But significantly, the choice I made was the choice that identified me as an Irishman, albeit not in most people's knowledge, a Northern Irishman.

In England they don't know the difference. Paddy is not my name; Jeremy is my name, the name my parents gave me and always called me. Paddy was what my nickname was at school. It's not a synthetic thing that it continued to be my name for the rest of my life, because so many of my school friends went into the same Royal Marines unit I went into, so the Paddy carried over. I've always found myself very content to be known as that. I am somebody who is proud to be associated with his Irish roots. They are Northern Irish roots in this case, so it has become internally, and I suppose externally, part of my identity.

But at some point you must have made the decision to hold onto the nickname and to use it as your name.

Yes. I never fought against it because I was content to be known by it and consciously preferred it to the name that my parents gave me, because I think it was a better description of me. Also, it was a sort of slightly rebellious determination to hang on to my identity in the face of all the forces which come from an English public school.

So what is the label you now use to describe yourself? When somebody asks you about your identity, what is it?

Well, this is the very interesting thing. There's a really big issue here. I mean, if you had asked me forty years ago when I was a British soldier fighting in some of those post-Imperial wars at the end of Empire in the Far East who I was, I'd have said I was British and that would have been sufficient. As a Royal Marines officer I didn't need anything beyond that. Now, I have to give you a much more complex answer. Now, I discover that I actually have several identities. I'm Irish by blood – part Northern Irish, part Southern Irish; Catholic and Protestant – with all that that means in this community in terms of identity and the clash of identities. I am also a part of the West Country of England. This is the place I chose to live, the place I represented in Parliament, and I'm proud of that too. I am also British and I discover that I'm also a European and perhaps, even, that I'm a citizen of the wider world. Unless I can use all those means to describe myself, I can't describe the space in which I want to live and above all, I can't describe the space in which I want my children to live. I am a passionate European because it's part of my identity – and here's the point: I think that in the modern age it's ok to have multiple identities. It's ok to associate yourself with several things. If you say to somebody, 'Look, I'm sorry you cannot be Northern Irish, British and Catholic,' you get blood on your streets. If you say to somebody on the streets of Savajevo, 'I'm sorry you can't be a Muslim in Bosnia; you cannot have that identity,' you get blood on your streets. So the concept of the multiple identity is not only, I think, a product of the globalised world which I feel very strongly, but also a safe presumption to make if what you want to do is have less conflict and more peace.

So you rail against those individuals who promote this notion of a single identity?

Yes I do. And I've seen them as the engines of conflict and the deliverers of blood across the world. I was four years old travelling with my mother when the British were leaving India after a hundred years there. We went through a station where there had been a massacre. I don't know whether it was Muslims killing Hindus or Hindus killing Muslims, but at four years old, seeing that sight is imprinted on my memory. And then I came back to Northern Ireland and found that same thing operating here. I knew very well, certainly by eleven, that the Troubles were coming. I knew it perfectly well, had an absolute clarity about what was going to happen, and what I've seen around the world since then – in the Far East certainly, in Northern Ireland when I was here as a soldier, and then perhaps most bloodily, most darkly and most dreadfully in Bosnia Herzegovina – is that those who propose the absolute, mono-identity of a singular faith or a singular race, prepare the way for persuading others that anybody else of another race or religion is sub-human and therefore, you can do terrible things to them. That's the mental preparation for something absolutely appalling.

So were you aware as you were growing up here that this place was effectively a single-party state with a largely disengaged minority?

I suppose the moment I started to get the small glimmerings of political ideas, probably around the age of ten or eleven, I was very conscious that it was a state where some were repressed according to religion. There are two democratic principles: one is that the majority has a right to rule, but the second is that no matter how large the majority, it doesn't have the right to crush out the rights of the minorities and that second principle was not being observed here and I was certainly very conscious of that. Here's a shocking thing to say – given my nature I'm a very fiery, passionate [man] – I get very easily involved in crusades and sometimes, perhaps, don't make the best judgements about them, but I have little doubt that if I'd been brought up in the Ardoyne in the '60s and '70s, you'd have found me on the Fenian side.

Really?

I should think so. There's accidents of birth all over the place. I would extend that further – and this will offend some of my God-fearing friends in Northern Ireland. If someone asks me what I am, I say I'm a Christian. If someone wants me to go further, I can't. I mean, I can't tell you and I find it offensive to be asked if I'm a Catholic or a Protestant. I'm a Christian and that's enough for me. That's probably because I see Christianity as a sort of convenient code with which to try to live my life in our place and in our time, but if it had been a different place and a different time, I would certainly always have felt a kinship with any of the Abrahamic religions. I spent the first three years of my life being brought up to the rhythms of Islam because my father was behind Chinese lines. My mother was waiting for him to return and I lived with the servants of the family who were Islamic. I could have easily been a Muslim, if I had been brought up in the Muslim community. There's a line in the Koran which says, 'There is one God but many ways to him,' and that's a fundamental belief that I have. So I'm a Christian, I've got Northern Irish blood in me, and I'm very proud of that. If you try to sub-divide that further I think I would resist the process. It is all an accident of time and place.

The irony, of course, about you saying you would very probably have gone down a different route if you'd been born in Ardoyne, is that you did come back here in 1970 in charge of a British commando unit.

Well, there's a double irony because, first of all, I came back to Flax Street Mill but even then, when I fought the little war we were involved in Malaysia, I remember thinking quite clearly that we were fighting on the wrong side. In fact, I thought the Malaysian rebels – those who didn't want to be part of Malaysia – had the right case, but I was doing Her Majesty's business. I didn't feel that, by the way, in Flax Street Mill, next to the Ardoyne. I didn't feel that because I felt that the legitimate claim for rights of the Northern Ireland Civil Rights Association – NICRA – had transmuted itself into something to do with violence, and violence has to be suppressed, because it produces only more violence, not solutions.

I remember rather a famous incident wandering out the back of Flax Street Mill, leaving my weapon and all my blokes behind, and wandering up the Bone [a small nationalist and republican area in north Belfast] and knocking on a wonderful man's door, [a man] I really admired. 'Hello. I'm the British company commander here and I gather you're the IRA company commander.' Bloody stupid thing to do and a very provocative thing to do, and of course the consequence of that was I was plastered all over the press the following day: 'British soldier intimidates innocent Irish citizen.' I was then put on the IRA death list and this had two further consequences. The first was that as a young, no-hope, Liberal candidate in 1979 fighting my first election in Yeovil, I had police protection because I was on the IRA death list. The result was the policemen who followed me around were significantly greater [in number] than any audience I ever got in any of the halls I went to. But it had another consequence as well; when I came back in 2007/2008 and Peter Hain, the then Secretary of State for Northern Ireland, asked me if I would negotiate the deal to see if we could solve the parades problem. I said, 'Yes, but you have to give me people who've got real clout on the streets. I don't want middle-class Northern Irish people who represent a Catholic or Protestant point of view. I want people who have clout on the streets.' And what I got was a very fine little group of people – six or eight of us – who worked for two years. One of them was Mervyn Gibson [a former policeman turned Presbyterian minister and leading member of the Orange Order], who I have a great admiration for, and the other was 'Spike' Murray [former IRA man Sean Murray], and those two were absolutely outstanding. I thought their capacity to understand each other's position and to reach a conclusion was extraordinary. I remember once accusing 'Spike' of being the bloke that put me on the death list. He said to me, 'You know Paddy I bet you never guessed you'd be wandering through Stormont with a member of Sinn Féin'. And I said, 'No 'Spike'. If I had seen you here thirty years ago, I would have arrested you on the spot'. 'I suppose I'd better not mention what I would have done to you if I'd seen you first!' he said. The important point was that here is the capacity of people who have been through the fire and done extraordinary things for their beliefs, but who nevertheless understand the moment when you have to build peace and are able to make the compromises. I thought that showed an astonishing nobility of human spirit.

What's been your personal experience of our politicians down the years?
To start with, I got so angry with them because it seemed to me, for a very long time, that the people were far ahead of their politicians. One of the things that particularly struck me about Northern Ireland – and it certainly applied in Bosnia as well – is you cannot reach a sustainable peace until the generation who had won the war had been replaced by a new generation. There was this thin crust of politicians at the top in Ireland and they just weren't shifting; they kept everybody locked into their tribal positions. They won their votes by frightening their people about the other side. I saw exactly the same sort of thing happening in Bosnia Herzegovina but yet magically, maybe just out of a process of time, in Northern Ireland, that crust has been broken. Finally, we're getting the new politics emerging and, for all my anger about the failures of leadership and vision of those who represented the people of Northern Ireland, in the end it happened – and it happened because of politicians. I mean, David Trimble – not somebody I had a particular admiration for when he was elected first – turned out to be extraordinarily powerful in this sense. In my view the greatness of a politician comes at the moment when they understand that to achieve what they want to achieve, the struggle is no longer an appropriate way and they are prepared to make the move for peace, and to have that vision is, I think, extraordinary. I would argue that, probably, Gerry Adams is the most effective party leader in Britain in the last fifty years from any party. For all people will say about Gerry Adams, the fact is that he has led his people to peace. No doubt there are things about him which are not, to many, personally attractive – but that was probably true of de Gaulle and it was

probably true of Churchill. I'm not making a comparison between Gerry Adams and Churchill, by the way, I'm simply saying that the politicians I admire are those who manage to conduct themselves as political animals, but also understand the historic moment that arrives when you have to turn from conflict to compromise.

Do you believe the process we went through here is a model of conflict resolution for other places?

Yes, but strategic patience is what you need to build peace – both those trying to build it from the outside and those trying to build it from the inside. Can you take a model and say, 'Ah, this is the solution?' Absolutely not. In Bosnia people used to come along to me and say, 'What we need is a Truth & Reconciliation Commission'. I said, 'Yeah. That'd be a really good idea'. So I looked into it and I discovered that the situation in Southern Africa was wholly different. You had moral leadership of extraordinary quality from Nelson Mandela – totally absent in Bosnia and probably largely absent here in Northern Ireland. Secondly, you had a clear victory rather than a suspended conflict. One side won and if one side wins it's much easier to be generous. If it's a stalemate, it's much more difficult to be magnanimous. And the third thing you had was that there wasn't a huge amount of violence, by and large. The black community suffered badly but nothing like Bosnia and nothing like Northern Ireland. Now, are there things we can learn from Northern Ireland? Yes. Is there a model you can propose from Northern Ireland that goes on to other countries with different cultures? I don't think so.

Here's the 'Ashdown theory' on multiple identity. I think the nation state is now under attack from two directions. First of all, I think people want power closer to them than the distant institution of their nation state government. They want the chance to be able to make their own decisions, and that's why you see all the advanced nation states going through a process of devolution of power. The second thing is that the most powerful things in the world now are not within the borders of the nation state – they're the global powers: the power of the internet, the power of satellite broadcasters, the power of the transnational corporations, international terrorism and international crime. So, the concept of the nation state is now being eroded and [that] leads to the necessity for multiple identities.

Is the solution for a Scottish identity the separation of Scotland from Britain? No. Alongside my British identity, I want a Scottish identity. If this thing leads to secessionism, if it leads to a different kind of unitary identity at a smaller level, well God help us, we're going back to tribalism. But if it leads to the understanding that I can be Scottish and British and European, then I can have all those identities and I think we've hatched something which moves us forward and not back. If you have not got into the habit today of accepting multiple identities for yourself, life is going to be very tough for you. Maybe that's the lesson Ireland can teach us: being able to look in different directions at the same time is actually a better way forward than simply looking at yourself.

Does it sadden you that your sister party here, the Alliance Party, although it now has two seats at the Executive table in Stormont, has for four decades been very much the squeezed middle of Northen Ireland politics?

You mean like the Liberals? Of course it worries me, because I have great admiration for them. They made the attempt to break out of the box and in the end they have been proved to be right and people have moved to their position. That's just the price you pay for liberal politics and being ahead of your time. Oscar Wilde once said that, 'In a democracy, the minority is always right'. I have to say it's a phrase that has given me much comfort as a Liberal Democrat over the years. It's not always easy to be a pioneer. There is only one reason to be in politics and that is to be in the government and inform the government of your country with the principles that you adhere to. That's a difficult process and it leads to the erosion of your identity, perhaps, which is exactly what's happening. That's the risk you have to take, but in the end, being in politics means being prepared to share the burdens of power and I'm glad they're doing it and I'm glad we're doing it and whatever the price for that, I think it's the right thing for us and the right thing for our country.

So why didn't you accept Gordon Brown's invitation to serve in his government as Secretary of State for Northern Ireland?

I would have loved to have done it, but in British politics, being in the Cabinet means having Cabinet solidarity and whilst that was a job which I would have liked to have done – not least because it would have enabled me to, perhaps, repay a little to the place of my blood – I couldn't join Gordon Brown's Cabinet because I didn't believe in what the government was doing. I said to Gordon when he asked me, 'Will you join my government in this capacity?', I said, 'No'. He said, 'Why?' I said, 'Because how can I join a government whose policies I don't agree with?' And he said, 'Well, could you not just keep quiet about it?' And I said, 'No, I couldn't keep quiet about it'. I could have joined three Cabinets and I said no to all of them, because, when Blair offered me a position in Cabinet, it was on the basis that the Liberal Democrats would become the same party as Labour and I said, 'Under no circumstances'. The preservation of the identity and independence of the Liberal Democrats is absolutely crucial to British politics.

So here we are meeting in Northern Ireland. Do you feel, when you come back here, any sense of being 'at home' now?

Of course I do. I remember driving with my dad over the Lagan, bringing lettuces to Belfast Market when his business was going belly up, before they went to Australia. And driving over that bridge yesterday, down towards the market, brought back all those memories. It's the place of my childhood, so every time I come back to Northern Ireland I feel that tug, of course I do.

PROFESSOR SIR GEORGE BAIN

Born in Winnipeg in Canada to parents of Irish and Scottish extraction, George Bain was the President and Vice-Chancellor of Queen's University Belfast for seven years until 2004. He studied at the University of Manitoba and at Oxford and, prior to his move to Queen's, spent eight years as Principal of the London Business School. A tireless and successful fundraiser for Queen's and other organisations, he also chaired the Low Pay Commission from 1997 to 2002 and again from 2009, and the Independent Review of the Fire Service which reported in 2002.

We meet in his County Antrim home.

George Bain:

I'd only been here a few months and I said to John B. McGuckian, who was Chairman of Senate at Queen's, 'When you're making a speech, how do you refer to this place without insulting people?' – because if you use the North of Ireland, if you use Ulster, if you use Northern Ireland, you'll upset somebody. He said, 'I usually refer to "this great country of ours".'

Mark Carruthers:

When you came to live here from London, did you feel that you had an affinity with the place?

Very much so. I suppose there's two reasons why I came. My dad was from Scotland and my mum was from here. My dad, perhaps like many men, wasn't much interested in family history or his origins. My mother talked about little else. In fact, she knew more about my dad's family than he did but she always talked about the 'old country' and although she was from a Protestant family – obviously a strongly unionist family – she was very proud of being Irish. Although the shortbread she made was traditionally good Scottish shortbread, she always referred to it as Irish shortbread and, from my youngest days I always knew what the 17th of March was and I was not allowed out of the house without a green ribbon or some piece of green on me. To her dying day, I would always send her a telegram wishing her a happy St Patrick's Day. Although I wouldn't use this phrase, she was almost stage Irish, in a way. She was so proud of it and actually she lived very little of her life here. She was born here in 1904, my grandfather went off to Canada in 1906 and in 1907 he sent for them. She came back and forth almost every year. He worked for the Canadian Pacific and they had a steamship line as well as a railway and must have had favourable fares. She was last here in 1919 and yet her whole life was Ireland. So, I had a very strong connection. I read quite a bit of history and I decided that I would start to do my family tree and, of course, collecting ancestors is a bit like collecting stamps, I think, unless you begin to put them in some sort of historical, social context, it's not very meaningful – so I started to read a lot of Irish history.

The second reason I came to live here was I'd had the job at the London Business School and I said to my boss there, when I took the job, I'd do it for eight years, nine years at the most and then I'd move on. So when I'd been there eight years, I went to him and I said, 'I haven't got another job, but I'm giving you my notice. I understand that there's a job coming up at Queen's; I'm going to apply'.

So you started the job in 1997 and found yourself stepping into the heart of a society which you had only ever really seen from the outside.
I took the job because I thought I'd learn a lot that I wouldn't learn at any other university – and that was true in spades. I thought I knew a bit about Northern Ireland having made all these trips over the years but, of course, I knew virtually nothing. Queen's was still seen then, pretty much incorrectly I think, as a Protestant university. Gordon Beveridge [the previous Vice-Chancellor] put into place a whole range of policies, for which he never got the credit, for making Queen's reflect the broader community. The composition of Queen's changed, so much so, that by the middle of my tenure people were claiming that Queen's was a Catholic university. I can remember speaking to a DUP politician and saying, 'You're right, 51% of the students now coming into Queen's are Catholic. But if you look at the last census, 51% of the eighteen year olds in Northern Ireland are Catholic'. We reflected the community.

Queen's had long been an institution, of course, which was right at the heart of the debate about what this country was and what it should be, and that hadn't really changed by the time you took over.

No, it hadn't. I also think I had a considerable advantage. First of all, I always describe myself as a Protestant atheist. Of course, as we well know, religion here in terms of the Troubles isn't about religion, it's about tribes. So even if I hadn't been a Protestant atheist, I wouldn't really count because I was an outsider and about as neutral as you can get here. I suppose I wasn't English, which is always an advantage here. And secondly, a good deal of my life had been spent mediating between unions and employers. The skills were the same: listening to people and acting on it. I once was speaking to George Mitchell, who was the Chancellor of Queen's while I was there, and he said to me, 'In these things you have to lead with your ears'. It's a phrase that I always remember. He meant you have to listen very carefully and do a lot more listening than talking, and then try to get people to work together. I think my background in labour management helped with this and I'm not averse to a pint or even two pints of beer. I used to go across on a Friday afternoon and sink a few pints with the Students' Union Executive and I think in my seven years at Queen's I got great respect from the Union Presidents and they were all extremely helpful. It was a question of encouraging them to take a more inclusive approach. I had no trouble but I just think it had not been the tradition for Vice-Chancellors to go the Union and have a drink with the students.

What's your sense of how this place is viewed internationally and how that might have changed in recent years?

I think during the Troubles, Northern Ireland was viewed as a bit of a basket case. When you'd go to Dublin, people would say, 'They're absolutely crazy up there' and wash their hands of it. Well, as a social scientist, I've never found craziness a very useful concept in trying to explain behaviour. My wife Gwynneth and I came here just at the right moment. When we came, the army was still on the streets. We came about a year before the Good Friday Agreement and all of a sudden, we had the renaissance of Belfast, the renaissance of Northern Ireland. The whole thing began to change. The rest of the world began to use us almost as a template for solving problems elsewhere.

Have you formed any kind of notion of what people here are really like – how much they have in common and how much they have separating them?

I'm not sure I have. First of all, Ulster people are very friendly – at least to outsiders. They may be at each other's throats, literally, but I've always found them extremely warm and generous. We decided to move out of Belfast and came to the edge of this small village, Glenavy, and people couldn't have been friendlier or more helpful – from Sammy Bickerstaff, the grocer, to our neighbours here who are all farmers or fishermen. I think the second thing is a certain amount of stoicism. I'd only been here a short time when Adam Ingram, who was then a [Northern Ireland Office] Minister, asked me to chair the Northern Ireland Memorial Fund, which was set up to help the victims of the Troubles. What a learning experience that was! There were people who had suffered greatly and yet were able to forgive, were able to take this very broad view and that's something that struck me. The third thing was the people who have a very quick wit and black humour.

And how do you now describe your sense of personal identity?

I carry three passports. I have, of course, my Canadian passport and many years ago when I thought I was going to head back [from the UK] to Canada, I thought I'd better get a British passport. So I got a British one and then when I came to Northern Ireland, I thought on the basis of my mother – who was born here in 1904 before partition – I'm eligible for an Irish one. So I got an Irish one and today I have three current passports. If Scotland goes independent, I'll probably get a Scottish one too! I think I'm actually a bit like how something like 25% of people here now identify themselves: not as Irish, not as British, but as Northern Irish. Malachi O'Doherty wrote a piece in the *Belfast Telegraph* recently saying that actually he was one of the people who returned himself [in last year's census] as 'Northern Irish' and I suppose that's probably what I think I am in a way now – albeit I'm a Canadian. I have clearly decided to end, with a small footnote, my days here. We decided to stay after retirement and I certainly can't face leaving, so I'm going to die here for sure. I hope here, actually, in this house, rather than elsewhere. The footnote is, I've decided to return to Canada after I'm dead and I'll get buried in the family plot back in Winnipeg – but until I'm dead, I'll finish my days here.

So you're adopted Northern Irish?
I'm adopted Northern Irish.

And does the notion of being an Ulsterman appeal to you at all?
It does a bit because I'm very interested in history and if you look back
on Ulster when there wasn't partition and it was unambiguously the
nine counties, Belfast and Ulster were the economic centre of gravity of
this island. Belfast was not just the greatest city of this island but one of
the greatest in the United Kingdom and in the Empire. Right up to the
First World War we were producing something like 10% of the world's
shipping capacity. Belfast was booming in terms of shipbuilding, in terms
of engineering, in terms of tobacco, in terms of rope making and in terms
of linen. It was just a fantastic city of Empire and everybody would have
known where Belfast was – the people who made the Titanic and all that.
There was, of course, a lot of romantic nonsense about it but, nonetheless,
Ulster does mean something to me.

**So was that sense of a special connection with this place partly why you
chose to stay here when you retired? Why choose Northern Ireland and
why, specifically, the village of Glenavy?**
Well, it's a very interesting question. A couple of years before I was going to
retire I said to Gwynneth, 'What do you want to do?' And so, we thought
about it. There was no question of me going back to Canada. I'd been here
too long, but if I'd had to put a bet on it, I would have said that Gwynneth
would say, 'Let's go back to Warwickshire, where we met'. We took a couple
of trips over there to look for places, thought about it and came back. She
said one day, 'You know George, why don't we just stay? We've really enjoyed
it here, we've met a lot of really interesting people and, you know, the society
here is interesting'. This was about 2002 when things were looking very
bright in terms of the future. You'd go to dinner parties and people were not
just talking about what are the good schools for their kids, which you would
expect to get at a dinner table in England, they were talking about how to
build a new society – so we stayed.

**But you particularly like what the Glenavy community has to offer as
well, don't you?**
I wouldn't make too much of it, but my mother was a strong conservative

and my father was a democratic socialist and I'm on the centre left. We deliberately did not want to live on the Gold Coast [affluent North Down] or places that were largely single-class communities. We set two criteria: one was that it should be a mixed community and, of course, when we use that phrase in Northern Ireland, people mean Protestant-Catholic and Glenavy is certainly that. It's probably become more Catholic than Protestant but it's still both and relations here are very good. The second thing I've always liked and admired, besides the beer, in a British pub, was the class mixture. Of course, class doesn't feature so much in Ulster politics as it does in other places – religion features – but this was a place where you could go and drink in the local pub and you could find yourself in mixed company, not just in terms of religion, but in terms of social class. That's why we chose it and that's why we thought it would be a good place. We can walk anywhere now in the village – into Bickerstaff's to get our newspapers – and everyone says, 'Hi, George'.

So if I walked into that pub on a Friday night I would see the retired Vice-Chancellor of Queen's, Knight of the Realm, having a beer with the local butcher and the local grocer?
Well you probably would – and certainly with the local farmers and fishermen. I'm glad to say there's not an academic anywhere in sight around here. My neighbours are farmers and fishermen. There's a civil engineer who lives across the way and there are schoolteachers – but not too many investment bankers!

LORD BANNSIDE

To many people, Ian Paisley is the very personification of Ulster Protestantism. He was born in April 1926 and built a political career on opposing Irish nationalism and republicanism in his native Northern Ireland. He founded and led both his own political party and his own church – the Democratic Unionist Party and the Free Presbyterian Church. After decades of opposition to sharing power, he entered government as First Minister of Northern Ireland alongside his long-time enemy, Martin McGuinness of Sinn Féin, in May 2007. He stood down as First Minister and leader of the DUP one year later. He became a life peer in June 2010. His son, Ian Paisley Junior, succeeded him as the MP for North Antrim at the general election in May 2010.

We meet, together with Ian Jnr, at his home in East Belfast.

Ian Paisley Senior:

I would say I'm an Ulsterman. People ask me, 'Who are you?' I say, 'I'm an Ulsterman'. To the ignorant, then, you have to explain what that means, but when I came into the world, the term Ulster was what you were. You were part of the original Queen Elizabeth settlement. I think there is a great interest among the coming generation on this whole issue because there is a change now. Ulster was looked upon as unionism and that is true – but not so much now. I mean, just take sport. Ulster people play rugby, for instance – and there's an Ulster contribution that we're putting into what is really an all-Ireland situation. I think there's a rapid change which really has come about *because* we have had Northern Ireland. If there had been no Northern Ireland, the battle would be still raging, very strongly, politically. But I think you get many Roman Catholics who boast they're Ulstermen. I hear them even on the TV saying, 'I'm from Ulster'.

Mark Carruthers:

Do you think Ulster identity was viewed differently, though, when we were in the depths of the Troubles? Ulster had a connotation to it which was uncomfortable for many Northern Catholics.

Well, I think the connotation came very strongly under Carson and it was aggravated by the fact that Carson really lost the three counties. If the three counties had been under the settlement, it would have been a different thing. That's what brought in the row.

That's interesting. You talk there about Carson losing the three counties rather than Carson saving the six counties. Is that how you see it?

Yes. Well, Carson said that himself. You know, he was very angry about that. I think Carson needs to be recognised by the Ulster people. He was a Dublin unionist.

He was very content with his Irishness.

He was, yes.

That's the interesting thing. Where does Irishness fit into the equation for you?

Oh, I would never deny I was an Irishman.

You wouldn't?

No.

Ian Paisley Junior:

You just wouldn't advertise it. I mean, before partition, before Northern Ireland, we were Irish unionists.

But would you (IP Jnr.) deny your Irishness?

IP Jnr: No, not at all.

Because there are people who might share your broader political world-view who would say they're not Irish at all.

IP Jnr: But my Irishness is mine. They're in denial!

IP Snr: But the person that says that, they are Irish and there have been more generations from Irish roots in them than they're prepared to meet. The English that came over here were 'Irish-ised' very quickly.

IP Jnr: I've never denied this is my island.

IP Snr: I think you've got to be honest that the South is not as Irish as it was. I don't think Ulster will ever be in a United Ireland in our day and generation. I mean, I would say there are more Roman Catholics today who are happy to be Ulstermen.

You think that's now settled?

IP Snr: I think it's settled. I do. Of course, you never know what's going to happen to Ulster with European politics. I mean, European politics has had a reflection upon the change in Northern Ireland. We used to talk about British Ulster. That's a term that's very seldom used today.

And a lot of the politicians back in the early days of the Northern Ireland state talked about Ulster. For them Ulster and Northern Ireland were interchangeable terms.

IP Snr: They were. Absolutely.

IP Jnr: That's the way I was brought up to view it. I think Ulster and Northern Ireland is the same place. Ultimately I think, for my generation, Ulster is the six counties.

When you first got involved in politics in the 1960s you were very concerned about opposing civil rights. What was your political understanding of what precisely you were doing and what you were opposing?

IP Snr: Well, the civil rights was a development of people who were really and truly angered by what Carson achieved. I mean, Carson wasn't happy with what he had achieved. There were people there that had good points which they made but the good points were destroyed by the fact that you had the IRA in the background.

They would say, of course, that what they wanted was equality – equal access to housing and equal access to jobs.

IP Snr: But sewn on to that were the people that were ready to take the gun, and the people that were really fighting the battle which they lost when division [partition] came.

So, you saw that movement as a threat to your Britishness and to your Ulster identity?

IP Snr: Well, a threat to what I believed had succeeded to a great extent in the Ulster settlement that saved Ireland from a lot of blood-shedding. The coming of the Great War, of course, was the thing that took all the fighting men from Ulster out.

So what did you make of those individuals who were on the extremes of loyalism who were prepared to take up arms to defend Ulster?

IP Snr: We were always bitterly opposed to that extremist element that we had in the tail of unionism. They were not only extreme in that way but they were extreme in other ways. It wasn't just anti-IRA, they didn't like the rule of unionism and they thought they could do better by doing what they did. But it was a terrible mix-up because there were very decent people at that particular time that got warped and they then got tied into it. It was a terrible, lop-sided thing.

How do you answer the charge that's been directed at you many times down the years, that loyalist paramilitaries listened to what you had to say and were inspired by your capacity as an orator to go out and do things they later regretted?

IP Snr: Oh well, that charge is absolutely, totally false. I mean, I was always very strong against any talk of killing people because I realised that when you read the history of Ireland, that's what wrecked the country. You see, there were people who started off on a good footing and were friends to what I was doing but then they got into this trap. They were trapped probably with guns and weapons in their home and then they were threatened: 'We'll tell the police if you don't go our way'. I mean, there was a lot of threats among the Protestant population and men were forced to do things that they didn't want to do. It was a sad time for Ulster.

So how uncomfortable were you, for example, that the UDA was involved in 1974 during the Ulster Workers' Council Strike?

IP Snr: Well, the UDA, at that time, were all for what we did. And I mean, I kept them on the straight and narrow as well as I could – and then it deteriorated. There was other people who wanted trouble and they looked at me as a great enemy because they felt that I had the majority Protestant people saying 'Amen' to what I was doing. There was a lot of bad boys on both sides and the bad boys on the Roman Catholic side terrorised their part but there was terrorism on our own side. The room next door to this was blown up by them, so it was.

So when you look at 'Ulster Resistance' and the 'Third Force', people have asked questions about how close you came to some of those organisations – how much you flirted on the edges of that world?

IP Snr: Oh, that's nonsense. You didn't flirt on the edges of that or they would have taken out a gun and shot you.

When we started off this conversation you said you were a proud Ulsterman. How far would you have gone to defend Ulster?

IP Snr: Well, I felt that we had to be shrewd politicians and we had to get the majority on our [side] so that we could sway the British government. The British government had to be swayed and they were swayed. I mean, Ted Heath sat in a room in Stormont and told us that he was sorry he couldn't drag Ulster into the middle of the Atlantic Ocean and blow it up! Thatcher was all right at the end of her days. I had her around to the right way [of thinking].

IP Jnr: It's a hard identity. I mean, the Ulster Protestant, the Ulster Unionist identity, is one of tough-nosedness, stubbornness, thran. It's all of those things – and why? Well, when your back is against the wall and you're not like that, you're crushed. And I suppose your political leadership can't be seen to be weak either.

To what extent, then, do you associate Protestantism with the Ulster identity?

IP Snr: Well, I think it has a very close identity because Ulster unionism is direct Reformation Protestantism, really. The history of unionism in Ireland has really been a history of Protestantism.

IP Jnr: But I think when you say you're an Ulsterman, it is shorthand for saying, 'I'm from Northern Ireland and I'm a Prod'. I mean, for example, if I met Alasdair McDonnell of the SDLP, he'd be telling me he's an Irishman before he would tell me he's an Ulsterman. Certainly, he wouldn't deny he's an Ulsterman but he would know that my interpretation when someone says, 'I'm an Ulsterman', is shorthand for a number of things. I think it's just a product of the Troubles and a product of the last forty years that that's what the shorthand is, but it has created an identity of its own and the new Ulster identity is starting to emerge with a Northern Ireland that is now more peaceful. The Ulster rugby team is now very much part and parcel of a success story. You have the yellow Ulster flag as well as the white one. I welcome the fact that people now are comfortable with the fact that we are a divided community and that's ok. We should be comfortable with the fact that we're all very, very different here – but at least we're sharing the place.

IP Snr: There's more uniting between Protestants and Roman Catholics in all walks of life in Ulster today.

And do you welcome that?

IP Snr: I do welcome it.

IP Jnr: That's what it was like when you were a boy.

IP Snr: Mind you, there never was a trusting in those days of the Éire government. But there is a trusting of the Éire government today. There's not the same hatred between them. I mean you can go down and you can talk to them. I mean, the last time I was Dublin, the new man [the Taoiseach, Enda Kenny] asked me to come and see him, which I did. He says, 'I want to show you a room', and he took me down to a room [in Farmleigh House, the official Irish State guest house in Dublin]. And he had a room shut off, packed from ceiling to floor with letters he'd received from all over the world for the bold stand he had taken against the Pope. He says, 'That's my recommendation to you'. Says I, 'Well, I have as good a room'.

Your public position has certainly changed down the years. Back in 1969, you were throwing snowballs at Seán Lemass's car at Stormont.

IP Snr: I would have thrown more than that at him!

And in 2007, there you were, taking on the role as First Minister alongside Martin McGuinness?

IP Snr: Aye. Well, Martin did what I wanted him to. I never had any trouble with him. I had never met Martin McGuinness before and I went into the room. I just simply said to him, 'Martin, you and me can fight like devils in here all night. We can pull down the curtains and wreck the place, but where would we be and where would the people that we're supposed to represent be?' I said, 'There are things which I will not do and please don't come and ask me to do them, for I'll not be doing them. You know the things I'll not be doing for you'. And we had a perfect meeting and everything we did was with the agreement of both of us. I mean, he's very strong. He says a lot of very strong things.

So how difficult was that for you to have to work so closely in government alongside someone with the history that Martin McGuinness has?

IP Snr: It made no difference to me because he was doing things and I was doing things that we both agreed on.

But it must have been difficult because you built a political career on wanting to 'smash' Sinn Féin. Yet there you were, accepting that it was right to do what you had said for so long it would never be right to do?

IP Snr: Well, he may be a Sinn Féiner but he's a different Sinn Féiner from the old Sinn Féin. I mean, you'll hear his statements condemning [someone] who was shot. You'd never have had that. They'd have had the flags out if a boy had been shot. We must give them credit for where they are. I mean, they have come a long way, so they have.

And you accept that at face value?

IP Snr: I accept that. But we have great differences still. I mean, the thing is far from settled because he wants a United Ireland. I don't want a United Ireland and, I mean, you're better not even talking about it. Better to leave it alone.

So do you see Martin McGuinness and Gerry Adams as fellow Ulstermen? Does that unite you at least?

IP Snr: Well, I wouldn't be so sure about Adams. Adams, I don't think, has the power within the party today. I think the other man *is* the leader of the party.

But now you don't want to smash Sinn Féin?

IP Snr: No.

IP Jnr: The fact is I grew up in an age when the actual emblems of the state were anathema to republicans. The fact of the matter is we are now in a state where they are uniformly embraced. Acts of the Parliament in Northern Ireland – whether it's a Sinn Féin Minister or a Democratic Unionist Minister – are enacted by Her Majesty, the Queen. The police are embraced by the nationalist community and they're embraced by the nationalist leadership. I mean, once you've done that, you are no longer the republican that I knew you to be in the '70s and '80s when I was growing up here. On that basis, who's changed in this relationship?

And if republicans have changed, maybe unionists have changed a bit as well?

IP Jnr: I think what we had to do at that point was mellow. I mean, at the end of the day, in stark terms, we won. I wouldn't want to tell a Shinner that to their face – but we won.

So, that line about the Good Friday Agreement – republicans were too smart to admit they'd lost and unionists were too stupid to realise they'd won. Do you think there's any truth in that?

IP Jnr: Well, I think we won at St Andrew's and we won once we got the policing issue resolved. That was the Rubicon. Once a republican says it publicly and takes an oath to support the police, that's it over.

IP Snr: And then there was something else that happened. His [Martin

McGuinness's] dear mother took very ill and he came into me one day and he was weeping and I said, 'What's wrong?' And he said, 'My mum is very ill'. 'Well', I said, 'you know what you do when a person's ill and they need to die', and then both of us knelt down and I prayed for his mother. And anytime I meet him, he says, 'Remember the time you prayed for me?' Says I, 'I'll never forget it'.

How easy was that for you to do, because you've always been outspoken against Roman Catholicism?

IP Snr: Yes, but I'm not against Roman Catholics. I've always been the friend of Roman Catholics. I have worked for them. I've visited them even in prison. I worked hard for them and they know that. 'You'll not shift the big man, but you can trust him. If he says he's going to do something, it'll be done.'

Do you regret any of your more strident pronouncements down the years?

IP Snr: No, I don't. I think that if I hadn't been known as a strong man, I could never have done anything. I needed to be strong and I needed to be strong with my own people as well.

But here's the question for a lot of people: was it worth sinking Sunningdale[1], with all the misery that came after that, only to come to the table again in 2007?

IP Snr: Yes because it would never have worked.

But if you could go back to 1969 and meet the young, vigorous, outspoken Ian Paisley of then, do you think he would feel betrayed by the Ian Paisley of 2007 who sat down in government with Martin McGuinness?

IP Snr: Not at all. It was the best thing we ever did, getting peace. Look at the lives have been saved through what happened and look at the way the Protestant population took it. No other person could have done that.

1 The Sunningdale Agreement was an attempt to establish a power-sharing government at Stormont. It was signed at Sunningdale Park in Berkshire in December 1973 but foundered the following year because of unionist opposition to its all-Ireland dimension.

Did you ever think that you would listen to the head of the IRA saying, 'You've got to condemn this shooting. This shooting shouldn't have taken place. Go and get the information to the police'? What would have happened if there'd been no Ian Paisley in the country? I have a very deep respect from the Roman Catholic population and always had in my own constituency. They came out and voted for me publicly – even in Ballycastle. It all worked out and I think we just need to let the thing sit. If more Roman Catholics joined the police, that would be good, so it would.

So how should history judge you and your contribution to Ulster?
IP Snr: Well, I think the judgment is the results. We have leaders that would have been rejoicing and marching when policemen were shot who tell the people to go to the police station and give information. We have a reasonable fellowship between both sides of the community. It's not perfect, but there's no country in which you get perfection after what we have come through and, as I said, we have come through well – very well. I think we've a lot to thank Almighty God for. I think there's a lot of work still to be done. We could be in places with blood running in the streets still, but it's not. Thank God for it. And Roman Catholic people and IRA people and Orange people – they are all talking together today. They're producing peace. They are working together and there's all sorts of committees through the country bringing them together. I went into a meeting six years ago in Londonderry and I met all the ruffians there and I went round and shook hands with them all and one man said, 'I wouldn't shake hands with you'. And I said, 'That's very good. Thank God for a hand that you won't shake hands with'. And all his mates laughed at him. At the end of the meeting he says, 'Mr Paisley, can I say something?' He says, 'I'm sorry I said what I did'. And he said, 'I'm glad you said what you said to me'. And that man has been a supporter of mine ever since. He was a very devout one on the other side, so he was. But he realised the day for the violence that we have had in Ireland is all over. There's no future for that. Everybody'll not be pleased but it'll be peace and it'll be prosperity for us. That's what we need. Look at all these young children that are growing up. They've all to get jobs. I don't want to see them leaving Ulster. I want them staying and making Ulster the place it should be. So, I think we've got a lot to thank God for – but the job is not finished and it's up to the people who have the responsibility to finish the job.

BARONESS BLOOD

The first Northern Ireland-born woman to be awarded a life peerage, May Blood was born in Belfast in 1938. She worked in a linen mill near the loyalist Shankill Road from 1952 to 1990 and has been a tireless community worker and campaigner for decades. She was a founding member of the Women's Coalition in 1996 and is a keen supporter of the integrated education movement. She sits in the House of Lords as a Labour peer.

We meet in her office on Belfast's Shankill Road.

May Blood:

Ulster means nothing to me; I would prefer to call this place Northern Ireland and I think when you say Ulster you're immediately putting people into a box. If I'm referring to home I always talk about Northern Ireland. I think it goes back to the days when I was a child. Ulster always seemed to be for the middle class; the people in working-class Ulster didn't matter. There was no such thing as an Ulster identity for the working-class and certainly at the outbreak of the Troubles that was proved to me. My father fought in two World Wars and we were burned out of our home by Protestants. When I was trying to get somewhere for my mum and dad to live, it didn't matter that we were from Ulster. It didn't matter that my dad fought two World Wars, we were told by the ruling bodies that we just didn't count.

Mark Carruthers:

Is that feeling partly because the established, unionist ruling elite often preferred to call this place Ulster rather than Northern Ireland?
Absolutely. My experience back in those days was you very much had to doff your cap. Working-class people just got on with life. When I went to work in the mill, it was owned by well-to-do Ulster people. On the floor of the mill you could have a mixed workforce, but in the offices you couldn't – everybody had to be a Protestant. 'Ulster' was always for the elite.

How do you think your early days helped to shape your sense of identity?

I was born off the Grosvenor Road in the shadow of the Royal Victoria Hospital and I was born into a mixed community. Our next-door neighbours were Catholic, people across the street were Catholic and we all knew we had different religions. They went to a different school, they went to a different church but we all played together and we had a sense of community. It didn't matter when it came to a crisis in someone's house that they were Catholics; all the women went to help that family and that's the way I grew up. My father was a great trade unionist and Labour man in his day and he came back very disillusioned from the Second World War. When he came home he taught us, as a family, that people were people. He was a staunch Protestant; he was in the Orange Order, but he left it because in his opinion, it had left my mother to get on with it while he was away at the war. But my father taught us to believe that the people next door were as valuable as we were because we were all working class. When I started to work in the mill I saw the clear division: on the floor it was all right to have a mixed community – Protestant and Catholic, working side-by-side – but in the office, the owners of the mill made it quite clear that they all had to be Protestant and that's where the discrimination crept in. They were a little better than us. They were middle class; we were just fodder. The office staff weren't allowed to speak to us on the shop floor; that was the division I grew up with.

So that experience shaped your political outlook?

Yes, absolutely. I always believed that you shouldn't judge people like that. If people had merit and had the capacity to move on, then I thought they should be allowed to do that. I think gradually, over the years, within the trade union movement, you learned to try and change those attitudes. We were burned out of our home by Protestants because we chose to help our Catholic neighbours one night but that never deterred me. I've never seen that as my community working against me, I just saw that as a bunch of idiots who didn't understand what was going on.

Were you always more interested in the idea of class politics than sectarian politics?

When I went into the mill to work my father gave me one piece of advice: I was not to join the trade union movement. My father believed in a trade union for men. Women didn't do that sort of thing and looking back on those days in Northern Ireland, of course, that's the way life was; women were always 'at the sink'. My mother had a full-time job and reared seven of us but, nonetheless, she was there running the house. I wasn't half an hour on the shop floor until I was asked to join the union because everybody was in the union – and I joined. Dad didn't need to know – it was only a shilling a week and he wasn't going to pay it. That's the way it was for five years and then I was at a union meeting during the lunch-break one day and I was standing at the back of the meeting. I made some comment and the union officer asked me to go up to the front and say what I had to say and he asked me to wait after the meeting and he says, 'You wouldn't like to be the shop steward?' I said, 'You've got it in one; I wouldn't like to be the shop steward!' He says, 'Would you take it for four weeks because this company is getting away with murder here?' I went back up to my workplace and was sent for immediately by the head boss and he said, 'We understand you're going to be the union representative. You'll do all that business outside the gate. You'll collect all fees outside the gate; all problems, outside the gate. You'll be allowed no time to deal with anything like that'. And I remember coming out of his office that day and thinking, if he's that against it, that's got to be good for the workers. That began my trade union education and it was the best thing that ever happened to me.

Do you look back on those days in the 1950s and 1960s as the glory days for the Shankill Road when there was full employment and a positive sense of community?

Yes. In the early '70s unemployment came on to the Shankill: the shipyard went into decline, Mackie's went into decline and the mills closed. I was in one of the last mills that didn't close until 1990. The second thing that happened was that our city fathers decided to take down all the little 'two up, two downs' and put flats in, and there was a huge outcry. There's a book written about it called *The Rape and Plunder of the Shankill*. They were taking down huge swathes of houses and moving people to Rathcoole, Antrim and Lisburn, and there were big gaps in the Shankill. In those days, there were 76,000 people living in the area; by 1990 there were only 25,000. The third thing that happened here, of course, was the Troubles and the onset of the paramilitaries. Those three things happened in the early '70s and they just took the Shankill away. I remember the area as a child when it was a very close-knit community and there was plenty of work. At the beginning of the Troubles that all stopped.

And to what extent did you feel that you had a responsibility to try to stand up to those paramilitary warlords at the time?

Well, it was extremely difficult. I remember I was coming up the Whiterock Road one day in the car and on the wall of the City Cemetery somebody had written in big letters, 'Is there a life before death?' It struck me that must be the way young people felt; young people who were corralled on both sides of the peace line into their own areas. Nobody gave a damn about them, nobody cared. People say, 'Where was your sense of identity?' But you were struggling to live, you weren't worried about Ulster or anything like that; you were just worried about how you were going to get through the next day. So, as a group of women, we set about trying to work with our Catholic friends on the other side. I worked with them every day but at night we all went our separate ways. We tried to work together and that sort of changed the system. And that has been going on ever since.

And did that experience alter your sense of identity?

Well, I suppose first of all I'm a Belfast woman; Belfast is very dear to me. And I'm Northern Irish.

What about the British/Irish dimension?

Well, it says British on my passport. I sit in the House of Lords among the elite in Britain, but I wouldn't say I feel any more at home there than I would feel in Dublin. I just feel at home in Northern Ireland.

So do you think the House of Lords is uncomfortable for you because you were a working-class activist all your life?

That, plus the fact that I think we just hang too much on this idea of being British. I can sit in the House of Lords and listen to people pontificating about abortion in Afghanistan or abortion in Uganda but if I mention Northern Ireland, people just collapse.[2] While we're British there is that difference and I just believe that's not right. I'm either British, and I get everything British – or I'm not. I have to tell you, the unionist peers in the House of Lords are probably more British than any of them because that's what they keep pontificating about. But we want to be part of the United Kingdom, so we can't pick and choose what we want to be and what we want to do within that.

How big are the challenges facing people on the Shankill Road at the moment?

There's been a lot of good progress here around a whole host of issues. When the Good Friday Agreement was signed [in 1998], people here imagined there'd be investment in the area. That's what they were told by certain political leaders. That investment never came and what's happening on the Shankill at the moment is down to individuals. During the years of the Troubles, instead of this being one community, it became six communities and you were very much identified by the paramilitary group that was in your area. I think the Shankill people themselves will have to come together and try and address this in some way and try and get young people trained to go out into the outside world. There's never going to be big jobs back in this area, it's just not going to happen.

Do you think the outside world has any real understanding of working-class loyalist areas?

No. I don't need a flag to know what I am but some people do. I always remember years ago I was interviewed by [the television presenter] Jeremy Paxman and he said to me in the course of the interview, 'Let's face it May, you Northern Ireland people are all a bunch of whingers'. And I said, 'Yes, that's quite true – but if you take away our right to whinge that's not fair

2 The terms of the 1967 Abortion Act do not extend to Northern Ireland.

because we'll become like the English and all we'll have to talk about is the weather!' In many ways that's true; there is a core of whingers in Northern Ireland and if you give them any excuse that's where they are. Unfortunately in Northern Ireland we still have young families who are being dragged back. I know one young family and they have kids aged from three to eleven and they took those kids religiously to the [flag] protests. I asked the mother and father why. They said, 'They have to learn about their culture'. Now, God help us if that's our culture.

What is the culture of people on the Shankill Road then?

Well, I think it's not just the flag coming down at the City Hall.[3] I think for a number of years here in the Shankill we've been told we're losing out in education and we're losing out on grants. Take underachievement in education: there was trouble here after a parade a few years ago and there was over one million pounds worth of damage done in the area at that time. One of the things that came out of that was underachievement in education and I was asked by the BBC what I thought. I said, 'Well, if somebody will tell me how destroying a million pounds worth of property is going to help education on the Shankill, I'd be pleased to know about it'. I was ostracised. I was called a Lundy[4], but it's true. When I went into the supermarket I was spat on. I pose this question: if we have been the ruling people for the last one hundred years, why are we the underdogs? Why is the Protestant community at the bottom of the pile? If that's the case, somewhere along the line somebody didn't bother. If you take the Catholic community, who at one time were the bottom of the pile, there's a confidence there now because their political leaders are telling them: we can do this, we can do that, we can do the other thing.

3 On 3 December 2012, Belfast City Council voted in favour of reducing the number of days the Union flag flies over City Hall to no more than eighteen designated days a year. This decision prompted weeks of protests by loyalists who interpreted the move as a diminution of their British culture.

4 A traitor, after Robert Lundy, the Governor of the City of Derry during the Jacobite siege of the city in 1689. Lundy was judged to have worked to undermine the defences of the city and, ever since, the term Lundy has been a byword for traitor by unionists and loyalists.

Do people here in this society feel they have a voice in the corridors of power or not?

No. People have lost all confidence in themselves, they've lost confidence in the system and they've lost confidence in the church. I remember a time in my church when you would have to go at eleven o'clock on Sunday morning to get a seat; now you could go at twelve o'clock and still get a seat. The church pulled away during the Troubles. The church didn't want to know on the Shankill and you only saw a church leader when there was a paramilitary funeral. And now the church wonders why they're sitting empty? We have a number of really vibrant churches beginning to try to make an impact but it's almost too late. There is good work happening here, and there's good work happening in the Lower Falls and in Short Strand, but it's all being done by local people. It's not being done by elected people.

What about the significance of the contribution made by women down the years?

The Shankill would have been way over the edge of the cliff if the women hadn't held the community here together. Women got on with what had to be done. The Shankill Women's Centre has raised education among women for years. I never believed in a women's party until we formed the Women's Coalition. I didn't want to get involved in politics in Northern Ireland because, to me, you had to be either 'orange' or 'green' and I didn't want to be either. I remember Bríd Rogers [a former deputy leader of the nationalist SDLP] asking me why and I said, 'Well, the Ulster Unionists are orange Tories and you lot are green Tories', and she nearly went ballistic but that is the absolute truth of the matter. We need to get women out to vote. I was speaking at a women's event recently here in the Shankill and it was interesting. It was a mixed event and we were talking about a border poll and there wasn't one Catholic woman in that room who said she would vote in favour of a united Ireland. They all said the same thing.

So, do you think their sense of identity has changed?

Absolutely. They all refer to themselves as Northern Irish and I think that's the way it should be. This is a very small part of the world and we're going to have to make it pay its way somehow. There is incredible strength here in

Northern Ireland, both in women and men working together, but we've got to get our act together. Nobody else is going to do it for us and certainly our political leaders aren't going to do it.

You talked earlier about how your father didn't think women should be involved in politics and how he discouraged you from joining the union when you started work at the mill. What do you think he would make of his daughter ending up Baroness Blood?

My father would turn over in his grave. My father would have been known as a communist. He believed Jesus Christ saved the world for everybody and the fact that I took a title and went into Parliament – he would never forgive me for that. My mother would have thought that it was absolutely wonderful, but my dad would never have agreed with it.

Do you not think perhaps he would be just a little bit proud of what you've achieved?

No. My father was an old-fashioned, dyed-in-the-wool man and there were certain things women didn't do – and certainly, you didn't accept a title. Believe it or not, when I got the title, I had three life-long friends and they've never spoken to me since. I got an e-mail from one, the day I accepted, to say, 'How could you let your class down? I will never forgive you'. I replied and I said, 'If you consider that your class is always going to be at the bottom of the pile, that's up to you. I do not consider that'.

You were the first woman in Northern Ireland to be offered a life peerage and presumably you accepted because you saw the Lords as a platform to use on behalf of the people you wanted to represent?

Tony Blair very kindly gave me three days to think about it. I did it, simply because all my life I'd been trying to promote people, particularly women. Women in Northern Ireland are 52% of the population but that's not reflected in power and I wanted women to grasp these opportunities. I went away and thought about it and, to be quite truthful, I believed it would have been churlish to turn it down. The Saturday before it was announced by the Prime Minister, we actually had a debate in the Women's Coalition about the House of Lords and how relevant it was. I always remember a woman at the back of the room saying, 'I don't know what we're discussing this for, because this kind of thing is never going to happen to anybody in this room'. I was sitting at the back knowing the next Saturday it was going to be announced that I was going to have this title. It was a hard time for the first year I was in the House of Lords; I don't believe I had ever experienced loneliness like it. I thought pride had led me to accept the title for my own benefit but it has worked out. You get asked to do the most extraordinary things because people think you have all this power – which you haven't. You can even see a little respect from the hardliners on the Shankill. In 1990 I ran a programme for long-term unemployed men in the area and one guy was a particular problem. He was in the UDA and he really was a hard nut to work with. We actually got him turned around in the project, and he came around to my house the day it was announced. He came in and he said, 'I just wanted to come and say I don't know what all the bloody fuss about you getting this title is – for you were always a lady'. That says it all.

Do you worry, finally, that we have a political system where it's arguably in the interests of the current crop of politicians to promote the idea of people being separate but equal?

Well, it's a valid concern in as much as I understand that if everybody loved everybody we would have real problems. We've got to get back to somewhere that bridges the gap between people on the ground and our elected leaders. The people 'on the hill' [elected representatives at Stormont] aren't listening and the people on the ground aren't talking any more because they think nobody's listening. We've got to do something about that and when I go to England or the South of Ireland I'm amazed how worked up people can get about politics. In Northern Ireland, some years ago, I wanted to join the Labour Party but I wasn't allowed. Then we got permission and I joined and I'm the only Northern Ireland Labour person in the House of Lords. We now have a vibrant Northern Ireland Labour Party here, but the party in England won't even let us contest council elections. Yet Ed Miliband, my leader, keeps talking about 'One Nation'! How confused must people be? Young people are the key to Northern Ireland and we've got to grow a new crop of politicians who don't have all this baggage on their shoulders.

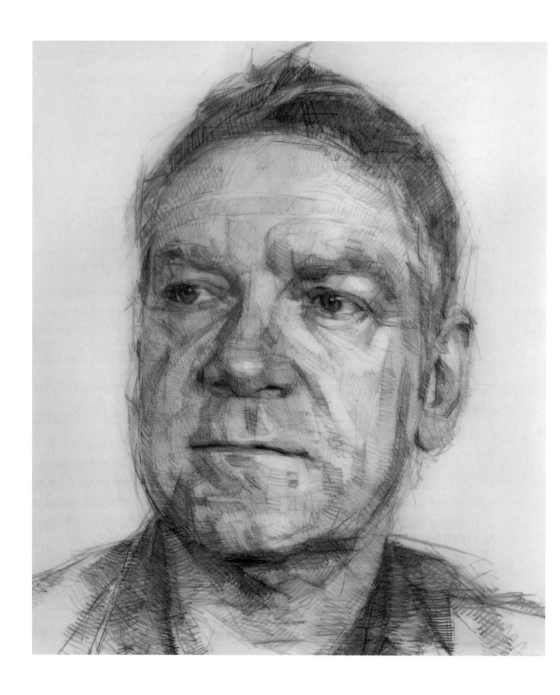

SIR KENNETH BRANAGH

One of the foremost actors of his generation, Kenneth Branagh was born in Belfast in 1960 and moved to live in England with his family at the age of nine. He trained at the Royal Academy of Dramatic Art and got his first break when he was cast as the eponymous lead in the BBC's acclaimed *Billy* plays written by Graham Reid and set in working-class, loyalist Belfast. Other television work includes *Fortunes of War, Conspiracy* and *Wallander*. He formed his own theatre company, Renaissance, in 1987. He has been nominated for five Academy Awards, the first man to be nominated in five different categories, for his work on films ranging from *Henry V* and *Hamlet* to *My Week with Marilyn*. In 2012 he was knighted for his services to drama and to the community in Northern Ireland.

We meet in his office at Pinewood Studios near London.

Kenneth Branagh:

When I think of Ulster, my mind goes to both the beauty and the grandeur of the North Antrim coast. I immediately think of something rugged, something bracing. I think of rain and vibrant, visceral things – the physicality of Ulster. I think the sound of my youth was a very elemental contrast between a very male world of clubs and drinking in pubs – not that my father was a huge drinker – and then females running everything else. My experience of Ulster is of men's voices and women's voices on the street on a bracing, very windy day. My sense of identity as a human being has never been as strong as it was in Ulster. I was growing up in the '60s in a volatile world, but my sense of security was total in the sense that it felt as though I could never get lost. I think it was highly likely that we literally knew everybody in the street and in many surrounding streets. It was a life built totally around visiting and mutual childcare. I remember years of coming home from school and going to my Auntie Irene's, who lived two doors down, before my mother came home from work. My granny gave me my lunch from school every single day when I was at the Grove

Primary School [in North Belfast]. I was walking to school on my own from a very early age because it felt entirely and utterly safe and I would always be falling into the company of other kids in the same street. We went to football matches with the school and it just seemed like you knew everyone, and the city had the feeling of a village. Large family gatherings was our entertainment – my mother doing her song, my father would do his jokes, other members of the family doing their thing – so there was the sense of identity inside a community that unquestionably was warm. I've never felt so secure, or as certain of who I was, since, to be frank.

Mark Carruthers:

But Northern Ireland was changing as you were growing up. Do you remember feeling a sense of that security blanket being removed?

Well, undoubtedly it affected things. Economically my father was doing better in a job that had taken him away, so from about '67 through to '69, he was travelling backwards and forwards from various places. My parents had considered, as many of that generation did, emigration both to Australia – where we had family – and to Canada. What made it not happen was my mother's sense of identity with the community. She was from the Shore Road and my grandfather was a docker. They had a lot of tentacles inside the Belfast working-class shipyard community, so I think it was very hard for her to go.

But eventually you did go to England. Was it a culture shock at that stage to discover that your identity was so different to that of the other children at your new school?

It was a complete culture shock because I came from a school environment that had four rows of formal desks and a system that had people tested on a weekly basis in Maths and English and that then graded them and put the people with the lowest results at the back. There was a tremendous strictness and formality to the life of the school. It felt very much rooted in its working-class community – and then I went to a school that was definitely, by contrast, middle-class. It felt literally like one had gone to a different climate. Everything about it was softer, including the classrooms themselves. I couldn't understand why they had a play corner in the classroom. There was a sand-pit and pictures and stuff on the walls. I had a good time at the Grove, but it was strict, and then I came to somewhere which was completely alien to me.

And did your new classmates regard you as alien? Did they tease you?

Yeah, they literally couldn't understand what I was saying from day one. They couldn't understand a word, not for days and days, and I didn't even understand what it was they didn't understand. I felt that I was being surrounded by people who spoke as if they were *Blue Peter* presenters. I don't know that they teased me in the first instance, but they certainly didn't understand what I was saying.

So that must have made you feel like an outsider right from the start?

I think inevitably you felt like a bit of an outsider because what you didn't have was a sense of place. The chief glamour for me was that we had a back garden, which we hadn't had before. When they first told us that we were going, I remember crying my eyes out. I couldn't understand it. The only thing that was really the lure for me was this bit of grass and the ability to play football in your own back garden. It seemed to me unimaginably luxurious. The thing that I found in Belfast was that we were just constantly on the streets and the neighbourhood network meant that you had very clear parameters about where to go and where not to go, in relation to the religious divide. And we did get stopped occasionally from playing with people.

So, you had a decade or thereabouts of a very comfortable upbringing in England and then suddenly you found yourself confronted with the part of Billy Martin in Graham Reid's first *Billy* play for the BBC, set in the backstreets of Belfast. How did you feel about that?

I went back with Colum Convey who played Ian in the piece and who was at RADA with me, just a couple of terms ahead of me. We were contemporaries for about half the time at RADA and we got on very, very well and were good friends and Colum, like me, had acquired and grown into a sort of suburban accent. That's where I had been brought up, so it was a suburban accent, and Colum was, I think, more London-based and he had a sort of London accent. I remember we got on the same plane on a Sunday to go to our first day of *Billy* rehearsals the next day. We'd done a couple of days in England at rehearsal rooms. It was October of '81 and as we got on the plane, Colum slipped back into his Belfast accent immediately and for the duration. But I found that I couldn't and it persists to this day. I was talking to an actor about it today, about what you do with accents. Do you stay in it all day? Some people are uncomfortable doing that and some aren't. Obviously I had been living with my parents most of that time and their accents were still as strong as ever, although, of course, family members said they weren't. I continued to speak in the way I'm speaking now because I felt that's who I really am and of course, many people would say to me, 'What happened to your accent? Why are you talking like that?' But, for me, it was more of a pretence to suddenly acquire and only speak in the Belfast accent because that's not who I was. It was interesting, of course, to be acting *Billy* that way, but it was kind of an escape back into that. I didn't pretend to have a Belfast accent when I wasn't actually playing a part there.

But could you identify with Billy as a character?
Definitely. There were lots of pressures on my family contemporaries, so I was aware that being a young man living through the Troubles in Belfast at that time was a very intense experience. I did have a lot of sympathy for Billy Martin and I did feel as though I knew who he was – there but for the grace of God I certainly would have gone. If we'd decided to stay where we were, my father wouldn't necessarily have had the kind of financial opportunity that he turned out to have.

The argument is often made that the *Billy* plays were the first time that particular Ulster identity – working-class, Protestant and loyalist – was portrayed to the wider UK audience. Does that ring true to you?
It does. It was my very first job and so my instinct was that I would show this script to my mum and dad. My father said, 'That's the last thing you want to do. You don't want to touch that'. He was quite upset about it and I didn't understand why. I realised that it was because it was so authentic.

It also came from somebody away from home who was very, very protective of the place's image and his concern was that it would somehow reflect badly on the people of Belfast and on that particular community. But in the end when they saw it, well, they both were amazed by it. Quite aside from me being in it, I think they felt that it did talk very powerfully about working-class life.

So, where does all of that leave you now in terms of your identity?
Well, one thing that strikes me is that I feel an intense admiration for the journey of the peace process over my lifetime. I was seven years old when I was first aware of what was a Catholic name and what was a Protestant name, even though my parents were absolutely and explicitly determined that we would take no exception to anyone because of their religious views. This was just something that they repeatedly said, even though they were absolutely from a Belfast, Protestant, working-class community. The street we lived in happened to have a mix, actually, but it was mainly Protestant with quite a number of Catholics. But from about '67, I feel as though I heard and saw the first television news reports of rioting in Derry. That's the connection that I make. When I went back to do the first *Billy* play, I think a bit of me thought as soon as I walk off this plane I'm going to have to duck in case bullets are flying around, because one had seen so much television footage. But across the subsequent decades, the incredible journey from the extremity of division and violence is an extraordinary achievement. So, I suppose when people ask me, I refer to myself as Irish – although I'm very, very conscious of being an Irishman from the North.

So it's an Irishness which is Belfast-based, rather than in any sense Dublin-based?
Yeah, but I believe there are many characteristics of Irishness up and down the island. There is much that is shared – but it's the wind of the North that I feel. I'm an Irishman who's got his collar up against the cold, as it were – the wind off the water, the wind off the harbour. My relationship to Ireland is that Belfast-connected, industrial, water-led thing – and also the cragginess of the North Antrim coast. These are somehow in the blood for me.

What about your sense of Britishness, though, which must be there after living in England for forty years, never mind that early experience of growing up in Belfast? You still reportedly support Linfield Football Club, for example…

I think the sense of identity that is so strongly implanted and imprinted is absolutely associated with what I would call the non-politically charged rituals of working-class, extended community life, which involves allegiance to a football team. I remember having a conversation with my father about names – about what made a Catholic name and what made a Protestant name. I heard various impassioned conversations in our household about the principle of treating everybody equally and the principle of equal opportunity. And cutting right across what could sometimes be these rigid, very imposing, fixed religious or political positions, was this incredible sense of humour, a sense of the ridiculous, a sense of the satirical. On the whole my dad didn't necessarily think it was a good thing to go and watch the parades and the bands. I think he basically felt that there were fringe elements that used the cover of that to, as it were, indulge in other things that he didn't really approve of. Certainly, running up to the Twelfth I remember, very clearly, having an up-turned box and a couple of sticks from the park, singing the songs and doing the marching. We would do that up and down that back entry in McAuley Street, no question. You heard the songs and you sang them, but you had no idea what you were saying. The idea of marching and the celebration and the ritual of it was definitely infectious.

The plays of Shakespeare have been a huge part of your working life, but how much interest do you have today in the great canon of Irish work?

Some people argue, and argue with some persuasiveness, that the Elizabethan dialect would have been pronounced much closer to a modern Ulster sound than the sort of mellifluous English tones that are sometimes associated with it. I've always thought that my interest and passion for Shakespeare comes out of an Irish love of words and literature. I still notice today, across Ireland, the breadth of conversation, the lack of nervousness or caution about talking about a range of issues, whether it be politics or football. There was never any embarrassment talking about poetry or music. There was no snobbery about being an intellectual, in a strange way. People in Belfast, even in our circle, didn't mind people talking 'big stuff' or being philosophical or metaphorical because that was meat and drink to everybody. Everybody had a view on that. Shakespeare wasn't hived off as something untouchable, so my connection was not to an English lyric tradition, it was to a gutsy, earthier, Irish tradition that just loved the sound of words for their own sake – that loved the music of words.

Does that, at least in part, explain the seemingly large number of actors from this part of the world who have been so successful – from Liam Neeson and Ciarán Hinds, through James Nesbitt and Adrian Dunbar, to Frances Tomelty?

Well, first of all, I like all those people. I like their work very much and what I notice is their acting is very full of curiosity. They combine a certain relish and love of performance with a very open-minded look out into the world. Their Irishness, I think, informs their work in certain kinds of ways that makes them quite distinctive and rich as performers. All those actors, I would say, have a tremendously soulful quality. I would say they've got a sort of poetic dimension available to them very easily in ways that other people don't necessarily have.

Despite the fact that you haven't lived in Northern Ireland for a very long time, do you still feel that it remains at the heart of who you are?

Even if I didn't want to acknowledge it or felt uncomfortable with it, it is. Going back to do *The Painkiller* [a Sean Foley play at the Lyric Theatre in Belfast in October 2011] it just felt as if the years had completely disappeared. It was as if I'd been there two minutes ago. It was the same when I got off the plane for the first *Billy* play. I hadn't lived there for any amount of time for eleven years and it was as if I had never been away.

It must be quite a burden, I imagine, when you are back there to see how you are regarded by people who want to claim you as one of their own?

Well, there's a tremendous sense of pride that people have. I share that about those other actors, for instance. I'm always feeling, 'go on Adie, go on

Liam'. I enjoy that. I'm proud in that way. I feel that about sporting figures. I feel that about any kind of success in the film industry. I feel that about Cinemagic [the Belfast-based children's film festival]. I feel that about the Lyric. I choose not to feel a burden. People care about what you do and are proud of what you do. What stops it from becoming a burden is that the people, face-to-face, will use the same sort of sense of humour on me. They don't get all churchy with me.

Well, if they thought you were getting too big for your boots, they'd soon tell you.

Yes, exactly. Part of their pride is if they believe you are still the same person and that you are all the things that you need to be, to be Northern Irish – which is you don't get above yourself. You've got to be down to earth. You've got to have that friendliness and directness. You can't be up yourself, as someone put it to me. You must be ready to tease and be teased.

JOE BROLLY

Well known as both a sports analyst and barrister, Joe Brolly was born in 1969 and brought up in a republican home in the village of Dungiven in County Derry. The son of politically active parents, he boarded at St. Patrick's Grammar School, Armagh and went on to study law at Trinity College Dublin from 1987 to 1991. In 1993 he was a member of the Derry side that won the GAA's Ulster Championship and the county's first All-Ireland Senior Football Championship. He now writes several newspaper columns on Gaelic football and appears regularly as a radio and television pundit. As a barrister, he specialises in criminal law and has been involved in several high-profile cases in the past.

We meet near his home in South Belfast.

Joe Brolly:

I have no hang-ups about anything. I would as easily go and watch Crossmaglen Rangers playing as I would go over to Ravenhill to watch Ulster playing rugby. I was brought up in Dungiven, where the GAA and republicanism were articles of faith. The GAA is like the Masons without the funny handshakes. It's a very close-knit yet very open community. My first sense of identity would be through the GAA. We would have been totally supportive of the Provos in Dungiven. We viewed them as 'ours'. I remember all the songs: 'Come Out Ye Black and Tans' and 'The Men Behind The Wire'. My father was interned. One morning he was taken away in a van and almost three years later our next-door neighbour, who had a phone, knocked the front door and said to my mother, 'Anne, Francie has to be collected at Long Kesh [also known as the Maze Prison]'. That evening he was sitting in the kitchen eating oxtail soup as if he had never been away. We were very small when it happened and although my mother must have been very lonely, we were cushioned from it and no fuss was made. There would certainly not be a week goes by, that I wouldn't think about the hunger strike [in 1981, in which ten republican prisoners died]. I daresay that would be the case for a lot of people; it was a very vivid thing for us because one of the hunger strikers was Kevin Lynch, who lived in the town and hurled for Dungiven and Derry. The surprising thing to me is how quickly society here has changed. My own children would not believe the way things were. As I matured, my own approach was transformed.

Mark Carruthers:

For the better?

For the better, of course. I chat to policemen all the time now. My club, St Brigid's in Belfast, was the first club to play a Gaelic match against the PSNI. There was a time when you wouldn't have spoken to the police. The old RUC were totally boycotted in Dungiven. I remember well, before I married Emma, who's a Ballymena woman, how she couldn't believe when she first came to Dungiven that the police weren't allowed into any of the shops. I never heard a sectarian sentiment in our house. Identity is forged in the North through your schooling system and your background. I've been privileged to meet, at very close quarters, people like Peter Robinson and Edwin Poots [the DUP Health Minister], people who would have been *bête noires* in our society in the past. Peter would have been seen as a Catholic-hater and a GAA-hater, but there we were, meeting in Stormont. And Edwin Poots seems to be, in all my dealings with him, just an ordinary, decent man. My experience wouldn't be typical, because I went away when I was eleven to boarding school in St Pat's Armagh before going on to Trinity. If you're in that sort of middle-class world you learn to mix more naturally. I learned a lot when I was in university. Trinity was the big turning point.

So that time in Dublin shaped your sense of identity in a significant way?

Trinity is very cosmopolitan, like Oxford without the snobbery. We talked and we had terrific debating societies and the prejudices that I had were swiftly banished. I used to suffer quite a bit of ribbing at the start. Opinions that went without question in the Dungiven changing room were held up to ridicule. I soon realised that 'Prods bad, Fenians good' was not going to cut the mustard in the real world.

And did that make you think again?

Oh yes, because you realise they're right. Things that would have been normal sentiments in your own community, that everybody subscribed to, suddenly people were saying, 'Catch yourself on. Do you know how ridiculous that is?' You're living in a community where everyone espouses the same view. There wouldn't have been a person in the Dungiven Gaelic football world who took a different view. We would have all just adopted the same view: the police were black bastards, Prods were a different breed than we were, all that sort of thing. That outlook was erased during the time I was in Trinity, because you could see, once you were being challenged, that those views were extremely silly.

What about your parents? They're both members of Sinn Féin and your mother is still a councillor in Limavady.

They are good Gaels: Irish-speakers, traditional musicians and so on, and they are very liberal politically. They would have a lot of Protestant friends. I remember one particular DUP politician on the council was very friendly with my mother and he used to come up to our house. They were very fond of him and he'd make regular visits, but there was a time when they were forbidden to speak. The word had come down from on high in the DUP that [its representatives] were forbidden to speak to the Sinn Féiners. This middle-aged man was sneaking up to our house on the understanding that nobody would be told that he'd been there. He'd arrive at Christmas time with a ham, like a smuggler crossing the border.

And how do you feel when you're watching an Ulster rugby match at Ravenhill?

Well, it's just, when they all sing 'Stand Up for the Ulstermen'. It's just instinctively...

Do you not feel like an Ulsterman?

Well, I enjoy going up there and people are polite and encouraging, and it's a very welcoming environment, but emotionally I wouldn't get the vibe that I get when I'm standing at a GAA match and they're playing 'Amhrán na bhFiann' ['The Soldiers' Song', the Irish national anthem]. It's a different vibe and I think emotionally, I wouldn't have the sense of belonging to that other tradition – because it is another tradition, and I have no sense of belonging to it. I don't know what it's like to come through the Protestant background and to be immersed in that different sort of culture, to be English in your outlook rather than Irish. I'd be Irish in my outlook. I still think that ultimately you're segregated via your schooling systems, and that's where the separation occurs. They're all great schools and I would have no difficulty if one of my sons wanted to go to Methody [Methodist College Belfast] or somewhere like that. But the more natural progression is to go to a Catholic school. My first son is in St Malachy's College. We like the ethos and all of that. Schooling undoubtedly segregates, but I don't think it presents a serious problem as long as everything continues to move the way it's moving. Society is changing. Think of the difference now versus twenty years ago – society here is unrecognisable.

But there are still problems where certain communities, rightly or wrongly, feel their identity is under attack.

All you can look for in any society is equality. I suspect that the vast majority of people in Northern Ireland give the notion of a United Ireland very little thought. I also suspect very strongly that Sinn Féin privately accept that – so the big thing in reality is equality. There's going to be an increasing homogenisation of society, the way it is homogenised in all civilised countries with the internet, Twitter and Facebook. People are increasingly internationalised. On a daily basis they're living in a bigger place than Northern Ireland and they're communicating instantly with other people all over the world and picking up ideas from everywhere. Young people nowadays I think, for example, don't have any issues about homosexuality or anything like that, which is about time. My kids don't know anything about the Troubles. They don't know anything about their grandfather being interned or their uncle being on the blanket and we'd never mention anything about that. If I started to explain it all to them they would think I was pulling their legs.

You've talked about your parents having quite an enlightened view nowadays, but if you wind the clock back thirty years, was that the case?

The Troubles were never ever mentioned in our house. Not a whisper. But in the town in general, there was no question whose team we were on. As a primary school boy, I can remember Lord Mountbatten being blown up in 1979[5]. The people in Dungiven saw it as a victory. Boys raised their fists at each other, saying, 'Did you hear, we got him?' Things like that would make your blood run cold now. It was a dreadful atrocity. Sitting here now, I think, 'Jesus Christ, what were we thinking of?' That's some mark of how things have changed in society. My son, Toirealach, for example, plays rugby for Malone and goes to the Cubs. Recently, he came home with a picture he'd drawn of the Queen. At Cub services, he sings 'God Save the Queen' with his pals. If I happen to be there, or his mother happens to be there, to pick him up and they're playing the anthem, we stand for it. These things are just a matter of simple respect nowadays. If I had announced thirty years ago I was intending to play rugby and arrived home from school with a drawing of the Queen, they would have been sending for the men in the white coats.

So in terms of your identity now, how would you describe yourself? Is your *Irishness* first and foremost what you are, or would you think of yourself more broadly as European?

No, I would say increasingly as I get older I'm a sentimentalist. I'm very comfortable whatever the tag is. I'm very comfortable with my life and who I am; I'm very comfortable with whoever I meet. I would say my first real love is the GAA, so I don't know whether you would call that Irishness or not. I think it brings a great sense of community and I feel very strongly part of that. The Catholic Church was once the glue of Irish society. Now it has been replaced by the GAA.

So, is that a strong sense of 'Ulster community' in the GAA?

Yes. There's a very strong sense of Ulster community in the GAA. If Ulster

5 Lord Mountbatten, the Queen's second cousin and former Viceroy of India, was killed along with three others when the IRA blew up his fishing boat off the village of Mullaghmore in County Sligo in the Republic of Ireland in August 1979.

are playing any of the other provinces in the GAA, I would be emotionally attached to the Ulster lads. This would be a common sentiment amongst Northern Gaels. We would say, 'Always support the Ulster team'.

So could you comfortably describe yourself as an Ulsterman?
I think so. I'm definitely an Ulsterman, more so than an Irishman. I do agree with the general sentiment that the concept of nationalism is outdated. I think there's a lot of people in the nationalist community who would say now, 'Well, I'm not that fussed whether there's a United Ireland or not. It wouldn't matter to me too much, but I'm very strongly wedded to the GAA'. The GAA is the big sense of belonging and the big sense of identity for Northern Catholics.

Would you ever describe yourself as Northern Irish?
I wouldn't baulk at that at all. I think there is a discrete Northern Irish identity. I like the North and I like the people here. I think we're not far away from being a civilised and decent society. I think we're modest and I think people are generally neighbourly, and I would feel more Northern Irish than Irish. I like Northern Irish society, I must say, and I like the long-term trend of it. I feel that I belong here. I don't feel any sense of alienation and I think that Catholics in general no longer feel any sense of alienation. It is ironic, is it not, that the sense of alienation that's felt is in some of the Protestant areas, but I think that's more about topical, private despair rather than any great philosophical issue.

Is it also about what they hear from their leaders?
Well, their leaders need to stop the pandering.

Their leaders tell them that their identity is being stripped away.
Yes, which is a big load of bollocks. I don't know how it's being stripped away, because Ulster Protestantism is a very strong brand. You've got the First Minister, you've got a very strong political party in the DUP, a very formidable party which can represent their people very well if they choose to. Ulster rugby is also a very strong brand now and it gives a lot of people here a lot of pleasure. The Ulster Catholic has got the GAA, which is voluntary and creates a very strong sense of community. The problem for

the Protestant working-class community is that they don't have a GAA. There isn't that cohesive sense of community that we have through the GAA. That's the one big identifiable thing that creates happiness and satisfaction amongst Northern Catholics. That's what creates cohesion and motivation. It is also a springboard for other things too, forging business relationships and the like. I would say, generally speaking, there's a contentment with being a Northern Catholic that there wasn't twenty years ago. People are very relaxed about their sense of belonging, and sectarianism – in the sense of 'a Protestant Ulster for a Protestant people' – has largely disappeared. The reality is that the vast majority of people here now are just getting on with their lives, and it's steadily becoming a damn good society, as good as you could hope for. I think that our political system has worked very well in the sense of forcing the parties to work together and has the potential to work even better as prejudice is eroded. I don't know what the DUP have to fear or what they think they have to fear. The big argument's won; they just need to show more confidence now and get on with leading. It's the same with Sinn Féin; their argument's won. It is time for these two powerhouses to get on with the real business of politics.

And you don't believe that things can go back to the violent ways of the past?
Not at all. Nobody wants that. The thing about the Provos was everybody supported them. They got cover in the nationalist community – emotional support and actual support. Nobody supports what's going on now.

In terms of the dissidents?
Yes. It's just a couple of hundred people, you know. It's pathetic stuff. Empty slogans and tired old lines. Pearse would be turning in his grave. It's just unfortunate that every now and again a family is going to have to experience a futile death because of them.

SIMON CALLOW

Simon Callow's connection with Ulster dates back to 1968 when he arrived at Queen's University Belfast to study English. Born in London in 1949, he is one of Britain's most distinguished actors, though he is also renowned as a writer and director. On stage he has worked at the National Theatre and the Royal Shakespeare Company and has toured internationally in one-man shows playing Charles Dickens and William Shakespeare. His film credits include *Amadeus* and *Four Weddings and a Funeral*. He has written biographies of Charles Laughton, Orson Welles and Oscar Wilde, and published several autobiographical books which have attracted considerable critical acclaim.

We meet in Belfast during the run of his most recent one-man show, *The Man Jesus*.

Simon Callow:

It's complicated, isn't it? Before I came here, I don't think I was all that aware even of the word 'Ulster'; I was much more aware of the words 'Northern Ireland'. If you mean Ulster very specifically, I think that's an entirely political phrase. I think of Carson and I think of 'Ulster will fight and Ulster will be right' rather than any specific culture or experience of people. My best friend's mother was a physiotherapist from Northern Ireland, a minister's daughter. She was an incredibly proper and uptight woman who, however, could be got to relax wonderfully with a couple of glasses of Irish whiskey. That was set as an image for me of what people in Northern Ireland might be like, which is that there was this quite severe exterior, which then melted a bit. Kathleen was the only Northern Irish person that I'd ever met and I was very aware that there was a big difference between the South and the North and it mainly meant Catholic versus Protestant, essentially. That was the sort of vague information I had in my head when I came to Northern Ireland. When I was working at the Old Vic and I decided I was going to become an actor, my plan was to get out of England. I thought, well, Dublin's the place. I'll go to Trinity, and I made a few investigations and discovered that I couldn't get a grant from the British government to go to Trinity and I thought, I'll go to Queen's in Belfast, it'll be much the same. Dickens, of course, adored Belfast. He read at the Ulster Hall twice. When he started doing the reading tours, Belfast was one of his first dates and he says that the Belfast audience was the best he knew in the world anywhere. Anyway, I didn't know, to my shame, very much about Irish history. It wasn't until I came here that I began to understand something of what it was all about.

Mark Carruthers:

So you must have got quite a shock when you arrived here in Belfast in September 1968?

Yes, exactly, and you must remember that I'd come straight from working at the Old Vic Theatre, at its glamorous height with Laurence Olivier, Maggie Smith, Bob Stephens and Joan Plowright and all of that lot. I went to school in Chelsea which, of course, was the epicentre of the Swinging Sixties. My way to school was down the King's Road and everything seemed to be blossoming in England into something completely unprecedented. We were in the throes of this fabulous sort of orgasm in London and then I hit Belfast and it did feel like travelling back in some sort of time capsule to another world and another time. It was night by the time I arrived; it was very cold and it was very wet. I came over on the boat and I do remember walking from the city centre, up through Shaftsbury Square and up University Road and all I could think was that everybody had died because there was nobody on the streets at all. The buildings all seemed black and one looked in vain for anywhere to eat, or any sign of life. There was that funny little Chinese restaurant on the corner of University Square which we later concluded was run as a political operation. There was a big picture of Chairman Mao in the kitchen and the waiters looked at us with such hatred, we were convinced that the monosodium glutamate was laced with some kind of killing substance. It was the only place on a Sunday night to be found open in Belfast. I went to the Students' Union. I had my first experience of the Ulster Fry, which seemed to be all that was available, and some chocolate – and something told me that this wasn't going to be a culinary heaven one way or the other. So, my first impression was pretty bleak. I saw the splendid

Lanyon Building, but otherwise it just seemed bleak. Then, of course, I rather quickly discovered a completely different Belfast: all the glorious pubs and the general warmth and wit of the people was just delicious. Of course the university is not representative of Ulster in general, or even Belfast in particular, especially since it was in the throes of a great political upheaval.

The university, of course, was at the heart of the emerging civil rights movement.

Totally. People's Democracy was in full flower and I joined it immediately. I went to meetings and all the rest of it. We had our orators, people like Michael Farrell, who was genuinely extraordinary. It was like being at the Easter Rising or something. He was just epic and visionary, inspiring; his eloquence was great. There was someone who was his sort of side kick, called Cyril Toman, who had a little beard and looked like Trotsky, and Eamonn McCann and Bernadette [Devlin, now McAliskey], who struck me violently one day. I've never quite known why, but I think it was probably just because my English accent grated on her ears. 'Oh you!' she'd say, and hit me on the shoulder, in the Students' Union Bar. I then discovered what the dynamics of the political situation were and I went to hear Paisley preach in his church. My God! I didn't think particularly of myself as a Catholic, but to hear Catholics spoken of as a sub-human species – or, perhaps worse, as the Devil's own agents – was quite an extraordinary phenomenon. That wasn't just like going back a hundred years, it was like going back to the medieval period! I found him utterly terrifying, but it was interesting. Then I began to understand some of the complexities of life. The bed and breakfast place where I was staying was run by Mrs Clark with her weirdly unsymmetrical eyes. She was an absolute Dickensian character, rather frothy and bubbly and lovely, but I went to see Paisley and I came back to her one day and I said, 'God, I've just heard the Reverend Paisley – that's awful'. She suddenly became very serious and she said, 'He's not wrong, you know'. And then I realised this woman was absolutely straight down the line and she just bought it completely, the whole idea that the Catholics were 'immoral'. I tried to argue with her; it was just absolutely ridiculous. Her house was a mad but rather wonderful place, though I was actually awfully glad to get out of it.

And by this stage you'd fallen in with the drama society crowd at Queen's?

I'd signed up with Dramsoc on the very first day and they were tremendously pleased to hear that I'd come from the Old Vic Theatre – albeit the box office. Neil Morton, who was then the president of Dramsoc, became a very close friend, as did Annie McCartney and Seamus McKee and Anna Carragher. Suddenly this idea that Belfast was some kind of an isolated place, culturally rather than physically, was quickly dispelled. There was a definite feeling of Queen's as a refuge for the slightly odd and out of kilter at the time. There was Marcus Wheeler, the Professor of Slavonic Studies. Marcus was a wonderful, sensitive, delightful man. I don't know how he came to be at Queen's, but there was something a little melancholy and distant about Marcus as well, which was delightful. Then there was this extraordinary figure of J C Herivel – John Herivel – who, I imagine, was everybody's ideal of what a tutor in a university should be. He always wore a three-piece suit and there was a fire on in his study and he'd toast crumpets for us and make us tea. He was a most charming, engaging man, and when I finally decided at the end of the year that I was going to run away to become an actor, John Herivel, who couldn't have been a less 'actorly' man said, 'You know, the way you speak about it makes me think I'd like to run away and become an actor too'. It wasn't until two years ago, when John Herivel died and his obituaries came out, that it transpired that he was one of the key code-breakers at Bletchley Park – but he never mentioned it; nobody ever mentioned it.[6]

So there was a traditional dimension to your Queen's experience and in sharp contrast to that there was your involvement in the People's Democracy march in Belfast in October 1968. You took part in that?

I took part in that and I, like many other people, had my shins whacked by the batons of the B-Specials, who were hectoring and frightening people.

6 John Herivel was born in Belfast in 1918 and attended Methodist College Belfast. He arrived at Bletchley Park in January 1940 and is remembered primarily for his discovery of what was soon dubbed the 'Herivel tip' or 'Herivelismus': an insight into the habits of the German operators of the Enigma cipher machine which bolstered the work of the Bletchley code breakers.

We all did speeches and so on, and I was there when we *summoned* the government to come and give an account of themselves. The Minister of Education was Captain Long – everyone was a captain in those days – a weasely, little man with spectacles, a little pencil moustache and a few henchmen. He was just about to start speaking and somebody shouted out from the back, 'Would Captain Long, as a token of his good faith, ask all the Special Branch men in the room to leave?' Captain Long said, 'As a token of good faith, will all the Special Branch men leave the room?' About a third of the room emptied out; it was just extraordinary. I was busily doing all the things one did: handing out leaflets and so on, speaking about the cause and the dignity and the equality we were fighting for, for Catholics, and so on. A woman came up to me and she said to me, obviously hearing my accent, 'Sonny, it's not your problem. Go home'. And I sort of thought, in my way, maybe that is right. I felt a little false suddenly. I believed in the cause, absolutely – but it wasn't my cause, it's true. I had no idea that it would turn to violence, but one knew that the genie was out of the bottle. By '69 we knew that it wasn't going to go away, that there wasn't going to be a wonderful accord and that everybody would say, 'Yes, we were wrong all along, we'll change'. But most of my days were obsessed by putting on plays and thinking about theatre. You can't live in an atmosphere like that and not relate to it, but while I wasn't washing my hands of it, I was suddenly realising that I was an outsider for the first time.

So was your decision to leave Queen's at the end of your first year about furthering your acting career, or was it about feeling uncomfortable with the way things were unfolding on the streets here?

A bit of both. Neil [Morton] and other people said if I wanted to be President of Dramsoc, the job was mine. I was full of ideas and it was a wonderful place in which to do all these things, but I knew that I had to train as an actor. I knew that I just didn't know what the fuck I was doing; I felt so dreadful as an actor. I felt so uncomfortable in what I was doing and I thought the only way through this is to train really hard, and also, I suppose, I had a certain nostalgia for the world of the London theatre. Although, the Festival was a remarkable phenomenon and this was in the early days of

Michael Emerson's creation.[7] The Chancellor of the university was no less a person than Sir Tyrone Guthrie whose work I had seen and who directed, at the Old Vic when I was there, *Volpone* and *Tartuffe*. I saw him striding around, this huge 6' 5" man, and Tony Guthrie, did a production here with Colin Blakely at the Grand Opera House, and that was a world-class production; it was absolutely brilliant. You'd walk into the Lanyon Building and there on the notices, it would just suddenly say that Sir Tyrone Guthrie would be reading short stories in the Science Lecture Room at five o'clock and so we'd all go along and Tony would be sitting there with twelve books in front of him. At five o'clock we'd all keep quiet and he'd say, 'William Trevor', and he'd read a short story by William Trevor. He'd read six or seven or eight short stories – nothing else, no commentary, nothing at all. It would just be done perfectly; wonderfully lucid and elegant readings; funny, beautifully timed. 'Thank you for your attention. Good night', and he'd go. Tyrone Guthrie was, at the time, a colossus of world theatre, one of the great directors of the twentieth century, and there he was in Queen's. He was an odd figure altogether, I suppose, but that was phenomenal; that was so exciting. It was absolutely formative for me in so many ways.

And you also encountered that other acting great, Micheál Mac Liammóir, during your time at Queen's.

When we came to do the Irish University Drama Association Festival, in which our contribution was *The Seagull*. They'd hired for £1,000 – I remember the amount, and everybody thought it was astounding – Micheál Mac Liammóir to come and adjudicate the festival and do two performances in *The Importance of Being Oscar*. As soon as I heard that, I went to *Gown* [the student newspaper] and I said I want to do an interview with Micheál Mac Liammóir. That was the first time I ever went to Dublin and I found him in his beautiful little terraced house in Harcourt Terrace and he gave me the most dazzling interview. I had some ancient old tape recorder and I came back and couldn't quite struggle through the process of transcribing it, and so I just did it from memory and wrote this rather glittering piece and I sent it to him and he said, 'Dear boy, this is one of the few times I've

7 The Belfast Festival at Queen's was founded by Michael Emerson in 1962.

been quoted correctly'. I don't know whether he said that ironically or not, but anyway that was also a big first for me because it was the first writing I'd ever done that was printed. Then when Micheál came up to do the festival I appointed myself his dresser and amanuensis, because his eyesight was so terrible. He couldn't write any more and so I would write down all his judgements. My housemate, Bill Mitchell, and I looked after Mac Liammóir, and that too was an absolutely transforming experience. He was a great raconteur, of course, but he was an Englishman who had chosen, as we all know now, to become Irish. He'd made up a name for himself, made up an entire history of being born in Cork – not a bit of truth in that – and he had elected not to be English. He elected to be Irish, to commit himself to this country, even though it was the South. He sort of took into himself what he thought to be the quintessence of Irishness.

And have you, after a long association with this place down the years, formed a notion of what the Ulster character is?

It's very interesting because, at heart, I would say that Micheál Mac Liammóir was right: the Irishness of Ireland goes all the way through the country. But people from here are Irish in many, many ways – in the sense of fantasy, the sense of humour, the sense of fatalism with a profound tendency to melancholy, a great obsession with alcohol, all of these things. But whereas in the South, it seems to me, there's a more bipolar tendency, rather like Russians – this kind of weird alternation between angel and devil, drunk and scholar, piety and debauchery, this sort of endless swinging back and forth – that's tempered here by the strong infusion of Calvinism and Scottish thinking. Although it's a strong infusion and it's deep, to me it's a kind of carapace which can quite easily be removed. It's very interesting, for example, that, generally speaking, people in Belfast would be much less expansive than people in the South. In the South they'll embrace you and if you give a good performance in Ireland – or if you give any performance in Ireland – they'll shower you with praise and hymn you to the very heights. In Belfast it's less; people are much more reserved and a little bit shy about that kind of thing.

Maybe there's an in-built modesty here.

There is a modesty – or you might call it an inhibition. It's a bit of both and I think there is a certain emotional constriction in many relationships that I perceive – and yet there's a kind of extraordinary good-heartedness about so many people that I know here.

Is that perhaps why there's a certain suspicion here of theatre, for example?

Yes, I think that's a very important and difficult aspect of the situation. There are two things that I'm very aware of: one is that sense of puritanism, shall we say; the feeling that the theatre is a bit extravagant, a bit over the top. 'Do you really have to stand up on stage and do that? Couldn't you just say those things in a drawing room?' There's a slight sense of that. The other thing is – and this is something that I've also noticed with my Russian friends – there's a kind of ingrained lack of optimism. I mean, God knows, you've been through a lot, but there's a feeling that it's turned out bad again and what else would you expect? It's not quite so bad as it is in Russia, where everybody says, 'Well, we Russians are just bad people, so everything we do will turn bad'. It's not quite like that here, of course. It's more a feeling that life is always going to be a struggle and it's very hard for people in Northern Ireland to celebrate. I've even noticed it at the Lyric. You have the greatest new theatre that I've ever been in and indeed acted in; it's a world-class building and you really would hope that people would embrace that idea and absolutely fill it, but there is something kind of standoffish about it – we mustn't get carried away, we mustn't go beyond ourselves or get big-headed about it. You really want the trumpets to blare in a situation like that – and that, I think, is something that's a little bit ingrained in the temperament. It's a sort of solid, put-your-heads-down, nose-to-the-grindstone culture. The theatre, I suppose we have to say, is a 'Cavalier' activity – as opposed to a 'Roundhead' one – and it therefore doesn't sit so well with Belfast or Northern Ireland, which is not a 'Cavalier' culture at all.

Which is why, arguably, any theatre that *is* here is so important?
Absolutely, that's right. There's another little thing that I've noticed more this time than I've ever noticed before: the use of the word 'wee'; everything is 'wee'. 'Would you like a wee cup of tea? Would you like a wee drink? Would you just wait a wee moment?' Everything is made a little bit small, cosy, comfortable, easy to deal with, and, of course, people are very, very nice, but sometimes one would quite welcome something a little more abrasive; a little more assertiveness. We're all dealing with recession and all kinds of other problems, but it seemed to me, about ten years ago, that Northern Ireland was really throwing off its past sense of not being quite in the first league, or not having the right to stand up and beat its chest. It was throwing that off and now, finally, the city shows all the marks of it – the fantastic new buildings and the wonderful restoration of the old buildings and the opening up of it all, which was so exciting and exhilarating. But the steam seems to have rather run out of that a bit and people are settling back into a slight feeling of 'it'll never get much better'. But it's just so immeasurably better than it was. I really would love to think that Belfast would see itself as a world-class city, which it really is. But maybe that's to do with economics, and still the absolute curse of Northern Ireland is that people want to get out all the time to prove themselves. The challenge is that you have to make it so exciting that people don't want to leave. So you've got to generate a sense, especially among the young generation, that it's up to them to make it; they can make this thing extraordinary. There's still a strong sense, much stronger here than in London, of a middle-aged hold on the central command points of the culture. The wonderful thing about England is that there is an unending vitality in the theatre of new writing and new directing – so you get plays by sixteen-year-olds at the Royal Court, and it's fantastic. Of course, they're not Shakespeare, but it's happening and they have a feeling that they're coming into an inheritance and that's something I feel very strongly isn't present here. I'm only an occasional, though regular, visitor, but this is my impression. I do love Belfast. I'm a great ambassador for the city. I sing its praises at all times – but with the reservations I've expressed.

WILLIAM CRAWLEY

The broadcaster William Crawley was born and brought up in North Belfast. Educated at Queen's University Belfast and Princeton Theological Seminary, he was a Presbyterian minister before embarking on a successful career in the media. He currently presents a range of religious, current affairs and cultural programmes on BBC Radio Ulster and BBC Radio 4. He has also written and presented several television series and documentaries on subjects ranging from the Ulster Covenant to the Vatican and from global warming to the history of Ireland's Presbyterians.

We meet in South Belfast.

William Crawley:

My relationship with the concept of Ulster has changed over my lifetime, because when I grew up in North Belfast during the Troubles in the 1970s, the word 'Ulster' was connected to a certain type of Northern Ireland, a certain type of hegemony and a certain type of paramilitarism. The use of the word 'Ulster' in terrorist-group names meant that I felt distant from it during my teens in particular. At that point, I'd been to the United States, where I'd lived with a Catholic family for six weeks on one of those deprived-children schemes and had come back with a mind that was willing to challenge what I was hearing in Northern Ireland more than perhaps my background in a working-class loyalist community might have prepared me for.

I also had a distance from the category of Irishness, which came from my background as well, because that was a sort of ingrained alien category within the household I grew up in. Britishness, I increasingly had a distance from, because I didn't really understand how all these things hung together. So over the years my attitude to all of these categories has changed and my attitude to the Ulster category in particular has changed in that, of all the things that we can describe ourselves as in Northern Ireland – whether it's Irish, Northern Irish, British, Ulster, European, citizen of the world, whatever – many of them are exclusionary, many of them cause problems for some section of the community. But there is a kind of unifying dimension to the term 'Ulster', when it is disconnected from some of those historical relationships.

Mark Carruthers:

What happened during your early years in working-class North Belfast, do you think, that meant you didn't quite see things politically in the way that most of your peers did?

I think one of the experiences I had was simply going with Project Children to the United States and living with a Catholic family in their home and going on holiday with them. At the age of nine that was a major transformation in my life, because when I came back I didn't believe a lot of what I was being told any more. Catholics were not demonic figures. The category of Catholic, for example, was completely humanised. When I thought of Catholic, I thought of that family, and I thought of the church they took me to and their friends, and I thought of the things we have in common. I also thought of the generosity of my mother in allowing me to go and spend a summer with a Catholic family at the height of the Troubles in upstate New York in the United States.

How big a challenge do you think that was for your mother and for your family?

It was a massive challenge for her. She had to really think about it. The way she reasoned it was, in her language, this was the chance of a lifetime. Of course now we all travel all around the world. It doesn't seem like travelling to New York is the chance of a lifetime any more, but in 1979 Northern Ireland in a working-class unionist, Protestant home, that was the chance of a lifetime in her world. My mother hardly ever travelled. She was over the age of sixty before she crossed the border and visited Dublin, and when she came back I asked her what it was like and she said, 'They're just like us'.

And was that a big revelation to her, do you think?

I think it probably was a revelation to her, and that again is an interesting aspect of this Ulster category, because there is something about the personality of people from Ulster, whether you define it as six-counties Ulster or nine-counties Ulster, that sets us apart from other parts of these islands. There's a kind of group identity that almost emerges – partly our argumentativeness or cantankerousness, and our sense of humour. We have more in common with each other often, I think, than people realise.

Of course, the reality is that you were changed by that visit to the United States, when a lot of your contemporaries might have gone on the very same visit and come back unchanged.

Another part of the mix was that my mother believed that education was the way in which you could walk out of poverty. I lived in a very impoverished home and had quite a difficult childhood with a father who was alcoholic and could be violent and a mother who was working as a cleaner with three different jobs a day. She believed that education was the way in which you could actually walk your way out of that and she was absolutely right. But, of course, the danger of education is that it makes you think and it introduces you to writers and thinkers who come from a different place, and that can change your own understanding of your place in the world.

Do you think some people who share your background are fearful of exposure to new ideas?

Yes. Bernard Shaw once said that travel was the greatest antidote to intolerance and whether you travel geographically, or whether you travel intellectually, through books and through education, that kind of journey can be threatening to some people. I embrace it; I'm open to the journey. I'm open to having all my ideas challenged; I'm not threatened by the challenge. But there are people, for sure – not just within unionism, incidentally, but within nationalism and republicanism as well – who might be threatened by that kind of travel. I met someone recently, a former IRA man who was still a very solid republican, and he struggles with this category of Northern Irishness. His daughter told him that she considers herself Northern Irish and he is offended by this. Why would you want to be called that? You're Irish! That was a journey too far for him.

It's almost a sub-division of Irishness. It's Irishness with a little bit added on for clarification, maybe.

And it all depends whether you capitalise the 'N' in 'Northern'. Northern Ireland is a political entity. Whether it should be is something people obviously debate, but it's a fact in law that Northern Ireland exists as a political entity and I am from Northern Ireland and I was born into this place and I sense my Northern Irishness, for sure. I talked to a woman not so long ago who told me why she had moved from describing herself as British to Northern Irish, and it's a very interesting story. She said that since the Good Friday Agreement of 1998 she had travelled more in Northern Ireland, been to places she would not have felt comfortable going to before, and had developed new friendships, particularly with Catholics and people from republican and nationalist backgrounds. One of her closest friends describes herself as Irish and she has learned a lot about her identity and her community in the last ten or so years. She has decided to call herself Northern Irish because that other person is now such a part of her sense of identity that she wants to include the word 'Irish' in her own sense of identity. That's a very interesting journey in itself.

But for her it still needs a degree of qualification?

Yes. It doesn't for me in that I'm sure everyone you've talked to is referencing John Hewitt and the wide spectrum of identities that people have here. I feel Northern Irish, I feel Irish, I feel British, I feel European and I feel internationalist, and I think growing up in a place which has a contested political identity has emphasised for me the liminality of our place. We're part something and part something else. We're in between all kinds of things – even in terms of our transatlantic relationship in Northern Ireland – we're historically in between the American and European experience. We can either embrace that or challenge it. I think it can actually be something that's worth exploring. I think all notions of political, national and cultural identity are fragile and they're not as solid as people think they are. What is Britishness? What is European-ness? These are things that we are still debating.

Do you feel more comfortable with the notion of Ulster identity now, though, than you did twenty years ago?

Absolutely I do, yes.

Would you describe yourself as an Ulsterman?

I'm definitely an Ulsterman, I certainly am. I'm an Ulsterman in the sense that John Hewitt was an Ulsterman or that C. S. Lewis was an Ulsterman. It doesn't have to be a threatening category. In fact, it's a bridging category because someone who is from a republican background in Belfast, who describes himself as Irish and wouldn't even go as far as Northern Irish, is still an Ulsterman or an Ulsterwoman. Whether they define it as six-counties or nine-counties is neither here nor there. We are of this place, we are part of this place, which is Ulster, and someone from a British background in Belfast, who wouldn't even describe themselves as Irish would, I suspect, not struggle to call themselves an Ulsterman or Ulsterwoman as well. The Ulster terminology has declined over the years in some circles, but if you go back and look at the old newsreels from the 1960s and '70s you hear the word 'Ulster' being used a lot. You don't hear it being used now. I mean, I work for Radio Ulster and yet the term Ulster would hardly ever be used in a news programme to describe Northern Ireland. It would be a fairly odd thing these days to describe Northern Ireland as Ulster, but that was very common in the '70s.

Living and working in Northern Ireland, do you look equally to London and to Dublin both socially and professionally?

I'm open to both directions. I've grown up watching *Question Time* on the BBC or *Yes, Prime Minister*. I grew up knowing absolutely nothing about the Republic except that it existed. At the age of ten or eleven at school I could have told you half of Margaret Thatcher's Cabinet members. I was obsessive about that kind of anorak political stuff at that age, but if you'd asked me about the Irish Cabinet, I couldn't have told you anything about it. The Good Friday Agreement is a big turning point in terms of these conversations. We know a lot more about the politics of the South now than we ever did. I'm not even sure how much republicans in Northern Ireland in the 1970s really knew about the politics of the South. They just knew that they didn't like the politics of the North, but now we know a great deal more about it.

What about the spiritual journey you've been on? You grew up in a Presbyterian household, you became a Presbyterian minister and then you turned your back on it and you now describe yourself as a lapsed Protestant.

Well, I wouldn't go as far as saying I grew up in a Presbyterian household. I grew up in a non-churchgoing household – nominally Presbyterian – that didn't darken the door of the church except at funerals or baptisms or weddings, so there wasn't a religious context in my home that I was aware of. There was a culturally religious context. The word 'Protestant' would have been used a lot. The word 'Presbyterian' would hardly have been used. I remember that being an issue for me when I was a kid, wondering why are people so wedded to this category of Protestant and yet they don't go to church? These were complex questions at the age of sixteen or so. I had an evangelical religious conversion experience which was not connected to my parents, needless to say, but was connected to one of my sisters and her husband, who took me to some events. I had one of those Billy Graham-type experiences, actually, where you walk up an aisle in the middle of a tent and kneel at the front at the altar. Then I became connected to a local Presbyterian church, which had very conservative ideas on just about anything. Women didn't even lift the offering in the church; Catholics were part of a non-Christian church and so on. The early fundamentalism that would have defined the character of my faith dissolved through my intellectual journey and was fully dissolved, really, by the time I got to Princeton in the United States in the mid-'90s. Eventually I worked in New York as an assistant minister in a church on Fifth Avenue and then I discovered that, actually, the Presbyterian family was not like the Irish Presbyterian family, but was a very broad church which had often revolutionary and radical ideas at the heart of it. I came back to Northern

Ireland struggling with an Irish Presbyterian church experience that didn't reflect the global experience of Presbyterianism. It's a church apart in many ways and eventually I had to make a decision about whether I was going to remain within that context or return to the United States. I made a decision that the next stage of my journey would be better lived out in the context of a journalistic career rather than one within a denomination that I was struggling to find my own place in.

So after that exposure to a breadth of thinking, you found it frustrating to come back here and be reminded of how fundamentally certain sections of the community hold on to more traditional beliefs?

Well it can be frustrating, can't it? At times I feel like we're isolated from the conversation that's going on in the rest of the world. It feels like we're cut off at times. When you speak to politicians about some of the cultural debates of our day, in private they can give you very different answers from what you hear them say on the radio and television. It's as if they have to play to the galleries of their own electorate at times and things are said in the media here which you know you wouldn't hear in London or Edinburgh. Some of the rhetoric about sexuality, for example, can be near-homophobic, or fully unreconstructed homophobia, and if it was said in other parts of the BBC in London or Edinburgh, I think there would be hell to pay for allowing someone to be on the radio for half an hour saying some of these things. But because of the context of Northern Ireland, and the fact that we have a very different kind of cultural context, there is freedom to express some of those views. I'm for free speech, for sure, but I do feel like we have an under-evolved conversation about many of the issues of our day – from moral issues like abortion and reproduction through to the creation-evolution debate. If you spent any time in Northern Ireland, you would think that no other religion existed in the world except Christianity.

What about the cultural journey that you've gone on in recent years? You've started to learn the Irish language, though there's nothing new in that as far as Presbyterianism is concerned, of course.

No, there's a long tradition of that.

But it's remarkable how many people, even within the Presbyterian Church, are not aware of that tradition.

I think you're right. I had a serving Presbyterian Moderator on my Sunday morning radio programme and I pointed out to him that in the late nineteenth century, Presbyterian ministers were required to be able to preach in Irish before they would be ordained, and that was news to him. So there is a kind of secret history here. It's a complicated history in terms of the Presbyterian relationship with the Irish language. There have been a number of books written telling the story of how Presbyterianism in Belfast and beyond saved the Irish language in many ways, but on the other hand there is that story of Presbyterians and other Protestants being threatened by the Irish language, especially in the period since the 1960s when the Irish language was seen as a kind of republican fetish that Presbyterians and Protestants couldn't generally engage in. That's changing. I mean, there's sixty to ninety Protestants as we speak sitting in East Belfast learning Irish on the Newtownards Road as part of a project run by Linda Ervine, the late David Ervine's [the former leader of the Progressive Unionist Party] sister-in-law. Brian Ervine, David's brother, is learning Irish as well. Of course, during the Troubles there were people like Gusty Spence learning Irish in prisons, but I think we're on a journey of the de-politicisation of the Irish language.

So is it about claiming the language back?

Claiming a part of it. It seems odd to me that we have this thing called the Irish language and we're on this island called Ireland and you could get through a lifetime of never exploring it. Michael Longley, the poet, said to me in an interview some years ago that it was one of the great sadnesses of his life that he had never explored the Irish language, simply for the poetry and the rich poetic traditions of it. That was one of the prompts to me to explore it. I want to be able to read Irish poetry in Irish, rather than as I do now in translations from other poets. I have a number of friends who are Irish-language speakers. One of my closest friends, Dáithí Murray, is my tutor. *Múinteoir* is the Irish word for 'tutor' and he is head of Irish in St. Paul's School in Bessbrook, near Newry, and he is a wonderful teacher.

I would have a drink with Dáithí years ago and Irish would come into the conversation and he would start to give me the etymology of a word or tell me this beautiful story about the history of a particular phrase or parable in Irish and there's no doubt in my mind it's a beautiful language to listen to when it's spoken well. When you listen to Michael D. Higgins, the Irish President, speak Irish it's just beautiful and I want some of that beauty. Why wouldn't I? So there's a kind of a cultural inclination towards Irish which comes from friendship, wanting to build on the friendships that already exist, wanting to reach out and explore parts of the territory that I haven't got into. I'm going to parts of Belfast to learn Irish that I didn't go to before, and that's great and I'm making friends there and I'm not threatened by that, not in the least. I mean, I'll get a tweet from Carál Ní Chuilín, the Culture Minister, in Irish and I'll respond to it and that's quite a nice thing to be able to do. I'm discovering an online community of Irish tweeters, which is fun, and I'm also developing a richer understanding of Ireland's cultural, political, historical and literary story through this.

And you don't sense any political dimension to that, do you, because there are people who are, for whatever reason, very hostile towards the Irish language?
Some people are. The politicisation of Irish has been there, there's no doubt about that. I think there were some unionists – and still are – who would hear a Sinn Féin speech begin with a little bit of Irish and finish with a bit of *go raibh míle maith agaith*, or something like that, and they would see that as a republican language. There's no doubt that has been there and is there for some people, but I detect that there's less of it. It's quite remarkable, actually, the number of Protestants coming forward in Northern Ireland to learn Irish. It simply can't be the case that all those people regard this as a republican language. That is playing into the de-politicisation of Irishness in the way that the term 'Northern Irish' is becoming de-politicised. Some people from an unreconstructed republican background might have thought the term 'Northern Irish' was an alien term or a partitionist term, but you can still be a republican and describe yourself as Northern Irish. You can still be Protestant and unionist and speak the Irish language.

And yet we had a very public and, many people would say, very damaging cultural battle recently in Belfast concerning the flying of the Union flag over the City Hall.

What we know about the evolutionary psychology of groups is that when a group feels under threat it will be prepared to do almost anything to defend its integrity. That's how groups survive and pass on their identity to another generation and the powerful voices within a group can signal that they are under threat and the consequence of that signalling is that the group responds in certain predictable ways. It will hit out or it will become defensive. What we have seen in the flags protest, really, is a signalling by some political voices that we are under threat. So if you don't want to see that defensive response, you have to have responsible political voices who articulate a different message that the group is not under threat – there's no need to be threatened by a new flags policy which puts the flags up at certain times of the year but not at other times. I mean, that was a big move for Sinn Féin, you might say. Sinn Féin actually voted to put the British flag on the City Hall in Belfast and unionism could have played that differently and said that's a success story, that's the first time that's ever happened. But no, it didn't play it that way. I've been at some of the meetings with protestors and I've spoken to people on the streets and it's clear that they are getting this signal that they are under threat: our identity is being erased, our Britishness is being taken from us. They are feeling vulnerable. In fact, on my programme we did a report with Eamon Phoenix, the historian, on how much Britishness is visible in Belfast in terms of symbolism, street names, memorials, all kinds of things. It's steeped in Britishness – and you've got the Good Friday Agreement, which has a double lock in terms of any possible reunified Ireland: it can't happen without the consent principle. There are all kinds of messages which can be signalled to a community which give them assurances that they're not under threat.

One of the great contradictions, then, is that within a mile of where those individuals took to the streets to demonstrate their fear that their Britishness is under threat, people from that very same community are sitting down to learn Irish.

It depends who you are taking your messages from, doesn't it? I mean, this was my story as well when I was a teenager growing up on the Mount Vernon estate in North Belfast. Some of the people I went to school with became murderers and went to prison, and they were obviously getting different kinds of messages to the messages I was getting. That's why travel is very important. Journeying, whether it's through books or education or geographical travel, is very important because you open yourself up to different messages and then you can hear a different story from different places which changes your sense of self and your sense of security in yourself. I think the people who are prepared to call themselves Northern Irish these days, for example, have less of a sense of threat about their personal identity than people who baulk at that term.

Do you find it frustrating that this place is perceived very often in a negative way by the world, when it has also produced some of the finest playwrights, poets, musicians and scientists who've lived?

It's undoubtedly the case that given the relative size of Northern Ireland, we are punching above our weight in many of those areas, from sport to science. It's a very complex story about Northern Ireland which is not often told because media representations of Northern Ireland will be visually driven and a riot is a better picture on a television screen than a picture of Ernest Walton [the Waterford-born scientist who studied at Methodist College Belfast] splitting the atom or winning the Nobel Prize for Physics. But those stories are there as well and it's a complicated mix that we should reflect. I think we bring it on ourselves at times, and our politicians don't help. I think we could do with some better politicians who are more willing to drive towards a progressive future which integrates every voice in Northern Ireland, rather than doing the easy thing, which is to work out what your cultural constituency is and play to the gallery in ways that replicate the status quo for another generation. We are a segregated community and that segregation can be cynically exploited by certain politicians – though not all of them, for sure. We need courageous, ambitious, forward-looking politicians who are prepared to say, 'I want a different kind of Ulster and a different kind of Northern Ireland experience' – and where is the evidence that we have these voices?

PROFESSOR GERALD DAWE

Gerald Dawe is a poet and academic who was born in Belfast in 1952. He studied English at the New University of Ulster in Coleraine, graduating in 1974. He then moved to Galway to continue his studies and to teach at University College Galway. He was appointed a Fellow of Trinity College Dublin in 2004 and is the inaugural director of the Oscar Wilde Centre for Irish Writing. He has published eight collections of poetry, most recently *Selected Poems* (2012), and several volumes of essays, including *My Mother-City* and *The Proper Word* (both 2007). Much of his poetry and prose reflects a deep interest in the diversity of Northern Ireland's cultural inheritance.

We meet on one of his frequent visits back to the city of his birth.

Gerald Dawe:

I have to think of Ulster historically in my own life. It didn't really exist when I was a young boy – I'd no consciousness of a place called Ulster. There was Belfast and there was England, and Ulster as an idea or as a place just didn't function. I suppose you thought about Ulster as something that was associated with the Royal Ulster Constabulary. It was a naming thing for horticulture or milk boards, but it wasn't actually a working, living, breathing idea. When I went to university in Coleraine, I became aware of an Ulster that was physical. As an actual place, it only really became meaningful when I left Belfast and started to experience the rest of Northern Ireland. Ulster became part of that. The other side of that story is that I also started to become interested in the Irish language and Ulster; *Ulaidh*, the notion of Ulster's roots in Gaelic culture, started to become interesting. Then, needless to say, the Troubles problematised the notion of Ulster. Was it the old Gaelic Ulster, or was it the Ulster of the UVF? Somewhere in between those two, Ulster evaporated in my head.

Mark Carruthers:

Would you ever have described yourself as an Ulsterman?

Never. Maybe in a joking way, but I've always felt myself to be a Belfast
man. It sounds parochial, but then I don't see Belfast as a parochial place.
I would have lots of difficulties in my head, irony being one, with calling
myself an Ulsterman. I see myself as a Belfast man and I see Belfast as being
a capital of Ireland – not the capital, but one of the capitals of Ireland. I don't
mean it in any kind of dismissive way, but I couldn't see myself as being an
Ulsterman.

**And if you have to take the next step in terms of your identity, do you opt
for Northern Irish, Irish, British?**

I'm very relaxed about all of that and I always have been. Half of my own
family grew up in London. We were back and forth when I was a kid.
London as a city-state influenced almost all my education; everything about
the clothes I wore when I was a young fellow growing up. The whole bric-a-
brac of my intellectual life, growing up, was all very much predicated upon
England. Whether or not that converted into seeing myself as being British,
I'm not sure. I've never felt myself defined by being British or wanting to be
British. I suppose when I was very young I had this emotional, idealistic,
nostalgic notion of Irishness, and that was the home I wanted to associate
myself with. But it was a wide church of Irishness and it was very much
a cultural identification with the literature and with the landscape that I
discovered when I was a young fellow going there in the early seventies, and
then ultimately settling there. I think if I was put to the pin of my collar, I
could never define myself as being British, and certainly not English, but
I see lots of connections with the place – emotionally, temperamentally,
economically – and I've never felt strained or uncomfortable in any part of
Britain. I've never felt I had to fake my way as an Irishman there. I never felt
I had to crawl across a bridge and say, 'Here, I'm British, and there, I'm Irish'.
It's always been a fluid thing and the notion that you had to define yourself
by a label is something I've always fought against.

So you don't buy the idea that identity is a fixed concept?

No, that's been the death of us here. The notion that you are defined by one block – that there's an equation or a fusion that you fit into from birth and that stays with you for the rest of your life and you can't work your way out of – to me that's totalitarianism and a form of dogmatism which we have paid for over many years in this country and in this city. It's actually possible to have a 'pizza' approach: a little bit of this and a little bit of that, because that's what we all are. If you go back into all our families I would say that many people in Northern Ireland can identify 'non' elements – 'non-Irish' elements or 'non Northern-Irish' elements – in their family make-up. So why should it have been frozen from 1922 on that if you're Protestant you must be unionist or loyalist and therefore you're British? That kind of lock put into somebody's life from an early age is a disaster – and it's the same from the other point of view. I know many Catholics from Northern Ireland who are very relaxed about the British elements of their upbringing from a cultural and political point of view.

You obviously have a very sophisticated notion of your identity and where you come from. Has it frustrated you that, despite that, people may well have made assumptions about you and about what you believe?

I'll tell you an anecdote that was a real eye-opener to me. There was a guy I knew professionally, and in fact I became quite pally with him. He has since died, but he was quite a prominent figure in the Irish cultural scene in the Republic and he was launching a magazine that I edited called *Krino* in Dublin. This was back in the mid to late eighties. He stood up and he spoke about the magazine and he said, 'It's so good to have someone from a unionist background, from the other side, here in Dublin, in Ireland, in the Republic, contributing in this way'. Now, I never, ever in my life voted unionist. I know my mother was a liberal unionist, but I never saw myself as being a unionist, whatever about the right of others to decide and so describe themselves. I was absolutely furious. It's not that I wanted to be described as a nationalist or a republican, that's not the point, but what actually amazed me was that this guy, who I knew and respected, actually still had the mindset that if you were from Belfast and a Protestant, you had to think and act in a certain way. That stereotype is still there in the South.

Something of a partitionist mentality, then?

It is, ironically. You can see the dead stare at dinner parties when the North comes into view and I'm banging on about this place and about how people's attention politically and culturally still should be focused here. It's as viable and significant and substantial a cultural part of Ireland as anywhere else on the island, and in a way I've been truly evangelical about it. I often felt that there's a kind of expectation in the Republic that if you're Protestant and from the North, you think and act in a certain way. Even your poetry and your art is of a certain kind, and for a short period of my life I devoted energy trying to challenge that. The reality is that stereotypes are conforming and consoling to people who don't want to think; that's basically it. They are a lazy man or woman's way of getting themselves through life. So, yes, I did experience that. It's not so prevalent now because the achievements of writers from this city have chipped away at those stereotypes. The clichés about Protestantism don't have the same potency as they once had, you know: business-minded, somewhat chaste in their attitudes to business management, unforthcoming, emotionally somewhat blunt. How we challenge that, I don't know. I think it's only ever going to be challenged politically, and unfortunately, politics lags behind rather than inspires. The lack of confidence and genuine self-belief in where we are in Northern Ireland you can see in Stormont. There's not a liberating sense of the future; it's two steps forward and three steps back, and there seems to be a certain degree of enjoying that too.

But do you get a sense when you come back here that society is generally better now that it was several years ago?

I think for the younger generation it's a much better place to live, particularly for those who are working and can enjoy it. I come back regularly. It's not as if I feel that I'm in exile somewhere else, but I have to say, looking at it with a really cold eye, that core problem of sectarianism has not been addressed and I think the reason why it hasn't is because there's a political investment in it remaining. So long as this society votes on a sectarian headcount, it's not going to change. The only other way it's going to change is through the people's will; through education and through active engagement with the other community. I just can't see how else it's going to happen. The big power blocks – Sinn Féin on one side and the DUP on the other – have too much invested in this society in terms of the control of the communities and consequently these pillars or silos, as everybody refers to them now, have remained in place. I was fortunate to integrate with other communities and see different ways of life here in Belfast, but also in other parts of Ireland and Europe, and that opens the flaps; you can actually see and experience things differently.

You've written quite a bit about two key cultural figures from this part of the world – the singer Van Morrison and the playwright Stewart Parker. Why are you so interested in them?

Well, Morrison is a huge figure. He's honoured in this city, but in Ireland he predates everything in terms of international achievement as a singer/ songwriter. The notion of a young fellow heading over to the States and making a reputation for himself in the hardest business imaginable as a twenty-one or twenty-two-year-old was a huge achievement. At one stage I thought it was taken far too much for granted and it hadn't been respected enough, so that's why I felt I'd throw in my ha'pence worth. I also thought there was something about his achievement in relation to the way he could bring together different elements of, shall we call it, cultural Protestantism. There's an almost Lawrence-like rapturous sense of language in his writing, as there is in his extraordinary theatrical performance. He seemed to me to be so true to this place, that on one level you have a sense of the buttoned-up-ness of Belfast Protestantism – it's very correct and proper, everything is in its place. Yet when you actually look at the language of the church here and the language of Protestantism outside the church, it's full of this extraordinary yearning and transcendent desire to understand nature and to understand the world. It's a very powerful language and it hadn't been recognised publicly in the wider community. To me, Van Morrison seemed the embodiment of a very powerful element of our culture which wasn't understood.

And what about Stewart Parker?

Stewart Parker is a different kettle of fish altogether. It's intriguing; they're a similar age and both from East Belfast. Parker's achievement as a writer seemed to me to be second to none, but he was not identified with any one place outside Belfast. In terms of his professional life, he moved around; he moved in and out of different kinds of stories and I suppose one of the things that he had, which is not to everyone's taste, was a wonderful sense of irony. That is a sophistication which doesn't sit so easily in the more caricatured versions of Irish theatre. It may be a Northern thing, I don't know. So those two fellows, Morrison and Parker, seem to me to be the foundation stones for a different kind of understanding of Irish literature and Irish culture. They brought to the table a different kind of reality, which is not 'Irish' and which is not 'not Irish'.

Not traditionally Gaelic Irish, is that what you mean?

Yes, exactly. To me, the whole thing that I've been banging on about for so long about Ireland and Irishness is that fluidity – that sense that there is mobility inside the country and there always has been, but which, for political reasons, was closed down. I do feel there's still an imperative inside the unionist community – and I deliberately say unionist, not Protestant, community – that if you concede, you're losing. There's a kind of cultural psychology, which I understand, that's almost like 'what we have, we hold'.

Is it a kind of siege mentality?

It is, and I defy anybody who grew up in that culture to say there's not an element of them psychologically that's still affected by that. It creates on the positive side a sense of persistence, consistency, commitment and engagement, but on the other side it can also produce fearfulness, intransigence, self-righteousness and a bullying nature. That has come out of that seed-bed of siege mentality.

Do you think, perhaps for religious reasons, it's also partly to do with a great suspicion of culture and the arts because they are challenging and they often ask difficult questions?

Yes. I've been thinking about that, off and on, over many years. If you think of the tradition of music in Protestantism in Northern Ireland, it's huge;

it's everywhere. The church itself, albeit with its chaste furnitures and its chaste interiors, is a theatre. The Methodist hall, the Baptist hall, the Church of Ireland, the Presbyterian Church – in all those sects, theatre is a part of Protestantism. But there's some strange kind of notion that the secular theatre is suspicious. Let me try to be direct about this: I think the class nature of Protestantism led theatre and literature to be identified with the middle class and the upper middle class. There were certain texts associated with the working class – *The Ragged-Trousered Philanthropist*, the work of George Orwell, those more left-wing texts – but the intellectual leadership of Protestantism in Northern Ireland didn't step outside its very safe and narrow confines.

Do you have a clear sense of how things might unfold politically and culturally here in future?
Yes, I think if we continue down the road of flags and emblems and marches, there's no future. If we go down that road we're going to corrode and we're going to end up back where we started; there's going to be flashpoint after flashpoint and there'll be some sustenance given to the nutcases and the violence junkies to come back out, though it won't be on any big scale. On the positive side, I think once you start to see the influence of the immigrant population beginning to force its way into society here culturally, that will start to break things up a bit. And I'm confident that the younger generation doesn't want to get involved in all the old arguments, though they're not politically influential yet. I think we owe ourselves optimism because if we don't have it, it's a great denial. I think we need to get away from the politics of identity and start recalibrating the culture in a different kind of way, so that rather than being pressed by these big pillars of unionism and nationalism, we actually start from the ground up to rethink our history. It's all going to be about how this generation and subsequent generations discover who they are; that's where the action's going to be.

BARRY DOUGLAS

Born in Belfast in 1960, Barry Douglas is a renowned classical pianist and conductor. He attended Methodist College Belfast and famously won the gold medal in the International Tchaikovsky Competition in 1986, the first non-Russian pianist to do so since 1958. As well as a busy schedule as a soloist and conductor, he is the founder and Artistic Director of the Camerata Ireland orchestra. Until recently he based himself in Paris, but has now returned with his family to live in Lurgan in County Armagh.

We meet for lunch at his home.

Barry Douglas:

Ulster for me is a kind of a melancholy term because the great history of this part of this island has, in a sense, been hijacked and used for another purpose. This is not a political statement. It's a shame that we can't just say we're Ulstermen, Ulster people, Ulsterwomen, without all of those other layers that have contaminated the great strengths of what Ulster has always been about. Even if you have a very definite, particular view on history and on identity, still the history of Scotland and Ulster and Ireland are so intertwined. It's a complete waste of time to worry too much about that because we're all Celtic people. I mean, the Scots actually came from Ireland first, then a few of them went back in the Plantation. Ireland was never really a united country anyway. It was always a country that was warring with itself.

Mark Carruthers:

So, growing up in Belfast, going to school in Methody – were you aware of what was happening around you politically, or were you sheltered from it?

I was aware of it. My mother was from Sligo and my father was from Belfast but I was so involved in music and I was so manic about working and practising and preparing and training that I didn't really get involved that much and also, I was living in a part of Belfast which was relatively unscathed, around the Botanic Gardens. We were at the top of the Holyland, which was anything but holy. There were the odd skirmishes down the lower Ormeau Road but that was way down there. That was a mile away, and a world away. My family on my mother's side is both Protestant and Catholic, so I've never had any issue one way or the other. I just think the whole thing is sad and tired and passé.

Do you think that your experience as an international concert pianist and conductor gives you a different perspective on things?

It will, but that's not the crucial element. I think the crucial element is education and, of course, the travelling is an education and living somewhere else is an education and when it comes down to it, we're all human beings trying to eke out an existence and then, one day, we die. Why don't we just get on and have fun? I know that seems a very trite way of putting it but living abroad, seeing how foreigners react to where you're from, is eye-opening. In Paris, when I speak French, I have an accent and they think I'm either American or German. And so I say, 'Look, I'm actually from Ireland'. Then some of them try to keep the conversation going, 'Oh, are you from the English part or the Irish part?' 'Well', I say, 'there is no English part'. I say I'm actually Irish but, yes, I am from the part of Ireland which is part of the United Kingdom.

So you say Irish rather than British? Would you ever say British, or is that just too complicated?

Well, actually, we are all British, even in the Republic of Ireland, because we're from the British Isles. And it's nothing to do with the United Kingdom – it's just this area is the British Isles. Technically speaking, going back to Roman times, geographically – not politically – it is actually the British Isles. Unfortunately or fortunately; I don't know.

Have you consciously sought to promote both aspects of your identity, then? With Camerata, for example, your joint patrons are the Queen and the President of Ireland. It's an all-island organisation working with musicians and young people from both parts of the island – so are you comfortable with both aspects of that notion of identity, the Irishness and the Britishness?

I am but I want to play to the strengths of both jurisdictions on this island. I want to find the positive links. It's always been about the border and differences and cross-community but I think that's the wrong way to look at it. I think we should build on the strengths. It's funny, I used to always be beaten up when I was a kid in Belfast and I've had two fingers broken by thugs who beat me up. They would say, 'Are you Protestant?' or they'd say, 'Are you Catholic?' and no matter what you answered, you still got beaten up. So, my mother sent me to judo and, after that, they didn't beat me up again because I knew how to defend myself. But after one particularly vicious thrashing, a policeman came and reprimanded the guy responsible. He was a Protestant policeman and he was actually a Gospel singer in his spare time. And he said to me, 'I don't know why people fight each other here. We've so much in common. The North has so much in common with the South – we should be building on that'. And I was really impressed by that. I was twelve, and here was this guy from a particular tradition who was this born-again Christian figure and he was talking about being friends and getting on. He talked about having more in common with each other than we have with English people and I was really impressed with that.

Some might say he was ahead of his time?
Yeah and he was in an institution which, of course, according to most people, was very much one-sided.

What about the adjustment your children have had to make? They spent most of their formative years living in Paris and they've now come back to a different Northern Ireland from the Northern Ireland you left.
When they came here they were the French schoolchildren.

And how did they feel about that?
They kind of like that, but they want to blend in just like any kids. They have lots of wonderful friends and it's going well but I did have to sit them down and give them a pep talk on day one on the dos and don'ts of living in this part of Ireland where you just have to be slightly aware of what it's possible to say and do and what's not possible to say and do – which is a shame. But I think that matures them. They see that there is good and bad in the world.

How interested have you been in the whole Irish canon of music and in particular, music that's been associated with this part of the island?

What I love about the contemporary composers, especially the younger composers, is that they're totally international. And they're writing great music. You may hate it, love it or be puzzled by it, but they're just following their own stars. I think that's great; they've no agenda. The one regret that I have is that we have not produced, North or South, any composer who's a Kodály, a Bartok or a Dvorak, who were able to marry the style and the essence of the music, their indigenous music, in a western European artform. Irish music is often just raw golden nuggets, but in terms of making some really sophisticated form like O'Casey has done in the theatre or like Seamus Heaney has done in poetry, we just haven't had that.

So the likes of Hamilton Harty and Charles Wood can only ever be viewed as minor composers internationally?

They did not have the far-reaching influence that some of the major names that we all are accustomed to have had. But they, nevertheless, made a very significant contribution and certainly furthered the reputation of the country, North and South.

Why do you think that is the case? Because, when you look at more contemporary, non-classical music, you can point to these impressive figures like Van Morrison or somebody like Gary Lightbody from Snow Patrol.

These guys have made huge reputations and done extremely well but I still don't see anybody who's been able to get the essence of what music from this island is about and express that in a really amazing and spectacular way.

And do you think there's somebody alive today who can do that – or have we missed the opportunity?

There may very well be someone. Certainly some people have tried but there is something about Ireland in this Western classical music form that has been very much an underachiever. I see it with young musicians that often – and there are several wonderful exceptions, thanks be to God – in general, Irish people, North and South, have a real problem expressing ourselves.

We are embarrassed by passion. We are embarrassed by direct, full-blooded expression. We go in on ourselves, we chop away at the edges. I don't know why that is. I see it all the time when I do masterclasses around the world and I say, 'Let go. Go for it'. We find that tough whereas in the theatre you see great Irish, Northern Irish, Southern Irish actors. They have no problem letting go.

People have talked about this notion of an innate Ulster reticence, a natural reservation. Is that what you're talking about?

I think it's partly tradition. We've never had a good conduit. We've never had a good development. We've never had a good system of enlightening people about what music is about. I'm not just talking about the narrow Western classical music, I'm just talking about music in general. So when we come to music, we don't go with our own instincts. We tend to adopt other people's.

And yet we have produced people who have achieved on the world stage in terms of playing and conducting – and apart from yourself, the other obvious person to mention is James Galway.

Absolutely. He's arguably the best flute player who ever walked the planet – but I'm talking about a composer.

So do you still live in hope?

I think it may happen. We may have missed the boat, though. The problem nowadays is that everybody knows everything all the time – and yet somehow, they don't know their own locale. It happened with the fall of the Soviet Union – the fantastic orchestras that existed there. Then the floodgates opened and conservatories around the world nabbed the best players and they started teaching and they started earning serious money. Now Russian orchestras are all diluted. Some of them are still wonderful, but they're all diluted. I think that's it. I think we're diluting ourselves because of the wonderful technology. It could have happened in the early twentieth century, but it might be much more difficult now to pin it down.

ADRIAN DUNBAR

The actor Adrian Dunbar was born in County Fermanagh in 1958. He co-wrote and starred in the 1991 BAFTA-nominated film *Hear My Song*. His other film work includes appearances in *The Crying Game*, *My Left Foot* and *The General*. His many television credits include *Murphy's Law*, *Cracker*, *Ashes to Ashes* and *Line of Duty*. He has worked extensively in British and Irish theatre both as an actor and a director.

We meet in Belfast's Lyric Theatre where his performance in Janet Behan's *Brendan at the Chelsea* was a recent critical and popular success.

Adrian Dunbar:

I find Ulster a very exercising question. It's a political question as well as an emotional question. When I grew up in Castle Street in Enniskillen, leading down to the castle, my first understanding that I was from Ulster was to do with facts that my father would explain to me: that this was Maguire's Castle originally, and he would go back into some of what was happening in Elizabethan times and the relationship between this part of Ulster and the rest of Ireland. Right from the get-go, I understood that Ulster was different from the rest of Ireland – and Ulster has always been different from the rest of Ireland. It's physically different. There would be a lot of artists I know who would say it's more masculine than the rest of Ireland. It's like the masculine head on this kind of female body. The south is this rolling land, whereas Ulster is a much tougher, harder place. It's got a different feeling about it and its borders are an abstraction as well. For example, Ulster once stretched nearly all the way into Sligo and down into Louth. It's a big part of Ireland. But because of what happened to Ulster – and the reasons for that are very well documented – we have become diminished in our influence over the rest of Ireland.

Mark Carruthers:

When you say diminished, do you mean diminished by the recent history of the Troubles or do you mean diminished by partition itself?

I think probably diminished since O'Neill. Since O'Neill and O'Donnell left and Maguire bought them the boat to leave on, our influence over the rest of Ireland has been diminished. And then reducing ourselves from those nine counties to six has also diminished our influence. Ulster is the sleeping giant of Ireland. That has always been my feeling.

But you always saw Ulster in an historical context and as a nine-county ancient province.

Oh yes, an absolute nine-county ancient province that fought for hundreds of years with Connacht and had a testy relationship with Leinster and Munster. Seeing Ulster beating Munster at Ravenhill is fantastic as far as I'm concerned. I understand where we're at in Ulster. I'm an Ulster person, that's the first thing I'd like to say. I am an Irishman and an Ulster person. The brethren of Ulster are my people. I understand them, I like them and they have informed me who I am. I'm different from people from Dublin and I'm much closer to people from Donegal than I am to people from Dublin. I am very proud of that melting pot and the influences of the Scottish Enlightenment and all those things that have gone into making me what I am. So I am very loyal to the idea of Ulster.

There are people, of course, who come from a similar background to yourself who might not so easily say, 'I'm an Ulsterman' because they would see themselves more as Irish.

I am an Irish person. I'm an Irishman, but I'm also an Ulsterman. I am absolutely an Ulsterman and I am reminded of that everywhere I go. I can't shake that in Dublin and I can't shake that in London – they are wary of us in both capitals. We are Ulster people and we kind of end up saying how we feel about things. We're straight and I think that the Ulster personality has always been there. We've always had the same sort of attitude.

Do you think there is one Ulster identity, or are there two Ulster identities, both looking in different directions? There is an argument that it's a Janus-faced place with half the population looking to London and the other half looking to Dublin.

Look, we're the same people. The incredible thing about being from Ulster is that there is no one more exotic to us than a Protestant and there is no one more exotic to us than a Catholic because we know so little about them. It's a bizarre place – and you know my feelings about education and things like that: I think being separated when we are very young doesn't help.

You are a keen supporter of integrated education.

I am a supporter of that because I believe in some way that could go towards us not having this separateness but that's the problem with the six counties as they have been set up. The unfortunate thing is that Ireland, by setting up the six counties, has been deprived. For very good reasons too – the fearful notion of what influence the Vatican was going to have on the Southern Irish government, which has been well-founded, and is only really starting to tease itself out over the last ten years. Those reasons were perfectly solid reasons for trying to stay out of what was going to become an independent Ireland. However it was the very exclusion of these six counties that has led to the twenty-six not progressing as quickly as they should have in the last forty or fifty years because I think the inclusion of the Ulster people would have made a difference. So for me it's a kind of emotional, spiritual and in some ways an economic necessity that we some day become whole, in whatever form, and find ourselves unified again and moving towards a secular, free Irish society that has a relationship with its neighbours in England. We've always supported and stood up for them whenever things get tough – and our friends in Scotland who we have a very close relationship with. And what is happening in Scotland is going to make us look at our identities even further, which is why a book like this will be interesting.

There was a time, of course, when Belfast was an economic powerhouse and Dublin looked north with envy but now that's all changed.

Well I'm not sure about that, I think there is a huge opportunity to get that back again. I think people in the South are desperate to do business here because business here is straightforward. People do things in a very straight and open way. Look at the two towns; they're like Rotterdam and Amsterdam as far as I am concerned. As they say in Holland, Rotterdam makes the money and Amsterdam spends it. And that's how it used to be here in Ireland; Belfast would make the money and Dublin would spend it. In my dealings with Dublin over the years, it's sometimes very difficult to get a deal done in the right way whereas Belfast is completely different. It's very, very simple in Belfast.

And is that to do with the two systems being different – or is it to do with that idea of the straight, almost abrasive, blunt, Ulster approach to things?

I think it is part of that. I think it's part of how the Protestant tradition has been brought up. It's the difference between having a singular relationship with God and having an intermediary – you know, the intermediary tends to let you off the hook, whereas if you have a singular relationship you are dealing with your own conscience and you want to sleep at night. I mean it's the Catholic Church here in the North of Ireland that has been the blunt instrument that has been stopping progress in my particular area of integrated education, for example. They want to hold on to that aspect of being able to, in my opinion, indoctrinate children in religion when they are very young.

You can say that as a Catholic.

I can say that as a Catholic. I can say I feel that as a Catholic and I didn't come from the social elite either. I came from a very working-class background, not very privileged.

Do you think leaving this part of the world and going to pursue your career in London thirty years ago helped you focus on your identity?

I think there is a great warmth between Ulster people because we know the kind of backgrounds we've all come from. We all know what it is we've had to get over to become the people we are. We all know we've had to sidestep prejudice, that we've had to sidestep sectarianism.

You use the word sidestep. If I was being unkind I might say it's not so much 'sidestep' as 'turn your back on'. Isn't the danger that you look back misty-eyed about how great home is – whereas actually for several decades you turned your back on that day-to-day sectarian grind?

Oh well, I am very pleased to have missed that. I have brothers and sisters. I have friends. I know what it is like to be under the pressure of sectarianism on top of the ordinary pressures of life and it just becomes unbearable. The legacy of what's happened over the last thirty or thirty-five years is going to be with us for a long time. There are a lot of casualties out there. But I don't think I ever turned my back on Ulster – how could you? It's so much of what you are, so much of what you are proud of.

Thinking back to some of the film, television and stage roles you've played, did you take a conscious decision to do work from here, by writers from here? Did you, for example, always want to use an Ulster accent rather than an English one?

Yes I take that decision all the time without any difficulty. The reason I did that was because I was very impressed by the likes of [the Scottish actor and director] Bill Paterson, whom I greatly admire, and 7:84, the great Scottish theatre company. I loved that they used the Scottish vernacular to tell all their stories – so I thought, right, I want to be like Bill Paterson. James Ellis and Colin Blakely were my mentors too. Jimmy drove Colin over in the car and on the way down to London they stopped off at Stratford and they went to see a play. They couldn't afford the seats and they got standing room at the back. Halfway through the play Colin turns to Jimmy and says, 'Jimmy, I'm going to be on that stage this time next year'. And he was – and very successfully too. They were my mentors. They don't come from my tradition. They are actors, they are not Catholics – but they are Ulster people and that is who I look up to. I am not looking at the Donal McCann, Tony Doyle experience. I am looking at the Colin Blakely, Jimmy Ellis experience. They are my people – and Jimmy was very good to me when we first met and helped me and so I made a decision: if these people are prepared to play me as the lead in this series I am going to do it in my own accent. If they're happy with that, I'm happy with that. It's not making a political statement about it or anything, though I did turn down some work because I thought politically it was incorrect. Most people would have just gone and done them and in the end these parts mostly went to English or American actors but I didn't want to sign up, and that was to my detriment you could say. But I have to say one thing: the best writing was happening here with the likes of Brian Friel and Frank McGuinness.

And why was that, do you think? What was it about this place that produced such a great roll call of creative talent?

There is something about the tension that's in this society between the creatives and the non-creatives. I remember what it was like here in the 1970s. I remember the excitement that was going on because we had these poets and writers and visual artists, and I remember people coming to Belfast for openings at the Ulster Museum, the frisson of excitement that was going on because of what certain people were doing, and all this against a really difficult backdrop. There was a huge burst of creativity here in the 1970s despite the fact that there wasn't a lot of money about for anything, but still it happened.

But Ulster also has a reputation for being a barren landscape full of proud Philistines who wouldn't be caught dead reading poetry or going to the theatre. That anti-arts culture is very prevalent. Can you explain that contradiction?

I've often tried to think about it. I've seen it in other places in the world. When I was in New Zealand I saw exactly the same thing – and it's like if you can't wear it or eat it or drive it really quickly, what the hell use is it anyway? Do you know what I mean? I think it's precisely drumming up against that that sets up the tension here. Frank McGuinness writing *Observe the Sons of Ulster* – the chord, the big bass note that resonated within it was that loyalist community seeing itself suddenly elevated artistically. That was a very powerful thing that happened here when that play came out. And those things really excite me: people don't think they can be overtaken by the arts, but they can. And theatre can do it.

Some people see it as subversive though, and if you think it is constantly trying to undermine the status quo, you are going to be nervous about it.
Well here's the problem. The problem is the six counties were built on a negative so there is really nowhere for us to go. For the Protestant community, any concession is the thin edge of the wedge. The Protestant community has a fearfulness. It was an extreme surprise to me growing up that Catholics hadn't cornered the market on guilt and that the Protestant community, although larger than us, could be just as fearful as us. I think that's one of the problems that we can't get past. We have to find ways of promoting ourselves and understanding ourselves in a positive light, moving forward together. I would be positive about here and I don't think it is time for Ireland to be united. I don't think that but I do feel that we might find ourselves a little more isolated if Scotland does vote for independence in its referendum. That would change everything here for us, because we are very close to Scotland [here].

There's so much focus at the moment on big cultural signature projects here. Do you have the sense that maybe, just for once, people here have the wind in their backs?
Yes, I agree and the people are more confident. I think we've all said we want to make this place work for us. We can make it work because we are smart people, we are intelligent people and we know that anger and violence doesn't work because we've been through all that. If we can really address the past we can say we are moving on. I do feel positive about the place. I think one of the things about us is that we will always remain united as a people – we are just too long together.

SEAMUS HEANEY

Seamus Heaney was born in rural County Derry in 1939. He attended St Columb's College in Derry and went to Queen's University Belfast to study English in 1957. In 1966 Faber & Faber published his first volume of poetry, *Death of a Naturalist,* to considerable critical acclaim. He published thirteen volumes of original poetry alongside many translations, plays and critical essays. A Nobel laureate and Professor of Poetry at both Oxford and Harvard, he was regarded as one of the finest English language poets of his generation and the most important Irish poet since Yeats. He personally prized the critic Karl Miller's description of him as 'a poet to be grateful for'. His sudden death on 30th August 2013 bore that out, prompting a great sense of loss and appreciation locally, nationally and internationally.

We met over lunch in his Dublin home.

Seamus Heaney:

For a long time the name Ulster was used by people of a unionist persuasion as a kind of signal that for them, Ulster was British. Ulster in that case stood not so much for the six counties bounded by the border, but for a Northern Ireland affiliated to the UK. l remember, for example, Joseph Tomelty's ironical parting shot to me when I'd be leaving his company, was always 'And don't forget you're British!' So nationalists had a standoff from that usage. At that time, if I described myself as an Ulsterman I'd have thought I was selling a bit of my birthright because I'd be subscribing to the 'Ulster will fight and Ulster will be right' tradition, and that was a different Ulster from the one that I was in, which was basically SDLP before the SDLP were invented – a nationalist, apolitical background, but with a kind of northern nationalism, I'd probably have said, rather than Ulster identity.

Mark Carruthers:

Did you feel that even pre-Troubles? Obviously as you grew older the word Ulster came to be used in a very political sense, but even as a younger man did it still have that connotation for you?

When I was in my teens there was a strong sense of the divide in our community, but there was also in my own case and in my family's case, and in the milieu I was in around home in County Derry, a very easy and well maintained relationship and friendships between, as they say, both sides of the house – farmers and so on. There was a lot of standoff from Stormont to put it mildly, but at a micro-local level everything was fine and continued to be so, despite a lot of things, with our own neighbour friends around there.

And was that very important for you – that sense of good neighbourliness in rural Ulster in the '50s and early '60s?
Well that was the life I knew there and I wrote about it. I wasn't at the time, I suppose, thinking about Ulster identity. In fact even though I declared my passport was green on one famous occasion, I had a British passport for the first while in my life and that is typical of the bind and the contradictions. I was going to Lourdes on a pilgrimage and I was getting a British passport – not that that should matter. I remember Ben Kiely saying that if you were living in the Republic of Ireland you didn't need a passport to go to Lourdes because it was part of the jurisdiction!

I was intrigued when I read that you had a British passport before you had an Irish passport. Do you think the notion of your northern-ness was awakened when you left the North?
I don't think so, no.

It was already there.
Yes. I remember in particular in the Irish class that we had in Derry at school in St Columb's picking out the Northern writers – Peadar Ó Doirnín, Cathal Buí Mac Giolla Gunna, Art Mac Cumhaigh – and hearing a different note, I thought, in them. Maybe it was only because I knew the actual Irish language better, but the sense of a Northern Irish identity was certainly there, as was the sense then of being a subject within a different North, one with a very different ethos. If I say subject, I am overstating it, I'm just using a technical term.

So if you were aware then as a young boy of your Irishness and your identity through your family, through your church, through your . . .
Gaelic football.

Through football – were you also aware that there was another identity, another community, living cheek by jowl who were different, but also there and part of the bigger community?

Oh yeah. Well there were of course the arches around the Twelfth which reminded you, around Castledawson, that there was a different community with different flags and emblems, as they say. All that was there, of course – but I should say that my family were kind of dormant in political terms. My mother was more alive to the overall political situation than my father. My father was brought up really by uncles – his mother and father died when they were quite young – and these were old bachelor guys and I think they lived in the world of the late 19th century. And he went backwards and forwards to England with cattle and so on, so I think he was indifferent to politics, but he was at ease. It wasn't an interest of his and so, for example, 1916 which was taken to mean so much, had very little purchase for me. I knew about it as a famous date, but to go back to Northern things, 1798 [the year of the United Irishmen's failed rebellion against British rule in Ireland] had much more sense of legend, drama, in placeness about it. I know that too much is probably made of that golden moment, but the memory of it was in the air as an imagining of a shared Ulster identity.

And that was a time when Catholic, Protestant and Dissenter were together on that issue and when Ulstermen were very much at the forefront.

That's right, and David Hammond used to sing the Henry Joy song – 'An Ulsterman I'm proud to be . . . ' – so all that was there. The idea of an enlightenment Belfast was with me early on. And also in the folk life that I was part of, things like 'The man from God knows where . . . ', that recitation about Thomas Russell coming up North, things like that were imbibed and imbued. And there were nights at home when elders gathered around Easter time, when there would be a party with songs and recitations and music – not party tunes, just tunes for a party.

Did the onset of the Troubles in the late '60s change your view of what you needed to be doing as a poet? Did your poetry knowingly shift from the rural, observational poetry to a more political commentary?

On the whole I didn't know how to handle the response, how to maintain a fidelity, if you like, to my own mythos – and at the same time to envisage a society where ethnic groups, religious groups, political groups would find a way of living a civic life. Actually, in 1972, which was four years after the Troubles started, a book came out called *Wintering Out*, and there is a poem there which looks back to the 1780s and '90s and it says 'take a last turn in reasonable light'. So the Troubles politicised me to the extent that when on the Wednesday after the turmoil started on the 5th of October 1968 with the baton charge in Derry, there was a big march of students at Queen's University where I was a young lecturer, I joined the march – which was a very unusual thing for me to do. We marched down towards Linenhall Street and the RUC had a barrier of themselves across the street and the Reverend Ian [Paisley] was in Donegall Square with supporters. So the police were kind of blocking or separating the two sides, I suppose, and I remember a couple of people wanting to run the barriers or crash the barriers – Bernadette [Devlin] and, I think, Michael Farrell and a couple of other people – but this young lecturer went up and said, 'Calm down'. I was being as mollifying as I could be. Eventually then they turned back and went to the Students' Union and that was the night that People's Democracy was formed. The next Saturday I went to Derry and there was a meeting there in the Guildhall Square and I wrote something for the BBC's 'The Listener' called *Derry's Walls* and that was the start of engagement, but actually I didn't go marching much after that.

So you were there mollifying, observing, trying to keep a lid on things – but that subsequently was perhaps misconstrued, was it? I'm thinking about some of what you wrote – *The Ministry of Fear, Act of Union, Requiem for the Croppies*. Do people look at those poems in isolation and conclude, wrongly, he's a nationalist poet – he's a republican?

There is no doubt you can't do anything with *Requiem for the Croppies* which was written in 1966, fifty years after 1916 – and again it was out of my dream life. It was pre-Troubles entirely and I didn't read it during the Troubles – but it was part of the '98 dream life. Actually I remember in 1968 when David Hammond, Michael Longley and myself did the tour called 'Room to Rhyme', I read that poem in different milieus. There would have been a very Official Unionist audience in Armagh Library, for example, and

I felt I was opening a space for this kind of identity within their Ulster, as it were, and that was certainly the thinking in choosing to read it then. That was the point.

Do you remember how it was received?
It was received perfectly all right. Now these were people – it was a self-selecting audience – people coming for the poetry and song and so on, so they would be fairly cultivated and fairly well mannered.

But there were those who were critical of some of what you wrote. Did that sadden you? Did it annoy you?
I wasn't that aware of it. Artistically maybe 'The Singing School' – which is the Derry, St Columb's stuff – is maybe that kind of partisan utterance all right, but it's based on experience. Conor Cruise O'Brien rebuked it, of course. But then there is one about the visit of the RUC man, you see, which I think is ok whichever side of the house you come from. It's called 'A Constable Calls'. There is one coarseness about 'the boot of the law' – but apart from that . . .

It's about filling out an agricultural form and it was the local constable who did that.
It was and he was well enough known. He was Constable Crawford from Castledawson Barracks.

But that wasn't the strong arm of the law. That was what we now call neighbourhood policing?
Exactly, yeah – but at the same time a slight frisson would occur. I remember his shiny baton case and the stitches on it. He had a revolver and so on. Just as with a doctor coming to the house, or a priest, in those days it was an occasion.

And do you remember feeling part of what is referred to as the minority community, which was separate from law and order and separate from policing? Because, of course, there weren't many Catholics in the RUC at the time.
Oh definitely you felt separate from that, definitely.

Did you feel vulnerable?

No I didn't feel vulnerable. I think we, the family anyway, didn't feel that. There was no, if you like, republican background in either my mother's family or my father's.

Do you think the fact that it was the 'Royal Ulster Constabulary' helped to distance you from that notion of Ulster?

I don't know. It wasn't particularly the Ulster that was the unease; it was the sense of the partisanship of the force. That was the thing that was most decisive in the standoff.

Did you feel as a poet that you had to speak up for the minority community – to ask those questions that don't get asked in newspapers or in current affairs programmes? Is that the challenge you and your contemporaries within the world of poetry set yourselves?

We weren't as clear as that about it, I don't think. I wasn't as clear anyway, but there is one poem which was meant to say something about how things were and how things could be, called 'The Other Side'. It was based upon a man called Junkin who was an elder – probably an elder of the Presbyterian Church too – but he was, like all our surrounding neighbours, the Steeles and the McIntyres, the Junkins, actually the Mulhollands too, very much at ease. There was no sense of political difference with them. So 'The Other Side' deals with that, maybe too optimistically, because there was something more noxious happening at the time – not that the Junkins were involved in it or we were involved in it. But if you are a poet, as you say, your writing has a duty to things larger than just the good message. I think I have said this too often but only because it is true: when I met the doctor who was the first Community Relations Minister at Stormont – Dr Simpson from Antrim, whom I met after the publication of *Wintering Out*, which had these poems in it – he said, which was true, 'Well it's good that you're writing because it shows what we have in common in Ulster is farming stock and this and that'. Naturally he was taking the good news out of it – and there was some good news there – but I thought, if that's what the poetry is doing there's something too consoling there.

So it shouldn't be a balm.

No, exactly. Not an emollient or a balm, no. So I suppose that's where *North* came from. It has more grunts in it, but it's not a very drum-beating book, really. I thought I really got able to deal with it a bit better when it came to the '70s and there's a book called *Field Work* and there are elegies in it. That's more like it, I think.

Because you did lose one member of your family and you lost friends and friends of friends. Sean Armstrong . . .

Sean Armstrong, that's right. Colum McCartney, Lewis O'Neill, Sean Brown. But also then there were people like Martin McBurney whom Michael (Longley) wrote about and whom I knew in the Arts Club.

And you've also talked about Willie Strathearn. So that pain was very real.

Yes indeed. The other thing that was real, I am astonished to realise, was [that] we took the death toll almost for granted, day after day, year after year, the news of those thousands of killings. When I looked at the book – one of the best books to come out of the whole thing, *Lost Lives* – I thought: we went through that every day! It scares you.

On the broader issue of identity, the poet John Hewitt famously wrote about being an Ulsterman, an Irishman, British and European.

I think that's fair enough.

Did you struggle with parts of it? Did you struggle with the British bit?

I think that was going a bit far. But John was British, by birth, by choice, by inheritance – so for him that was absolutely in order. My problem came clear in one simple way, the time that Thatcher was in power and there was talk of going on a British Council tour and I said, 'No, I am not going to go on Margaret Thatcher's tour at all'. I suggested that the tours be co-sponsored with the Irish Cultural Relations Committee and I think that was done a couple of times, which was fair enough, but that kind of partnership has now come into political reality and in the new conditions there is co-sponsorship, if you like, of identity.

Did you feel uncomfortable at that time, because of course you wrote your famous *Open Letter* against being included in *The Penguin Book of Contemporary British Poetry* which was edited by Blake Morrison and Andrew Motion?

Two friends, yes.

You knew them very well. Of course you became Oxford Professor of Poetry, you'd been included in other collections . . .

Well, very early on, Hobsbaum got us all shoehorned into a book called *An Anthology of Commonwealth Poetry* and then there was another compilation called *Young British Poetry* – early on.

Why did that one in particular – the Blake Morrison, Andrew Motion anthology – tip you over the edge?

Because it was the 1980s, not the late '60s, and the violence had been going on for fourteen years – and it was about nomenclature to some extent.

And it was a difficult climate.

Yeah, it was terrible. Also I was part of *Field Day* and it was decided that the poets on the board should write something. Seamus Deane did a pamphlet titled *Civilians and Barbarians*. Tom Paulin wrote about 'the language question', so I felt I had to write one and I thought that doing it in verse would be fun.

Do you regret that now at all?

No, I had to get through it. In the context of identity, it was the old standoff with the Ulster-British, you know. On the other island, it didn't matter much one way or another.

So was there a sense of imposition – that the Britishness was imposed in Ulster?

Yes, that's right.

But that it was more *laissez faire* in GB?

That's right, absolutely. So I felt I was being dishonest if I didn't say something. It may have been wrongly expressed, but that's another matter. At any rate, something had to be done which is why I used that epigraph from Gaston Bachelard[8]: 'What is the source of our first suffering? It lies in the fact that we hesitated to speak. It was born in the moment when we accumulated silent things within us'.

And that famous line of yours: 'Be advised my passport's green. No glass of ours was ever raised to toast the Queen'. Did people overplay the significance of that line?

The Queen thing – green, Queen – it's a rhyme. I mean, truly, there's a bit of a spring to it. I didn't want to sound a bigot in the pamphlet. At the same time I wanted to address the breach in the community at that stage.

Were you aware of how that was received by unionists on the ground in Northern Ireland?

Oh I can imagine.

There was that and then there was the idea – was it ever formally confirmed? – that you'd turned down the Poet Laureateship.

Never formally.

But there was the sense you may well have done.

I thought another Ulster poet should have got it. Funny, I wouldn't have thought that would have affected opinion. You see, to put it this way, people would say that would have been a great symbol of a reconciliation – and I kept saying, symbols we don't need. We need reality.

But that whole situation has now changed hasn't it? Because you used that line: 'No glass of ours was ever raised to toast the Queen' – and then there you were, sitting beside her at the state dinner in Dublin in 2011. So has your view changed on that?

No. 'No glass of ours was ever raised to toast the Queen' – I meant to characterise a culture. We at home in the house would never have lifted a glass to toast the Queen and I suspect manys a one in the other tradition wouldn't be doing it at home either. On the other hand, I have always felt the courteous thing to do when you were at a formal event or dinner was

---

8 Gaston Bachelard (1884-1962) was an influential French philosopher who wrote widely on poetry and the philosophy of science.

certainly to stand and toast. So whatever the impression came out of the words, which I can understand entirely, whatever the reading of it as 'a bitter word', it was meant to have a bit of merriment in it too, coming as I say from the rhyme. Of course those lines were quoted gleefully when Her Majesty and Prince Phillip came to Ireland, partly, I hope, because it is a nifty couplet – 'My passport's green. No glass of ours was ever raised to toast the Queen' – very quotable. I had met Her Majesty before in Belfast and, in fact, before that again in Buckingham Palace a few years ago. She gives these lunches, every month for a few months of the year, and invites various persons. Twelve guests from different sectors. The time I was there, for example, there was an engineer from Cardiff University who had done something with motor engines and the Duke was very interested in that. There was a woman from the Prison Service and Sir Christopher Bland who was head of the BBC at the time. Anyhow, Christopher Bland was on the Queen's right-hand side and I was on her left-hand side. This was a few years ago. Ted Hughes had just died and the Good Friday Agreement had just come in to force, so at that time I thought – come on now, do the decent thing here.

So there was no doubt in your mind that was the right thing to do?
No. None at all. There was a world change as far as I was concerned. Then too, I had been to Buckingham Palace when Ted Hughes was Poet Laureate because I was on a committee with him for the awarding of the Queen's Gold Medal for Poetry. So when Marie and I were invited to the event in Dublin Castle, I was happy to say yes. We didn't realise where we were going to be placed until the afternoon of the dinner, at which point a friend of ours in Protocol in the Foreign Service rang up and said, 'You're at the top table tonight'. So what were we going to do about that? I assumed it was going to be like a college top table or a wedding top table – a long board for the Last Supper, as it were – but when we came to the door of the big hall we realised there were only ten people's names for Table C and truth to tell, I swore when I saw I was placed between the Duke and David Cameron. Nothing political in the worry, you understand - just sheer social anxiety. Marie was in a little bit more of a homely situation. She had the Taoiseach and Cardinal Brady, so she was between Mayo and Cavan. But Mary

McAleese was beside Cameron. I actually got on easily and merrily with the Duke.

And are you happy now about the symbolism – the Queen being in Ireland, you being at the table?
Yes, that was fine by me.

So you are now cast in this role as a great man of letters and, to some extent, a spokesman for the peace process. 'Believe that a further shore is reachable from here'; where 'hope and history rhyme' – those are the watchwords of that process. That's what people quote – that's what Clinton quotes.
It is indeed, yeah.

Are you comfortable with that?
I am, yeah. The only uncomfortable thing is that people disagree with the actual lines; hope and history, they say, don't rhyme! But the line was never of course meant as a phonetic aspiration, it was meant as a political one. But yeah, I am content. What might make me uneasy, or give me pause, is the fact that it is such a 'good' news message and so you think, am I just assuaging something? Avoiding the actual conditions? But no, it came out of a context and it came out of the play, *The Cure of Troy* and it came out of the conditions we were in, in 1990. 1990, '91 were savage times with a lot going on, still three years before the cessation. But there was hope in the air as well, in the bigger theatre, what with the fall of the Berlin Wall and all those Eastern European Soviet regimes.

So not only are you comfortable with it, you're happy about it – but your innate modesty, your Ulster modesty, means that you don't want to overplay it?
My Ulster – what's the word? – not tight-fistedness, but scepticism, maybe, would worry about a message like that being too positive. I must illustrate this by telling you that when I was a student, or shortly afterwards, there used to be a café at the far end of Botanic Avenue, opposite the then Arts Theatre. I was in it one night with Marie when we were courting. Two fellas came in – they were coming from a mission hall somewhere close by – and

one says to the other, 'What did you think of that?' He says, 'All right, but I thought the message was a bit soft'. So at times I too wonder if the message might not have been a bit soft.

You've talked about that famous Northern reticence before. Is that part of the Ulster identity, or part of *an* Ulster identity?

No, I think it *is* the Ulster identity – speech and manners. I mean anthropologically, the Ulster identity's alive and well. If people meet from different traditions, even if you throw two hot sectarians together, they could find a lingo that would be sharp, merry, oblique. But Ulster people, despite all that, are very sociable and manageable.

The reputation they have, though, is for being dour and not much craic and, perhaps the phrase you used yourself a moment ago: tight-fisted.

Well, I'm reluctant to go too far in the optimistic vein, but between themselves I think they can get on fine – at a personal level and at a community level. So yes, there is an Ulster speech, an Ulster idiom and an Ulster sense of humour.

Have you thought about why Ulster, which is such a small place on the world map, has produced so many significant poets and writers and actors and musicians?

Well I think that people were craving a way of making something coherent for themselves in an incoherent situation. To make an inflated comparison, think of Russia from 1880 to 1930, think of Dublin from 1890 to 1930, think of London from 1580 to 1620 – places where nothing was concluded and history was in the making and there was an unsureness about how to proceed and then a settlement of sorts. I think that in the North, the blueprint of the divided loyalties was in every psyche, and so the need to do something about it was strong. I think the Northern writers, the poets of my own generation, weren't satisfied to live in a divided society; they wanted something better. And we thought the ironies and the generosities of the art would help. Not that we set out deliberately to preach or convert, but there was an unconscious need for some kind of freedom, inner freedom, because you were hampered by the habits of mealy-mouthness and evasion and all that went on to keep realities under wraps. Not that we set out to write political poetry but I think the sense of escape into something that was jubilant and different and free was important and it was in reaction, in some way, to the psychic, never mind the political conditions that people lived in.

So that notion of a specific identity was there.

I remember when I was doing a post graduate year in a teacher training college up in Trench House, St Joseph's, I produced an extended essay on Ulster literary magazines. I read there John Hewitt and Roy McFadden, Robert Greacen and John Gallen. Greacen and Gallen were writing as undergraduates in a Queen's magazine called the *New Northman* which was trying to establish a literary culture in the North. And similarly with *Rann*, a magazine in the 1950s, edited by Roy McFadden and Barbara Hunter. So I was interested in Hewitt's regional idea but it still seemed a way of cutting things off at the border.

What seems so strange now is how easily people like Terence O'Neill and Brian Faulkner used the term Ulster when they were referring, in fact, to Northern Ireland.

Yes, I know. That's what got the nationalists' goat – and now as a concession or realisation of the new times I call it Northern Ireland.

And you're comfortable with that?

Yeah.

But you would always regard yourself, and want to be known as and remembered as, an Irish poet? The moniker Ulster would make you a little uncomfortable, would it?

It would, yes. Irish-Ulster, Ulster-Irish. I think my identity is Ulster-Irish or Irish-Ulster, take it one way or another.

Either way is fine?

Probably. But you would have to keep the options open.

CIARÁN HINDS

One of Ulster's most successful and versatile actors, Ciarán Hinds was born in Belfast in 1953. A keen Irish dancer in his youth, he gave up his law studies at Queen's University Belfast to study acting at London's Royal Academy of Dramatic Art. On stage he has performed with the National Theatre in London, the Royal Shakespeare Company and the Glasgow Citizens' Theatre and to considerable critical acclaim on Broadway. His television credits include *Prime Suspect*, *Rome* and *Game of Thrones*, and he has also won acclaim for his film roles in *Road to Perdition*, *Munich* and *Tinker Tailor Soldier Spy*.

We meet in Belfast.

Ciarán Hinds:

When I was younger, I wasn't aware that the place I was growing up in was called Ulster; it was called Northern Ireland. The word Ulster, when I was a kid, wasn't really in the vocabulary and then later you found out the difference between Northern Ireland and Ulster. It was only probably when I was in my teens, in the mid-'60s, that we heard things like, 'Ulster will fight and Ulster will be right'. In the '60s everything started changing here in the North. The civil rights movement kicked off into what we know as 'the Troubles'.

Mark Carruthers:

Would you have thought of yourself as an Ulsterman at any stage in your life?
No. I think my identity would be as a Northern Irishman as opposed to an Ulsterman, but it means the same. When people don't know who you are and they can't pronounce your name, they say, 'British actor'. Then they say, 'Well, he could be British but he's sort of from Ireland. He's from the North of Ireland'. So all these other people are having a row about your identity.

If people say to me, 'You're English', I say, 'No, I'm not. I'm Irish; I'm from Northern Ireland'.

When you're in the United States, do you find people think of you as an Irish actor?

I think they do but I don't know why. I think maybe it's because when they first saw me I was playing British [characters] and I came from the British Isles. They would have been aware of things like that classical stuff I did, like *Jane Eyre* and Jane Austen, so they assume I'm an English actor or a British actor.

You made a decision to live in Paris some years ago and you also spend a lot of time working in the US. Do you think having that external perspective on this place has altered the way you see it?

I think it probably has but I think it's probably the same for anybody who goes away to live. I had the opportunity to work with Peter Brook [the English theatre and film director who has been based in France since the 1970s] and he put us in a company with fifteen different nationalities. Now, that's insane. Your moral compass, your religious persuasion, your sense of perspective, it's all different and that was such an eye-opener for me. I worked in Northern Ireland and in Scotland, and I felt at home in both places. I felt at home in Dublin and in Galway, and then I went to London to work and that felt a bit strange. When I was working in Paris with all these different nationalities, it just gave me a completely different perspective.

Let's talk about your very comfortable upbringing in North Belfast.

I did enjoy growing up here. I was lucky because I was loved and we had good friends. I was fifteen or sixteen before things got really hot here. It was a normal childhood. We were in a mixed area – Catholic and Protestant, middle-class, untroubled. Of course, everybody looks back on their childhood with rose-tinted glasses in a way. I've always been against segregation in education which has been one of the pitfalls here. I was lucky because of my involvement with Irish dancing. Patricia Mulholland, [the celebrated dance teacher and choreographer] was absolutely adamant that it was not pure Catholic, Gaelic culture – it was for people from this island who would dance together and weave patterns together, and that's where we got mixing. I would only have known the word Ulster from Irish dancing, I suppose, and Patricia's old storytelling myths. One of the big ballets that she did was *Cúchulainn*, who was the warrior king of Ulster. That's the way the word sticks with me.

So, as a child growing up you weren't particularly aware of any idea of community division?

I'd spend holidays down in Ballycarry [a County Antrim village midway between Larne and Carrickfergus]. It's a little loyalist village and I'd go there every summer and spend a week with my best mate, Peter Sturdy, who was a great Irish dancer from a Protestant family. Every July we'd go and help with the harvest out of town and there was King Billy painted over the village and the big bonfire in the middle of it. That was the ritual and there was no wrath about it – maybe there was somewhere but I didn't come across it. When we were young, I suppose in the early '60s, we were taken down to watch the Twelfth of July march – all the colours and the music and the drumming. I was at a Catholic school but I don't remember that any of our teachers infused us with any sense of wrongness that they thought might be in the system.

So you didn't grow up feeling part of a disenfranchised minority?

No, because I really didn't know about it – and I don't think I was.

What about your experience of student life at Queen's University in 1972?

My sister Bronagh was the first woman President of the Queen's Student Council. She was pretty radical. She was in the People's Democracy, and when I got there she was still in her last year. The civil rights movement was still in full flow. We were studying the Northern Ireland legal system – and it had just been abolished[9]. Of course, Belfast has got better since then, there's no doubt about it. The question is how we all continue to progress it, I suppose. Chekov was good at that – if not for us or for our children, then for our children's children.

9 The unionist government at Stormont was prorogued by the Westminster government in March 1972 in the face of a worsening political and security situation in Northern Ireland.

You mentioned Chekov there and I wonder to what extent you think figures like Van Morrison, Stewart Parker and Brian Friel have given people here a voice?

I don't know if it's unique, but what Brian Friel, Van Morrison and Stewart Parker do have, is that they write from a real sense of place. There's a world in their heads and with their imagination they interpret that – some with humour, some with irony, some with passion, and they identify with their own humanity. And then there's the poetry of Seamus Heaney and Michael Longley, of course. People feel rooted here and feel there is a value to it. And these people who write also look outwards as well as looking inwards. They're not trying to say that this is just about us. Although Friel locates his work in Ballybeg [a fictional Donegal village where many of his plays are set], we know that he's writing about the world. That's why Brian Friel's plays are staged all over the world. The writing, I think, will be there forever because the heart of what they all write about is so deeply felt.

Do you have a strong sense of wanting to share your identity with your wife Hélène and your daughter Aoife, who have never lived here?

Hélène knows the family and she's been over here. She sees how different it is but she's all right with that. I remember it was quite a shock when Aoife and I drove here from London, just the two of us, up to Stranraer and across to Belfast. I'd forgotten the date but it was the Eleventh of July and we were on this boat from Stranraer to Larne. Aoife must have been six or seven and when we got into Belfast the first thing she noticed were all the kerbs painted red, white and blue – and she just says to me, 'Oh Papa – le tricolore !' She was seeing a French flag on the kerbstones and that did make me laugh. I thought, well, I'll just leave it at that. She's studying international relations at the minute and I think she has to look at things in a way she's never looked at them before. She was educated through the French system completely because we were living in London and then we went to Paris. The thing is, she has an Irish name, I always played her Irish music and she went to Irish dancing for a while in London. Her mother is Vietnamese and was also dislocated from there when she was three and brought up in the French countryside. So you say, what's my daughter's identity? She's already been a child of several cities and with both parents from such different places, I don't think she'll ever have an Ulster identity – apart from maybe her stubbornness.

JENNIFER JOHNSTON

Jennifer Johnston is widely regarded as one of Ireland's finest writers. Born in Dublin in 1930 and educated at Trinity College, she has lived much of her life in Derry in Northern Ireland. Her 1977 novel *Shadows on our Skin* was set in the city and was nominated for the Booker Prize. *The Old Jest* won the Whitbread Novel Award. Much of her work is set in the period of the First World War, though she dislikes the suggestion that she is a 'Big House' writer. She has also written several stage and radio plays.

We meet over lunch in her home overlooking the River Foyle.

Jennifer Johnston:

Ulster is one of the four provinces of Ireland and that is what I would like it to be. I don't want it to be anything other than that and I think it has got, sort of, too big for its boots. I think it's pushing above its weight and I don't think it's good for the people who live here. I just want it to be what it ought to be – the same as Munster, Leinster and Connacht.

Mark Carruthers:

Ulster is an ancient province of nine counties, but some people here do tend to think of it as the six counties of Northern Ireland – that's their definition of Ulster.

Well, it isn't mine; that's all I can say to that. I really wish it wasn't and I don't see any way of stopping what is happening to it now. I think they have awful plans in their heads, you know, when the Scots get their *freedom*, if that's what you like to call it – I don't necessarily call it that – but I think they've got awful thoughts in their minds, those people who look after us. I think people's thinking about the North has hardened. Somehow or other the disappearance of the violence, or so-called disappearance of the violence, has made people turn in on themselves. Instead of looking out and saying, 'Ok now. Where do we go from here? What are we going to do with ourselves and our compatriots?' they're looking after themselves, only themselves, and it's only their own tribe. I don't like that at all. Perhaps I don't get out and talk to people enough. I used to get out and talk to people an awful lot and I can't be bothered any longer because I feel these barriers going up all the time.

And you feel that's specific to the North?
It's specific to the North.

And even more specific to this city?
Well, this city is another little island inside an island, which is a very difficult thing for anybody to be, but they're rather proud of it and they wouldn't want it to be any other way, I don't think.

And when you came to Derry from London in 1974, was that an enormous culture shock?
It was a culture shock in that I had never lived in the country before. I sort of threw myself into the whole thing with a certain amount of abandon and for about five or six years you always had the feeling, everything's going to be ok if only they'd all stop killing each other. But then, of course, they did stop killing each other finally and everything hasn't been ok. Everything seems to have regressed rather than gone forward.

And do you think that comes down to a lack of political confidence or cultural confidence?
It seems to me to come down to that, for a long time, the two tribes filled themselves with a sort of loathing and hatred of the other tribe. You go on doing this for a long, long time and it becomes part of you and you've frankly got to get an axe to get it out of you. And there were not enough people – there were, of course, obviously some wonderful people and, when I do make statements like that, I'm not talking about everybody – but the main body of people in the country, I think they have no imagination. I try and work out why. Is it the church? Is it their mad politicians? I mean, such a bunch of mad politicians we have here. They don't do anything for the people who live here. They don't suggest to them gently but firmly, 'We don't have to sit here and moulder', which is what it seems to me we're doing. We're just sitting here and mouldering. We don't do anything else at

all. We occasionally have a little bit of a shout about are we going to pay for water and things like that, but otherwise there's nothing exciting happening in the way of political movement at all. I think they're all too frightened. I think the politicians have it embedded in their heads that, if they put a foot wrong, they'll lose their seat – and they don't want to do that. Politicians all over the world don't want to do that, but they never say anything. They never say anything that's worth listening to. When did you last hear them saying anything that's worth listening to?

Is that because there's so much talk about the past? Because the past hasn't been fully resolved, even now?

The past has not been fully resolved and, until it is fully resolved, we cannot go forward. I would totally agree with you there, yes.

Is it also because, as some people claim, too many of our politicians aren't perhaps as widely read as they might be?

No, I'm afraid that doesn't wash because I don't think politicians anywhere necessarily read books or paint pictures or play the fiddle – except in a very sort of a cavalier and superficial way. They have no imagination and that is what is happening here. Every child is born with an imagination. Everybody has an imagination in some little corner of their brain and unless you cultivate this thing, it will just die off and drop out of your head. I do honestly believe that with great vigour. Our children's heads are all being scrubbed of their imaginations and so they grow up to be people who don't have imaginations and they cannot see how life could be different, how life could be better, how life could be more entertaining – anything like that at all.

And yet here we are sitting in a city which is the UK City of Culture in 2013 – and the politicians will be very quick to take the credit for achieving that.

Indeed. I just think that's slightly ludicrous, if I may say so.

Why?

Why do I think it's ludicrous? Well, there was a wonderful time in Derry. I can't remember exactly when – it was the early eighties – when suddenly the city became alive and there were about four years when there were wonderful things happening and it was absolutely amazing and you enjoyed going into the streets and there were plays being put on, there were theatre companies coming, there was music, there were painters painting and great exhibitions here in the art galleries and suddenly, just like that, somebody switched a switch. It stopped and it has never come back, and there is not even any sign of it coming back, and I don't quite know how that happened. I sit here and I ponder over it. I don't ponder all that much over it, because I'm busy writing books, but I do ponder from time to time. My grandfather, my father's father, Mr Justice Johnston, was a man from Magherafelt and his father had become a very wealthy tea merchant. My grandfather was a Home Ruler and he stood as a Home Rule candidate for Derry at one stage in some election or other, and he was a splendid man. He was a wonderful, liberal Presbyterian and when his career took him to Dublin, he went and lived there for the rest of his life very happily. He was a very kind, gentle and funny man and my view of the North has always been that it's full of people like that. And then, when you come here, you find it's not.

But there are people like that.
There are people like that.

Maybe they just don't say too much in public?
But they need to, that is the thing. That is one of the big differences between the North and the South. In the South, everybody says things all the time and it may not make them happy, but it makes them more approachable, more likely to change their evil ways than keeping it all inside yourself. Being kind and warm and wonderful in private doesn't do anybody very much good at all, except possibly your immediate family.

To what extent has that whole experience of living here influenced your writing?
Not all that much, I'm afraid. I just keep on plodding along and I've only written one book that has anything to do with the North at all really.

Yes, *Shadows on our Skin*, which some people would say is your best book, and yet you dislike it very much.

I don't dislike it very much. I am embarrassed by it because it is so full of clichés and it is written in a sort of 'Dubliny' idiom that I should never have done. But I'd only been here two years or so when I wrote it and I didn't have the real voice of the people in my head at all in any way and it's a bit of romantic rubbish. I was very lucky because it got on the Booker shortlist simply because of the attitude of the English to the Northern Irish. They don't know anything about the North of Ireland at all.

And did you subsequently take a conscious decision not to write anything else set in this place?

Well, I knew I couldn't. I knew I couldn't write positively about the Troubles. It always had to be a step removed because once you get yourself emotionally involved in what you're writing about the book becomes skewed, always. Around that time I saw a play by Ben Kiely at the Gate. I can't remember what it was called but it was about the Troubles and I couldn't bear the way he'd written this play and at that moment, I thought, 'I'm not going to write about the North. I can't do it'. I suppose every hour you spend on the earth influences you in some way, even if you're just sitting there. In the book that I literally have just started, I'm going back to the last war and, without any problem, to the way people lived then.

Is it set in Dublin?

Set in the country somewhere in Ireland, not specifically anywhere.

But not the North?

No, not the North because the North immediately hands you problems that you've got to face. You couldn't write a book about the North without facing those problems. Perhaps that is why I don't want to do it, because I don't want to face those problems. I don't know how to face them. Nobody else does either as far as one can see.

And yet you've written quite a bit about that notion of Protestants in Ireland.

Well yes, because I am a Protestant and it is what I know. I'm a Protestant very mixed up with a whole lot of Catholics because my mother's family is totally mixed and I could have been either of those things. It was just the luck of the draw. I now technically am nothing, but I couldn't look at it in the same way as people look at it up here. I could take a whack at them in the South and I enjoy doing that, but I couldn't really take a big enough whack at them here. That was what was wrong in *Shadows on Our Skin*, you know. It really was a nice book. It was a tidy book. It didn't take any great whacks at anybody at all.

Are there other writers from this part of the world whose work you particularly admire?

Longley and Heaney are now the sort of grey-haired druids of poetry; Stewart Parker was the last splendid playwright. Brian Friel, as far as I'm concerned, wrote one truly great play and that was *Faith Healer*, which I think is an absolute icon. I thought it worked absolutely beautifully. It was a great, great play. Frank McGuinness has turned to England. He doesn't have his plays done in Ireland any longer. His last two plays have both been done in London. He comes from the province of Ulster and has energy in what he writes. But it's that imaginative energy that is sort of just decaying away. I feel very embarrassed when I say this because I feel I shouldn't be saying it – but you've got to say it.

But if it's a problem, it's not necessarily a problem unique to the North?

Well, it is unique to the North. It's a sort of bleeding away of energy. Ok, they've been through a war and you're tired and you're exhausted and you're mournful because what you fought your war for, hasn't happened – hasn't happened to either of them. What frightens me is that the violence will come back again and it'll be horrific this time. Maybe it won't. I hope it doesn't, but I just have this feeling because nobody has sat down and said, 'Now, we're going to talk about why we are the way we are'. What makes us like this? It can't just be chance. We have made ourselves like this. Our parents have made us like this; their parents made them like that – and what are we going to do about it? Because we've got to do something about it, otherwise this little wretched corner of the earth will just sink into the sea.

Do you think that artists, whether they are playwrights or poets or novelists or visual artists, have a responsibility to help lead that conversation?

They haven't got a duty to do anything except paint or write books or whatever it is. They can infer, but the minute they start being polemical it becomes useless.

So it's wrong for them to have a manifesto or an agenda?

I think so. Yes, definitely.

How much have you been affected down the years, living in this beautiful house just on the edge of the city, by those very public demonstrations of political and cultural allegiance?

Well, I hated those early months of summer when they did bang their drums because there is something terribly menacing about the sound of the drums coming across the water. In the evenings they used to practise, or whatever it was they did, but you used to hear them thumping away and it was totally unexpected. I didn't know that this sort of thing would happen, and it went on year after year after year, and you get used to it. I didn't like it much. Drums are very menacing. Those people who sang hymns outside the Catholic church [in Belfast] last year said, 'Oh, we didn't realise it was a Catholic church', which was a patently obvious lie because of course they knew it was a Catholic church. They all lived there, so they knew it was a Catholic church. You're trying to – well, to put it very mildly – you're trying to pull someone's leg and it's not kind. It's not the way we ought to be living.

And those people would say, of course, that that is an expression of their culture and that's something to celebrate.

Celebrating singing their songs outside Catholic churches? Well, you know, that's a poor sort of culture to have.

So you're not persuaded?

No, not at all. And this goes for any country where you do that. It's a sort of blatant provocation.

Because it has a sense of triumphalism about it?

Yes. It's coat-trailing. It's a bit negative because I feel helpless. I fear very much for the next twenty-five years. I'm not going to be here but I would be very troubled because it is terribly easy to roll into violence, you know? There are little indications that this might just happen. I don't like that. I was told literally three days ago about some people who live on the Waterside. There's a place called the Brow of the Hill, which is a Catholic enclave. There's a family with two boys who live there and the boys are going to secondary school and they're having to move because the boys are wearing the uniform of one school and walking up the hill to their parents' house. They get abused and they get things thrown at them by other boys who go to another school. Well I mean this is ridiculous, absolutely ridiculous. I mean how can you allow your children, whether they be Protestants or Catholics, to throw stones at other children just because they have a uniform on which says, 'I am the opposite to you'? That is absolutely dreadful and it should not be able to happen. People shouldn't even conceive of that sort of thing happening – and this is now! This wasn't last year or the year before. These people are selling their house at this moment because they're afraid that their children are going to get seriously damaged. How can you be anything except negative with that sort of thing going on?

Overall then, how would you think of yourself in relation to this place that has become your home?

Well, I'm in my own country. I'm in Ireland, so I'm happier than I would be if I was in another country. Sometimes I think it would be quite nice to live in the South of France, mind you, but that's for different reasons. If I'm happy, I'm a happy outsider. I'm definitely an outsider here – but that's just here, in the island in the island.

MARIE JONES

Born in 1951, Marie Jones is an actress and playwright whose working-class, East Belfast roots have heavily influenced her career. She was a founding member of the all-women theatre group Charabanc, which toured widely and to considerable acclaim in the 1980s. In 1991 she co-founded another successful company, Dubbeljoint. Her best-known and most popular plays are *A Night in November* and the award-winning *Stones in His Pockets*. She played Gerry Conlon's mother Sarah in the film *In the Name of the Father*.

We meet near her home in South Belfast.

Marie Jones:

Always for me Ulster is the six counties. I never think about it being further than that, although I know it includes Donegal, Cavan and Monaghan. I think it's probably because when I grew up, that's what Ulster meant to us. Ulster meant being Protestant; Ulster meant being from Northern Ireland, and Northern Ireland meant six counties, and that's exactly how I felt. Still when I hear 'Ulster' I think: well it's these six counties and those other three are joined on. I know they are Ulster – but I never think about it like that.

Mark Carruthers:

So when you think of Ulster, do you tend to think of Northern Ireland post-partition?

Yes. I think of it from when I was born – that's what I think about because that's what I knew. That is what I've grown up with and that's what I feel very much a part of. It doesn't bother me to say I am Irish at all – in fact I am very proud of that – but definitely I would say I am an Ulsterwoman.

Would you say that first?

No. I would say I was Irish first and then I'm from Northern Ireland. I know there is that whole debate about the North of Ireland or Northern Ireland, but it's just what I am used to, it's just what we said. I know that it's a huge debate and I know nationalists have difficulty saying it because they can't recognise it, but it's just semantics really. I just always say I am from Northern Ireland and that's how I say it.

So you would say you are Irish, Northern Irish and an Ulsterwoman, but do you ever say British?

Very, very seldom.

And is that making a point?

I am probably making a point, but I think that is the way we have always really been. When we said 'British' when we were kids it was because it was drummed into us, although we didn't feel any connection whatsoever. No connection at all. We were saying we were British, but we had never even been out of Belfast! You think it is so, so far away. Britain to me was like somewhere away over there, when we were kids. I remember one time doing a play in Ecuador, which was a fantastic opportunity. We were invited over by the British government and the British Ambassador was our host; it was *Stones in his Pockets*. I went with my friend and we went to a party with him, and he introduced me as Marie Jones the British playwright – and I thought it was so unusual to hear that. It seemed wrong. I don't mind 'Irish' or 'Northern Irish', but 'British' just didn't feel right for me.

Though you were awarded an OBE ten years ago and you accepted that.

I was happy to accept that. It was for services to drama. My name was put forward to the British government from here, from our government, so I was absolutely happy. I have a son who was in the Royal Navy and I was very proud of him. In fact he came that day to the Palace in his uniform with my other two sons and we were very proud of him. I have nothing against being British, I just never think about it. I never say it. It doesn't feel right for me.

Do you think people have tried to pigeon-hole you? One of your best-known plays, *A Night in November*, drew criticism from some people who felt you'd abandoned your working-class Protestant background and written a play that was critical of where you'd come from. How difficult was that for you?

I was quite defensive about it because I was criticising a certain kind of Protestant. It is very clear through the play that I am criticising the kind of people who discriminate because they can do it discreetly and without anybody noticing. It's actually an attack on that middle-class kind of Protestantism.

The central character in the play is Kenneth Norman McAllister. He's a Protestant and he works in the dole office. He has a very closed mind, he's very anti-Catholic, and then all of a sudden he goes on a journey and ends up supporting the Republic of Ireland football team, which is playing in the World Cup Finals in America – and his whole world changes, his whole identity shifts. Was there a bit of you in that?

There certainly was. It was something I had thought about for a very long time – and also with Dan Gordon the actor. I think both of us had come from that background and had made the journey through our experience with theatre, through culture, through just opening our minds to that. I also made the journey myself to New York and the whole second half of the play is based on the experience that I had in that pub, watching that match, talking to those people. But I remember at the very end of the play it was exactly what happened at the end of the night after the match, and we were celebrating. I felt it doesn't matter that I am from the North or that I am a Protestant. I feel Irish tonight – a great, great feeling, as the character felt, because he had made that journey as I had made it. As we were sitting outside, everybody was celebrating. It was just so funny and wonderful – and then the policeman came up because he heard my accent and he said, 'Are you from the North?' And I said, 'Yes, I am from Belfast', and I was so proud supporting the Republic of Ireland. I was feeling the camaraderie. It was wonderful. And he said there'd been a terrible shooting there that night.[10] Six people were shot dead just watching the game on television. I just sat there and cried, just like Kevin McAllister does at the end of the play. But the good thing about it was that I felt exactly how the character does. The character says at the end: 'I am not part of that; I am not part of these people

10 Six Catholic men were shot dead and five others were wounded by members of a UVF gang in the Heights Bar in Loughinisland in County Down as they watched the Republic of Ireland versus Italy match in the football World Cup in June, 1994.

any more'. At one time I felt guilty that I was part of them because of where I grew up, but I could distance myself, and that was a great moment for me. It was the revelation, if you like, for me, that I am not part of those people any more. It was a journey that I suppose at that point was very powerful for me – so any criticism of the play I could always defend because I had been through it myself.

So you opened your mind to a new idea of identity – but you never felt you sold out?

Never, no. I mean some people might have said it, but what does selling out mean? I am still part of here, I still contribute to the cultural life of here. It doesn't matter to me if I play the Shankill or the Falls or wherever. I will go anywhere and respond to people if they have positive things to do and say. I suppose you could say it's extreme, but I decided I should speak the language, so I took myself off to Gaelic classes. I went for a couple of years.

And can you pass yourself now?

Maybe not so much now. I did it for a couple of years. If I had a couple of vodkas in me I'd be fluent! *Cad é mar atá tú* – I'd do all that bit. When I went to night classes I was there with a Professor from Queen's, a bus driver, there were two mothers whose children were going to the *Bunscoil*, there was a guy who worked in a restaurant in town and there was my friend who was ex-UDA. It was just a mix of people saying we are from this place, let's find out more. I found the language fascinating.

Do you think that people in this place can actually co-exist alongside people from a different part of the community and never really have any real contact with them whatsoever – and never really fully understand who they are?

Absolutely, there is so much of that. I see it all the time. There are people who are challenging their communities, but there are still people who just don't want to know. I think there is a big effort to do that, but then you think sometimes it's two steps forward and one step back – that's how it always will be, but at least it is two steps forward.

One of the things you have been very associated with – in the early days of your career, in particular – was finding a voice for women. Is that something you still think needs work?

It's not finished business, but I can only talk about the area I work in. I did a play recently with two actresses who came to me – Katie Tumelty and Tara Lynne O'Neill. *Fly Me to the Moon* is the play. They don't want to leave here; they want to work here. They are so much a part of this place and they want to contribute to it. They love the theatre here, they love the audience and they love the people, and they are good at what they do. So they came to me in total frustration that there are no really good roles for women, and I thought, 'Oh my God, thirty years ago that is exactly what we were doing – and these women are the same age as I was then'. And I thought, 'Ok girls, let's go. Let's do it – let's do what I did then'. So that's exactly what we did. We did exactly what we did thirty years ago: we talked. In fact you could actually say it was exactly the same process. Thirty years ago we talked about our recent history: who are the women who are underpaid and undervalued and have no voice? In our time it was the mill workers. They were still there at the time and we could still talk to them about their lives. So again, thirty years on, who are the women in society who are underpaid or undervalued and doing the work you wouldn't even think of doing yourself? Community care workers and community nurses who work for very little, and if they are looking after your parents you appreciate the work that they do. So that is what we focused on, those women and their lives and who they are. When Charabanc started off there were two reasons for it: to give us work as women and to create an audience for community theatre – theatre that is relevant to the people. At that time there was really only the Lyric or the Arts Theatre, so Charabanc did achieve what it set out to do in one sense because you can't move now for community theatre companies. Drama can be very important to a community in terms of expressing itself and I think Charabanc started that off.

Do you think people on the rest of this island and on the rest of these islands really understand or care about the notion of Ulster identity? Or do they just look back and see thirty-five years of the Troubles that they don't want to think about?

I think the majority of people would think like that because it is not about them. The more thoughtful person would actually understand it and probably, I think, in Scotland they are having that big debate now about their identity. When I go to Glasgow I actually feel – for some reason much more than I ever feel in any other city – part of this place. I don't know why. Maybe it's because obviously with a name like Magowan – which my maiden name is – they were probably Ulster Scots anyway. So somewhere there in the back of my mind, I don't feel uncomfortable, in it. I feel relaxed in it, whereas I wouldn't in any other city.

So those links are important?

I think they are important – but it's just a feeling that you get. Any big city apart from here makes me feel uncomfortable and when I am coming back home, when I get to the end of the motorway at Balmoral Avenue, I feel relaxed. I need the breath of this place. I know how people talk and feel and think. It's part of my identity as well. It makes me feel so safe and I never want to leave it. I feel very much a part of whatever you want to call it – Ulster, Northern Ireland or Ireland.

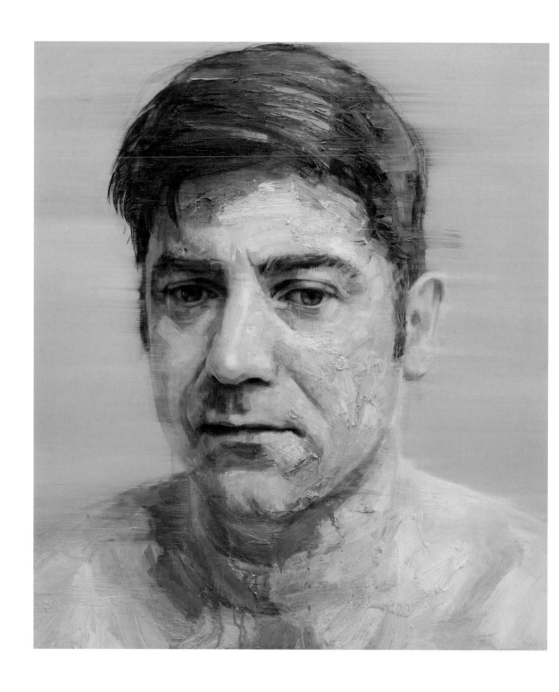

BRIAN KENNEDY

Brian Kennedy is a singer-songwriter who grew up on the Falls Road in Belfast and now lives in Dublin. Born in 1966, he has forged a successful career as a solo artist. He tours and records extensively and for six years appeared alongside Van Morrison on stage and in the recording studio. He appeared in *Riverdance* on Broadway in 2000 and represented Ireland in the 2006 Eurovision Song Contest in Athens. He has published two novels, *The Arrival of Fergal Flynn* (2004) and *Roman Song* (2005), and is currently writing his autobiography.

We meet in his Dublin home.

Brian Kennedy:

I didn't really know what Ulster was. It was just a word, a strange word. Then slowly but surely, of course, Ulster became this word that was full of politics, full of murder, and then the next thing is that Ian Paisley 'Ulster Says No' thing. That was the constant mantra where he's suddenly seen to represent Ulster, in its entirety, according to him. And of course it couldn't be more Irish in a sense either – one of the four Irish provinces. So, it just seemed to be really schizophrenic in the end and, therefore, because it was never clear what it was, it was the kind of thing that I sort of embraced and ignored in equal measure.

Mark Carruthers:

Your background couldn't be any further away from Ian Paisley's and his idea of identity, I suspect. Are you saying that as a young boy growing up on the Falls Road, the notion of Ulster had a negative connotation for you?

Most certainly. The negativity being that anything that was remotely Irish was basically illegal. You kind of felt like you were illegal. And I certainly felt like I was illegal in the sense that everywhere we went we were dogged by British soldiers. I was telling people recently that when we were kids and you wanted to go into the city centre, you were met with barricades and turnstiles and the men queued on one side and the women queued on the other. And so I would queue up and eventually in the lashing rain get up to the turnstile and, before I could go through, this guy was saying to me, 'What's your name? Where do you come from? What's your address? Who are your parents? When are you coming back? How long will you be in the town for? What are you going to the town for?' All this interrogation before you even get through. Now, of course, what's interesting is that that was only happening on one side of the city. If you were coming from the Malone Road or somewhere like that, or any other part of our city, nobody else had to encounter that. So later on, when we described it as a ghetto, people thought we were really exaggerating – but for me that was completely and utterly normal. So my version of feeling a sense of identity was absolutely coupled with the fact that you're in Ireland – but it's occupied territory at the moment. What was really interesting recently when we met Queen Elizabeth – *Éilís a Dó*, as they call her in Donegal – I was really struck by how when we left the Lyric Theatre and I went down to sing at Stormont, just how British it was. It was really interesting to suddenly get into a little cart to go up the driveway to the Stormont building to get to the stage where I was singing – and it was flanked by twenty-two thousand people waving red, white and blue flags – and I could have been in Windsor!

Did you feel uncomfortable?

Not at *all*. That's what's really interesting about it. Not at all. I felt certainly like I was celebrating someone else's identity. You know, I didn't feel British. I didn't think, 'Oh, I want to be part of this'. I didn't think, 'Oh, this is awful'. I thought to myself, 'Wow, this is really amazing! It's brilliant energy'. But it was really a moment when I just thought, 'This is very clearly for all of these people – Britain'.

And they gave you a good reception?

Oh, they gave me a gorgeous reception! I have footage of it.

So, they were delighted to see you – but they know who you are. They know your background.

Yeah. The cool thing about it is, they know that I'm from the Falls Road, they know I'm gay, they know all these things that would have been absolutely the reason why I *wouldn't* have been invited. And all of a sudden, it's actually the reason that I *am* invited. What I love about what's happened with identity in our culture is that it's absolutely flipped on its head; it has done a complete U-turn. Actually, in the middle of Stormont someone said to me, 'Will you take a Union Jack?', and I said, 'Of course I will, absolutely. Come on'. And I put my arm around them and they held the Union Jack and we took photographs. I wasn't remotely uncomfortable because it would be like me being in any other country and somebody saying, 'This is our flag. Will you celebrate my identity with me?' Of course.

So it wasn't that you felt in any way British yourself?

I never have!

It was that you didn't feel threatened by it . . .

Not at all – and that's the thing. Even though my identity was absolutely on shaky ground from the moment I could step on the ground, it never occurred to me to not have an Irish passport, for example. It never occurred to me – even though a British one was cheaper, by the way, in Belfast. I could have had both, as you know, and I still could if I wanted to, but I'm not a political person particularly. I'm political by definition, by birth, by my accent, by being a gay person, all those things. I immediately have to wear all these layers of politics without my permission. What does it mean to be Irish? I have to tell you, no more than it took me to live in the country to realise I was a city person, it took me to live in England to really discover what it was like to be Irish.

That's a very interesting point. Now that you've chosen to live here in Dublin, has that helped you define your Irishness? Do people here regard you as being as Irish as they are, or do they look at you and think – that's that guy from the North?

It's like that's my surname. It's like I'm not called 'Brian Kennedy'. I'm called 'Brian KennedyfromtheNorth'. It's funny that my geography is the thing that is my identity – and if you look at the geography, it's not even that north! It's north-east and, in fact, the reason why my sense of direction is so fucked up is because our teacher at school would refer to Donegal and say that it was in the South. Donegal's in the South. So, in my mind, even though I know, there's still that weird thing that it's in the South!

Some people would say, of course, that the biggest display of a partitionist mentality is here in Dublin rather than up in Belfast.

Well that's interesting. I think a lot of people down here, whether they're politicians or other creative people, have a sense of shame, in a way, that they didn't do anything, that they didn't get more involved. We were like the handicapped cousin that nobody spoke about, you know. Now, because I've become well known in the field that I'm in, I was asked to represent Ireland in Eurovision. A very interesting thing happened. I went to do a record signing somewhere and this little girl comes up with her family – quite a well-to-do, well-spoken girl – and she said to me, 'Why don't you represent Britain?' And I said, 'Well, because no one asked me'. But it did get me thinking – what would I have said if someone had asked me?

Well, what would you have said?

I wonder.

Or what would you say if someone does?

Oh, perversely, I'd do it. I mean, come on, I love a challenge.

Let's go back to something you touched on earlier, then – your sense of Irishness being shaped by living in England.

When I moved to London in 1985, that was a dangerous time to have my accent, to walk around London, especially as a relatively poor person on the dole, you know, in very working-class areas of London where it was dangerous enough to be different. Johnny Lydon's book, which I have upstairs on my shelf, is called *No Irish, No Blacks, No Dogs* for a reason – because the first people they didn't want to consider were Irish people. So, in '85 and '86 I was called a terrorist. I was called everything you can imagine. I was chased down the street. I was beaten up a couple of times.

This was just by people on the street?

Yes, when they heard my accent, absolutely. Any time there was any kind of flare-up in the media about a bomb being planted somewhere by the IRA. I went to a party one time, I remember, and these girls literally had to just get me out of there. A guy was going to kill me. His brother had been shot by somebody and he basically decided in his drunken logic that I had shot him. And then the next thing, of course, is any time I ever came through the airport. Now, one of the up-sides of being poor is that I couldn't afford to travel very often, but when I did I was always detained. I was held for hours. They would be checking and I was saying, 'Look, we've done this before. I've done this every time I've come through this airport'. But I said it in this accent, probably even stronger, and it just meant nothing. Your man would just be like, 'You just sit there now and don't speak until I speak to you'. They literally would treat you like that. But then when I started getting well known as a singer in my middle to late twenties things began to change because I could say, 'Oh, look – I'm a singer. I've made this album'. So I wasn't going, 'I have a gun'. I was saying, 'I have a *record*. I have a voice. That's my ammunition for the world. It's not anything else'. Do you ever watch [the BBC sitcom] *Outnumbered*? There was a brilliant episode recently where the brilliant wee girl called Karen talks to her mother. She somehow uncovers on the internet that Irish people used to be considered as terrorists and she goes, 'Irish people are terrorists? So does that mean Graham Norton and Jedward are terrorists?' She was like, 'What?!' That's how much we've changed in terms of the public perception of what it is to be Irish. It really summed it up for me right there. There's a wee girl who's smart as a whip and she just doesn't get that Irish people could be terrorists – that's not possible.

That's quite a journey to come on, isn't it? To be held and questioned about your identity – and then to end up singing at the Queen's Diamond Jubilee event at Stormont.

And, as you know, to be introduced to her and to shake her little gloved hand.[11] I remember looking into those sparkly wee eyes and thinking, 'My God, here is this moment that I never thought I would ever be in'. I was

11 Brian Kennedy attended an event hosted by Co-operation Ireland at the Lyric Theatre in Belfast in June 2012 at which the Queen also shook hands with Northern Ireland's Deputy First Minister, Martin McGuinness. Later that day Brian Kennedy sang at a Diamond Jubilee event at Stormont's Parliament Buildings.

looking at an old lady who sort of looked a bit like my granny – just a little lady, except a much cleaner, much more privileged version of my granny. And so, if you had said to me, you know, in those moments on the Falls Road, or in those interrogation rooms in Heathrow Airport, when I'm nineteen or twenty or twenty-one, 'Ah, don't worry. You'll grow up and you'll be a singer and it'll be fine. And, in fact, the Queen of England will shake your hand' – I mean it's unthinkable, but here we are.

And that's good?

It's not good – it's great!

What about those early days growing up on the Falls Road? You must have been at school with people who got involved . . .

Of course. The guy that died in Gibraltar was in our art class. I remember very clearly. He was a great drummer. When one of the first hunger strikers died, my dad was a marathon coach. Francis Hughes – I remember his brother being in our house when that happened and, God love him, the devastation of all of that, and his wife, and how dangerous it was. Everything seemed so dangerous all the time that, at any point, you just expected that you were going to be next. My next-door neighbour had his leg blown off. I saw people shot dead right in front of me – right in front of me.

So that story is true?

Oh God, yeah. I'll never forget it. Beechmount Avenue. There was another riot of some kind and I was standing outside my best friend's house and this guy comes belting round the corner. And then right behind him, a few seconds later, a soldier in loads of gear and a big rifle comes round and he just takes a stance and then shoots him a couple of times in the back. So your man obviously just hits the ground ten, twelve feet away – and you can imagine. It's just like, 'Oh fuck!' I mean you don't know what to do. Do you move? Is he going to turn around and start shooting other people? You don't know what's going to happen and the loudest thing of all is the silence that happens after a shooting – and you can't imagine how loud an actual gun is in front of you. It's like everybody's just held their breath and then, finally, some more soldiers appeared. This woman appeared three doors up. She thought it was her husband. The weirdest thing in the world happened. She, like a Tasmanian devil, lost her fucking mind – screaming, crawling on the ground to get to him, crying, calling her husband's name. And she turned him over – and it wasn't her husband. She suddenly just went, 'Oh'. It was like a play. She just suddenly snapped out of it and fixed herself and walked back to the house, which was only a few feet away. It was a bizarre thing and then, of course, eventually, more army come and people get the word that somebody's been shot. A few guys gather, people start throwing bricks at the soldiers, petrol bombs, all of that. Now, we're sort of in the passageway. It was a real dangerous thing to do but it just happened. What do you do? You can't practise for a moment like that and, eventually, the army came and managed to get his body into the back of a Saracen and off they went.

And what age were you at that point?
Eleven.

And did you read about it in the papers?
Ah well, no. I mean first of all, we didn't really have newspapers. I mean occasionally the newspaper would end up in our house, but it would end up in the back of the fire. It was used to light the fire. But what did happen to me, which is another memory – I remember our riot was long over. We were just like, 'Can we get on with it now? Is the riot over now? Can we play? Can we just get on with being kids?' – and this group of journalists arrived up too late. Obviously, they'd missed the whole thing and this English guy said to me, 'Any of you boys want 50p?' And back then 50p was a fortune. And he goes, 'Look, all you have to do is throw a few bricks at that burnt-out car'. So a few of us pick up a few bricks and he takes a few photographs of us doing that. Now I'm a kid. I don't know what's going on, but, of course, as an adult, I think, 'Oh, I see'. So he gave us 50p. Fair play to him and off he went and those photographs appeared, versions of them anyway, a day or two later – 'RIOT IN WEST BELFAST: YOUNG KIDS THROWING BRICKS AT A CAR'. The whole thing was set up and clearly what had happened was he had missed it. He was probably down in the 'Whip and Saddle' still necking a brandy or he just couldn't get through the riot. But I have first-

hand experience of that, where it was absolutely staged and used as proof of a riot. So, somewhere in the annals you might see me.

So if you felt a bit of an outsider growing up in your own city because of where you came from, what did you think about the idea of being an Ulsterman?

It's funny, when I first heard that term 'Ulsterman' I understood it to mean Protestant. I didn't understand it to mean anything else.

You didn't think you could be an Ulsterman?

No, not at all, because it was already the property of the Protestant community. 'Ulster says No'. When Ian Paisley said those words, he basically was saying, 'Ulster is me. I own Ulster – and we say no!' And the really interesting thing about the difference between the Irish language and the English language is when you might say to me, 'I'm hungry'. Just two words, 'I'm hungry'. If you say it in Irish, you say, '*Tá ocras orm*', which means, 'The feeling of hunger is upon me'. It's as if, hunger visits you and then leaves again, but actually, in English, you are hunger – 'I'm hungry'. You own it. It's not something that comes and goes and I think that's really interesting. It really is fascinating. Cathal Ó Searcaigh, the wonderful poet friend of mine, explained that to me one day and I just remember thinking, that's it! That's the difference between these two identities – between being Irish and being English.

So things have changed a great deal politically in the last twenty years. Things have also changed as far as your sexuality's concerned, because we've come a long way in twenty years on that front, North and South.

I know, and the greatest thing that happens to me now – somebody stops me in the street, like they did yesterday, and very warmly said hello and asked could I be photographed with their little children. One of the other things that's happening there is that they're also saying, 'We know you're a gay man and it's absolutely cool'. They wanted me to hold their baby. They were happy to tell me that their cousin was gay – or not. I mean sometimes I meet people who have never met a gay person before, so yeah, of course, we've made massive strides and I think that one of the things that makes that possible is people like me coming out and leading a healthy life and saying, 'Look, there isn't one way to be gay, first of all'. Just as there's not one way to be Irish, as we know. I sang at 'Newry Pride' in the summer and it was a really fascinating thing to see how far it's come. First of all, as you know, I sang at the inauguration of Newry as a city about sixteen years ago and then here I am at 'Newry Pride', the first ever 'Pride' there, and the fact that, first of all, they can have a 'Pride'. Second of all, all these families came along and when I arrived I had to walk a good distance to get into the field and, Jesus, the amount of people saying, 'Hello. Delighted you're here. Can't wait to hear you sing' – and that was unthinkable not very long ago.

Do you think your notion of identity has been shaped, as well, by that international aspect to your life – living in London, singing in Eurovision, and that whole American experience?

Riverdance on Broadway, of course. Look, I honestly, hand on heart, think it should be compulsory that when you get to sixteen years of age, you have to travel around the world for a year and you have to cope by yourself, more or less. I think the greatest thing that you can do to discover what it's like to be a being on this planet is to go round the planet. I remember the first time I ever went to the Shankill Road to sing. I was invited to sing. No one like me had been invited before and there was all sorts of discussion about do I wear a bulletproof vest? I mean serious conversations, and a few people who were close to me were very worried I'd be shot and I was going to be used as an example, as sometimes these things bizarrely happened. But not for a second did I feel afraid, not for a nanosecond, and I'm not the bravest guy in the block. I am a lover not a fighter, as I always say – but I remember thinking, 'Look, I've been invited by these fairly high-up political people to come and sing in the Shankill Leisure Centre'. And so, along I go, and I decided not to wear a bulletproof vest. It was offered in great seriousness and I turned it down and I was asked did I need anybody to come with me, an armed person or a security guard? I turned it all down and I went along – and guess what happened? I had a brilliant time. It was like a film where, when I stepped out on stage, there was maybe about fifty photographers because I suppose it was a big moment and there was all these flashes and it was slow motion and it was like the perfect moment for a lone gunman to just go 'bang' and I'm dead – if we were making a Hollywood movie. But we weren't. And then of course, I did the concert. It was gorgeous – and guess what happened? I'm upstairs and I meet all these wee women and wee men and they're exactly the same as all the wee women and the wee men I grew up with. All the same craic, the same boldness, the same kind of warmth, a bit of suspicion, whatever. Exactly the same. It was absolutely summed up in that moment and I just thought, as Bono would say, 'We're one, but we're not the same'. Yeah, we're one and we *are* the same. In fact, we *weren't* one and we *are* the same. It was like that phrase turned on its head. I met all these people that I could have grown up with. They're exactly the same. It was like there was a wee factory somewhere and they just spew out all these little people. I'm from very little people. So I think the greatest thing that any young person could do is travel the world. I would say to any young person out there that it's really important to experience what it's like to be a minority – before you can feel properly part of any majority.

So you've travelled a lot, you've lived in different places – but you're settled in Dublin?

I always say, if I was a stick of rock and you snap me in two, it would say, 'Made in Belfast' right in the middle – probably in pink letters. But, at the same time, I am a forty-six-year-old consequence of my childhood and it's extraordinary to me to be able to stand on Grafton Street in the middle of Dublin and switch on the Christmas lights and a couple of thousand people are cheering and singing along with me. And then I go into the Shankill Road, into that leisure centre, and sing there, and sing for Georgie Best at his funeral up in Stormont – it's really extraordinary when I think of it.

So, as far as your identity is concerned, at this point in your life, how would you describe yourself?

There's not one way to be gay. There's not one way to be straight. There's not one way to be Irish, just as there's not one way to be British. I wrote an essay about this many years ago which you've just reminded me of. It was called 'Being Irish in the Year 2000', and the thing about the word 'Irish' or the word 'British', it's like you're saying something is 'small-ish' or 'big-ish', you know, it's not quite complete. I don't think the identity is really ever complete until you get to the end of your life and only at that moment can you look back and say, 'Ok, my identity is now this . . .' and boom, you're dead. So I think it's ever evolving. It's 'Ir-ish'. It's 'Brit-ish'. I'm 'ish', I would say. Yeah, I'll settle for 'ish'.

GARY LIGHTBODY

Born in Bangor in County Down in 1976, Gary Lightbody is the lead singer and songwriter with the alternative rock band Snow Patrol. A past pupil of Campbell College in Belfast, he moved to Scotland in 1994 where he studied English at the University of Dundee. Though Snow Patrol's success was slow to come, the band is now one of the most successful in the business with hits like *Run*, *Chasing Cars* and *Just Say Yes*.

We meet over lunch in Belfast just before he heads off to Los Angeles to record the band's seventh studio album.

Gary Lightbody:

Ulster isn't a word I use that often. I use it to refer to the rugby team, of course, but I wouldn't use it to describe myself. I say I'm from Northern Ireland. In Northern Ireland the word Ulster has a lot wrapped up in it. It's a tricky word to get your head around. I think part of what we need to work towards in a modern Northern Ireland is a language that isn't full of trigger words that set people off. I know the word Ulster means a lot to some people North and South and I respect that but I'm not sure what it means to me. Northern Ireland, though, means everything to me.

Mark Carruthers:

So if you're asked how you identify yourself, do you automatically say Northern Irish?

I say Northern Irish. Sometimes I say Irish. When you travel a lot, it's just easier sometimes to say Ireland than Northern Ireland. Explaining the difference to people around the world can lead to long conversations that I'm maybe too jet-lagged to get into. It's not really a statement of anything other than geography for me.

And what about the British dimension? Do you ever say British?

No. I think we, as a people, need to start being ok with being Northern Irish. How about a united Northern Ireland? That would be a lovely thing, just forgetting for a minute Britishness or Irishness and just being proud to be Northern Irish. I'm very proud of being Northern Irish. I think there's so much greatness in this country and if we want to cast off the past, we need to be ok with being Northern Irish – whatever our background.

You grew up and went to school here but then you chose to go away to Scotland to university.

I think as a kid, I just looked to get away anywhere. I wanted to leave. Everything that was happening in the country was upsetting me. It upset me from a very young age. I didn't understand it at first. To be honest, I'm not sure if I understand it now, because I never was deeply religious or political and growing up in Northern Ireland put me off politics completely until I actually moved to Glasgow. Not because Scotland is a utopia – there are the same problems there, especially in Glasgow with Rangers and Celtic – it's just about seeing things from a wider perspective. At the time in Northern Ireland, everybody was looking inward rather than outward and I think that's the difference now – Northern Ireland's become a part of Europe, whereas before it didn't feel like that. It felt secluded, isolated – certainly to me – and that's why I wanted to leave. But at the same time, leaving made me realise what I appreciated about it – so I'm glad that I got away and got a different perspective on home because I fell back in love with it again.

So did being out of Northern Ireland help to define your Northern Irishness for you?

Yes, I think so – although literally fifty percent of the people in my class in Dundee were from Ireland, North and South. It was my first time experiencing life with Southern Irish people and realising that everybody's just the same, there's absolutely no difference between them. That's the first time I actually realised that in practice. I thought maybe there's something missing from my life, maybe I need to go out there and explore because there must be some other type of people on this planet – but there's not. We all have the same insecurities and we all try to find the same joy when we can. I really appreciated Northern Ireland for the things that I loved about it and didn't realise that I loved. It made me the person that I am.

Were you shaped, do you think, by your experience in this part of the world when you started writing music?

I had grown up reading Heaney. I had a great English teacher called Mark McKee who's still teaching at Campbell now. He introduced me to Heaney, Bob Dylan and Van Morrison, so it was a big moment going into his class in fourth form. It was literally just like a saloon door was kicked open. The posse had arrived and there was a new sheriff in town and it was just music and poetry. I became obsessed with Heaney and Van Morrison and that set me on the path that I'm on today. Mark McKee pretty much is the catalyst for the path that I took. That was twenty-two years ago. He was able to relate to us in a way that none of the other teachers could. His classes were always so much fun and he had such a great sense of humour. Classrooms aren't normally filled with laughter and if they are, you're told to shush or you're reprimanded in some way. School was tough for me up until that point but that really got me engaged.

And you wrote a song called *Reading Heaney to Me.*

Yes, it's just a song about a beautiful night with my now ex-girlfriend. It was like something off a greeting card – a roaring fire and jumpers at Christmas time. It's pretty clichéd, even in my mind, when I'm thinking back. It was a beautiful night and we were literally reading poetry to each other and it was very lovey-dovey but it was really awesome. I love people who aren't afraid to just crack a book open and start reading it out loud – that's one of the great joys.

Have you thought much about why there is such a rich vein of writing talent in this part of the world – from Heaney and Longley, to Brian Friel and Van Morrison?

We punch well above our weight artistically. I think great tragedy and great pain always lead to great art. It's not that I grew up in the worst of the Troubles but a lot of those guys did, and I think that out of the darkness comes this extraordinary wealth of poets and writers and thinkers. I think most of the time people are just trying to make sense of what's going on around them. I'm going to get into trouble for this since I live there now, but not that much great art comes from LA because it's sunny all the time. Surfer dudes aren't going to come up with *Digging* [the celebrated Seamus Heaney poem]. The Irish – North and South – tend to be reflective. America's more often about what happens tomorrow.

Which can be a good thing but it can also be a bad thing.

Of course it can be a bad thing but when it leads people to make great art, it's a great thing, even if it's terrible at the time. As far as politics goes, it's a bad thing to get completely wrapped up in what happened in the past. We have to let these things go or else we'll never get out of this. Maybe the American idea of looking more towards the future might, in fact, be of some benefit to us in a modern Northern Ireland.

So you subscribe to the view, do you, that the artist has to suffer a little to produce his or her best work?

Yeah, I think so. Certainly, the best things that I've ever done artistically have come from heartbreak. Some of the worst things that I've done have been wrapped up in that too, but certainly the best music or writing that I've ever done have come from moments of pain and reflection. There's not that many truly great songs about just being happy – not really. Marlena Shaw's *California Soul* – there's one, a great song. But, again, California – it's sunny there. What are they going to write about? Music and sunshine. Here there's a darkness and it's what, I think, I was afraid of as a kid and what eventually lured me back – this great mystery that is Northern Ireland. It's a very unique place to be. I've never found anywhere else like it in the world, in terms of how great we are as poets and how bad we are at moving forward.

That's quite a contradiction, isn't it? How do you feel about the politicians, then, who want to meet you and associate themselves with your global success?

I've met Martin McGuinness quite a few times now. I met Peter Robinson recently and various other politicians over the years. They're all great craic and they seem like nice men but it's very hard to have anyone agree with anything in Northern Ireland. You don't hear 'yes' an awful lot, which is why using [the Snow Patrol song] *Just Say Yes* for the [2013 Derry/Londonderry UK] City of Culture was a great triumph. The word 'yes' is a really important word in the new Northern Ireland. If we don't trust it and we don't own it it's going to be hard to shake off that big, massive, gigantic 'no' that has been Northern Irish politics for such a long time.

So, you would give the politicians quite a bit of credit?

I think it's an extraordinary thing to do, to want to be a politician in Northern Ireland. It is a great service to the country because it's a hell of a thing to undertake to try and rebuild the confidence and the trust of so many people who have had their hearts broken in so many different ways. I have an awful amount of respect for anyone that tries to do good in this country. It's a phenomenal thing to do. I just want everyone to stop fighting and I want everyone to stop rioting and I want everyone to realise that it affects the whole country. It affects people's hearts and souls and people's businesses, and every facet of Northern Ireland is affected detrimentally by violence and bomb threats and all these things that have reared their heads again in recent times. It upsets everybody who has Northern Ireland's best interests at heart.

So when you're on the road with the band, do you find people asking you what's happening back in Northern Ireland?

Very, very few people ask me what's happening. Lots of people tell me what's happening, which is the most frustrating thing in the world because you want to just scream at them, 'If you're not from there, if you never lived here, you cannot possibly know'. Because *I* barely know what's going on! I mean, it's nice to have perspective as a Northern Irish person, leaving the country and then being able to look back and see a little bit more clearly how I feel about certain things. But to have no direct experience of it and yet to have a definitive answer is ridiculous, really. Not that it's not great to meet Irish people all over the world. Of course, it is. We have wild craic with most of them but it's when it comes down to the inevitable talk of politics – it's difficult to take from people who haven't experienced it firsthand.

Do you feel comfortable with being cast in the role of a global ambassador for Northern Ireland?

Yeah, I'm ok with that. I think our music and the new talent that's coming through are ambassadors for Northern Ireland. On that stage last night [at a music event at Parliament Buildings in Stormont] I didn't ask people what religion they were. I know that some were Catholics and some were Protestants but not ever would I ask anyone that in my life – and nor have I ever had it asked to me in a music situation in Northern Ireland. No one ever asks that question. It doesn't mean anything. It doesn't matter. You're never judged by your background when you're in a band, so that is a great way to show a different side of Northern Ireland – the side of Northern Ireland that it doesn't matter where you're from. It doesn't matter what religion you are or what you think about certain issues. It just matters if you're a decent person. That's a really important thing, I think, for anybody I hang out with or am friends with.

So at this stage, do you see Snow Patrol as an Irish band, a Northern Irish band or a Scottish band?

Well, three of the members are Scottish. If someone says we're Scottish, I would say, 'Well, most of us are from Northern Ireland, actually, but we do have some Scottish members'. Dublin embraced us before Belfast did. Belfast took a little bit of time but then when it did embrace us, I mean the love that we get here is extraordinary. Other bands from other places have said how jealous they are of how loved we are in our own country because not that many bands get that same sort of love. Generally, in your own country, you'll get shit for being a big band, whereas here, for the most part, people are very proud of us. It's lovely to have that and I do feel very proud to be Northern Irish. Even with the riots and bomb-scares, there hasn't been a dramatic shift back to the dark days. It seems very far from ever shifting back there. I think the overwhelming majority of people want the peace to hold and to move forward and that's just extraordinary. That's one of the reasons why I fell back in love with the place.

Have you thought much about how your relationship with this place might change in the years ahead?

I don't think that we're ever heading back to the way it was but if it did, it would break my heart. It would break everyone's heart. I guess that would change my feeling for the place but it wouldn't change my love and my connection to the place because I want to be among the people who try to keep spreading some kind of joy here. If you desert a place that badly needs your help, then you're no great shakes. I would never desert Northern Ireland, ever. It would just break my heart a little bit if it did go bad again but it would take a hell of a lot to change my love for this place. I do love it, heart and soul. It's too good a place for me to ever fall out of love with.

ANNA LO

Anna Lo is an Alliance member of the Northern Ireland Assembly. She was born in Hong Kong in 1950 and has lived and worked in Northern Ireland for nearly forty years. A former social worker, she was the first ethnic-minority politician elected at a national level in Northern Ireland, and became the first politician born in South-East Asia to be elected to any legislative body in Europe.

We meet in her office at Parliament Buildings in Stormont.

Anna Lo:

I would rather use the term 'Northern Ireland' than 'Ulster'. 'Ulster' always seems to me to be a more Protestant term. I try not to use it. I would rather use a more neutral term – 'Northern Ireland' – and I try not to say 'the North' or 'the South' as well.

Mark Carruthers:

And do you think that more and more people are now doing that? In the latest census, a lot of people seemed to be moving towards a notion of 'Northern Irishness'?

I think particularly young people. I know my two sons who live in London will not call themselves English. They will not call themselves Irish. They call themselves Northern Irish. Very clearly they say, 'We are from Northern Ireland'.

So what do you call yourself at this stage in your life?

My passport is a British passport, but I don't see myself as British. I still feel very strongly that I'm ethnically Chinese. My partner once said, 'You're more Chinese than you think you are', so I would see myself as very westernised and I think my Chinese friends would say I'm not really quite Chinese, so I'm kind of in between. I'm not totally Chinese in terms of my thinking maybe. My upbringing is still very much Chinese, but I've been very westernised after living here for thirty-odd years. I see myself very much as a mixture of East and West.

And would you regard yourself as Northern Irish at this stage?

Yes. My identity would be Northern Irish. I would very seldom actually call myself 'Northern Irish'. I would say I live in Northern Ireland, rather than saying I'm 'Northern Irish'. I don't see myself as Irish at all. I still see myself as Chinese with a British passport, with a British nationality, living in Northern Ireland, in a part of Ireland. But I think I still feel very much an ethnic Chinese person. That would rank top for me.

Do you feel that gives you a special voice as an elected representative in speaking for other people of different ethnic origins who also live in Northern Ireland?

Not really, no. I have been elected as a member for South Belfast so I represent all nationalities there. The only criterion is that you live in my constituency of South Belfast, and so we have turned away, unfortunately, people from different parts of Northern Ireland asking for help. They say, 'Well, you are from an ethnic-minority background and you know about ethnic minorities and we want your help'. I say, 'I'm sorry. You live outside my constituency. You've got to go to this or that person. If it's an immigration issue, go to your own MP or MLA'. It's amazing that people think that because you are an ethnic Chinese, you should know about anything Chinese or anything Oriental.

But are you not active in the Northern Ireland Chinese community outside politics?

I'm not. I have never been accepted by many Chinese as a member of the Chinese community in Northern Ireland. It's more people from outside the community who say I am a member of the Chinese community. I suppose it's very loose. How would you say you're a member of the community? It's difficult to define that. It's very much a social construct in a way, but certainly I know Chinese people, particularly first-generation Chinese, who come from Hong Kong, where I actually came from, who would say, 'You're not part of the Chinese community' – in an affectionate way. I've always been their helper rather than a member of the Chinese community, because I came from a different part of Hong Kong. I'm a city person, as they would call it, in Chinese. My educational background would be very different from them and I'm too westernised for them to call me totally Chinese.

And is that because you married a man from Northern Ireland and came to live here?

Well, I was educated in Hong Kong in English. They are from the very rural part of Hong Kong called the New Territories, which is really the buffer zone between mainland China and the British colony of Hong Kong. That's an area that had been left behind, really, for many generations. Hong Kong was given to Britain in 1841 in perpetuity. But the part of the territory north of the island of Hong Kong was on lease to Britain, so the majority of the first-generation Chinese people came from that area called the New Territories and they had been left behind when Hong Kong developed very fast into a world trade centre. It was out of neglect on the part of the Hong Kong government, and on the part of the Chinese government – which in those days had no jurisdiction over it – that that area became really very deprived, and a lot of people left that area to come to the UK in the 1950s and '60s. So the majority of them would not have had a lot of opportunities for formal education, and so I would be quite different in terms of background.

So their journey to this part of the world was very different from your journey?

Yes. And they laughed and said, 'You're not Chinese! You've never worked in the catering trade!' I'm not a good cook, so that bars you from being a member of the Chinese community for the first-generation Chinese. But I've worked as an outsider in many ways and I think that works better for me to help them, because I was a social worker and I was a community worker. I was the person outside looking in and helping them.

What do you remember about coming here first in 1974?

They were very dark days. It was a total culture shock. It must have been horrendous for a woman in her early twenties coming from a very vibrant city of Hong Kong and London, places that were alive day and night. After being here two weeks, I took up a position working as a secretary for the *Farm Week* editor and I asked my colleagues, 'Right, where do you all go out for a meal at night?' And they said, 'No, we don't go out at night. All the restaurants are being bombed out!' In Hong Kong and in London we would go out to eat in a not-expensive restaurant very often, so eating out was very much part of my life, and being told you don't go out to eat was hard – you only go to hotels to have dinners for birthdays and wedding anniversaries. I was thinking, 'I don't believe it! What sort of life have you got?' And then I realised also there were no cinemas here in those days. They were all bombed in Belfast, anyway. Going to cinemas and theatres was also very much part of my culture and my background, and that was a total culture shock too. Also, I remember the accent here was so difficult for me, and the only person I could understand a hundred percent was not my husband, but my mother-in-law, Trudy Watson, who was very kind to me. Trudy taught French and Communication, so she pronounced her words really well. She didn't shout at me or speak very loudly to me, but she pronounced words properly and she was the only person for months I could understand every single word of.

And how difficult was it for you to get an understanding of the nature of the conflict here back in 1974?

I was thrown in at the deep end. My first husband, David, died a few years ago. He was quite involved in politics. David was very friendly, for example, with Gerry Fitt. I did meet with a lot of politicians so I did learn about who's who, which side is which, and also then I went to work in the BBC. I worked in the World Service in Belfast, so I did pick it up quite quickly. I think I have to say, if anything, at the very beginning my sympathy would have been more towards the Catholic community – these were the oppressed people – but the more you learn, the more you try to balance it out. But certainly my initial sympathy would have been very much with the Catholic community about housing issues, job issues and job discrimination. I would be from a background that's quite strong on equality. There were no politics in Hong Kong; it was total direct rule – absolutely. When we talk about direct rule in Northern Ireland, you don't know what direct rule is like in a British colony. When the Governor of Hong Kong arrived in his fantastic uniform with those feathers on top of his helmet, nobody would have heard of his name until the day he arrived. He was appointed by the Queen, generally from diplomatic circles, so politics were never encouraged. But I was quite active in school and I was quite strong on equality issues. I was in a very good government school, but at seventeen I was made to leave school, although I absolutely adored it. I left mostly because of economic issues, but also a bit of gender equality. The Chinese tradition would favour boys, and I had three older brothers, two of whom were still in education. So my parents said, 'You have to go and work and help pay for the education of your brothers'. So that to me was maybe my first real experience of discrimination. It's not race discrimination, it's gender discrimination, and it left a big mark on me at the age of seventeen, being the brightest in the family. I totally loved school more than anybody else in the family and I was made to leave, and it left a big mark on me. So I think equality has always been in my blood and bones – to fight for the underdogs.

But many people in your situation in a place like Northern Ireland would step away from politics and avoid expressing a political opinion. They wouldn't want to get involved in any way – but you did the opposite.

Yes. Part of what motivated me was ethnic-minority issues at the beginning. That was part of the reason for wanting to join the Alliance Party. It was the only one I felt comfortable with because I really don't want to be labelled 'orange' or 'green'.

And much has been made about you breaking new ground as a legislator in Europe with an ethnic Chinese background.

Yes. There are some ethnic Chinese politicians in Europe but that's third- and fourth-generation. I'm the first China-born legislator in Europe. In reality, it doesn't mean anything. It doesn't matter at all, but if you say it made a bit of history, then yes. It was a positive story for Northern Ireland to show respect for diversity.

And did that tie in with the kind of positive response you got in 1974? Were people generally welcoming when you first arrived?

The majority of people were very welcoming. If anything, they were more curious about me. I did get a bit of hassle. There were two types of racism I experienced. You have the very middle-class reaction, a bit patronising. I also had some nasty experiences where, for example, I was kicked on the street in broad daylight. There was a group of young people walking towards me and shouting abuse at me, and after they passed me one of them kicked me from behind.

But that was quite some time ago?

Oh yes. That has changed a lot. I still get it now and again – for example, with each election I would get something. The first election was the worst. The first election I did get phone-calls, 'How dare you? You could not represent people in Northern Ireland. You are from China!' That was in 2007, when I first stood.

So how do you feel about people in this part of the world feeling so passionate about their sense of identity? Do you feel baffled or bemused by that?

Yes. I do understand where they come from, where they have this very strong sense of identity. I think when they've been in a situation like it's been in Northern Ireland, you do make people feel the need to uphold their identity. I do understand the background and I think people from outside would say, 'Oh, these people are just mad'. But until you know the history of Northern Ireland, you cannot really criticise people for being so hung up about their identity. I think young people are not subjected to the same sense of threat and fear about their identity being eroded or diminished. They don't feel the same sense of threat against them and I think younger people are less concerned about the symbols of identity. I think young people are beginning to see themselves more as a multitude of identities, and not as either just 'orange' or 'green'. I think younger people are less hung up now about their identities, but I can understand why people who've lived through the Troubles feel their identity is so important that they need to defend it.

You've got two sons. Their father was Northern Irish, their mother's Chinese, they grew up in Northern Ireland and they live in England. How do they regard themselves?

My younger son, Owen, regards himself as European. He's an architect and he lived in Switzerland for two years and he has friends all over the world. He went to Cambridge and he speaks two or three European languages. He sees himself as European and not British or Irish. But then, within the UK, my sons would say they are Northern Irish. And also, with my influence, they would have the Chinese heritage as well. My other son, Conall, would have less of a sense of whether he is European or not, but he is very much an environmentalist. He's involved in a really worldwide project now. They really don't like limiting themselves to being one thing. I see myself as having so many different identities. Why should you just be so hung up on your national identity? You have your identity as a mother, father, son and daughter.

Are you content that your journey in life brought you to live and work in this part of the world?

Yes. I made a very long journey. I like it here. Sometimes I wonder what would have happened to me if I had stayed in Hong Kong. What would I have become? But you've only one life to live and I'm happy with the life I've lived so far, and that I've chosen to live it in Northern Ireland. I love the open space. I love the green space here. I love the people. I could have gone back to Hong Kong, I suppose. We had thought about it, but David wasn't keen to go back. Hong Kong is very different. Hong Kong is exciting. So I did make a huge – I wouldn't call it a sacrifice – a huge set of changes. I remember one incident, right after we got married. We were still on our honeymoon. We didn't have money to go anywhere, so we were in Belfast for the first two weeks before I started work. David, my husband, said one Saturday, 'Let's go to the city centre to McGlade's Bar for lunch'. We got off the bus in the city centre and walked all the way up Royal Avenue. David had just come back from two years in Hong Kong. He met so many people that by the time I got to McGlade's Bar I was nearly in tears because I suddenly realised I was nobody except David's bride. That sudden sense that you know nobody, and nobody knows you, was really upsetting. Suddenly it felt like part of me had gone. It suddenly hit me, and just that one incident of half an hour down Royal Avenue made me realise I was a total stranger here.

But if you walked down Royal Avenue now, everybody would know you.

Yes, it's true. I hadn't thought about that.

MICHAEL LONGLEY

The poet Michael Longley was born in Belfast in 1939 of English parents. He was educated at The Royal Belfast Academical Institution [RBAI] and Trinity College Dublin where he read Classics. A close friend of fellow poets Seamus Heaney and Derek Mahon, he received the Queen's Gold Medal for Poetry in 2001. His 1991 collection, *Gorse Fires*, won the Whitbread Poetry Prize. *The Weather in Japan* (2000) won the T. S. Eliot Prize and the Hawthornden Prize. His collection, *A Hundred Doors*, won the *Irish Times* Poetry Now Award in September 2012. He was Ireland Professor of Poetry, 2007–2010.

We meet over lunch near his South Belfast home.

Michael Longley:

Ulster is where I was brought up and the first thing it means is home. I see it as a very particular part of Ireland but increasingly I see Ireland as a whole. I would like to think of myself as a pan-Irishman with an Ulster accent. Sport, in a way, brings out the true self. I wouldn't cheer for anyone else but Ulster in rugby. I wouldn't cheer for any country other than Ireland. But Ulster means, for me, complication. If I'm abroad, the word Ulster makes me smile inwardly. I'm loyal to it because of my history.

Mark Carruthers:

So, to what extent has that history shaped your sense of identity, do you think? Your father came to Ulster as a commercial traveller from Clapham.

Yes, from Clapham Common. He and my mother came to Belfast in 1927 and they just stayed. I don't know whether they were ever what you might call 'honorary Ulster folk'. They remained fairly obviously English but they clearly were committed to Ulster as their second home. My father was extremely popular, much loved, and people still, when they hear my name, mention Major Longley. It's not that common for English people to be popular in Ulster, as you know. Loyal Ulstermen are not among the leading

Anglophiles. Because of my parents I remain unshakeably an Anglophile. I'm true to that side of my background. How could I not be true to what I think of as the Britannic tinge? My father fought in the First World War gallantly and then joined up again as an old-fashioned patriot in 1939. He was a great supporter of Churchill, I remember. So I am an Anglophile, but then I went to a fairly rough primary school in Balmoral Avenue, my twin and I. Many of my school friends lived down the Lisburn Road in the small two-up and two-down houses to the left as you're going into town. Peter and I fairly quickly, in order to survive, became Belfast boys with Belfast accents, much to the alarm of my gently spoken parents. It's funny how one's sense of oneself is relative. When I was visiting my friends in Hugh Street and Melrose Street, streets off the Lisburn Road, I felt tremendously posh. I was embarrassed by my poshness, by the fact that I would wipe my nose on a handkerchief and came from a, relatively speaking, large and comfortable home – a middle-class home – and I never really thought of myself particularly as an Ulster person until I went to Trinity and then I realised, yes, I was a Northerner. I was an Ulsterman.

So, do you think that your Trinity experience helped shape that Northern-ness?

Yes. In those days the major grammar schools in the North would send their classical students down to Trinity, so there was a little group of Northern Irish classicists. I think we were aware of our Northern identity. I took to Dublin like a duck to water and I wasn't bothered too much about matters of identity. That all came much later but Trinity, of course, had a profound effect on my sense of self and I think I'm still shaped by it. I think, over the years, right up to today I realise that I'm of the Anglican tradition, you know? When I was a schoolboy most of my friends went to Malone Presbyterian Church or to McCracken Memorial [Presbyterian Church]. I was baptised and then later confirmed in St John's, the Church of Ireland church. There are intuitions and shadings which make me realise that whether I want it or not, I'm Protestant and, in the more refined definition, Anglican. All of that was coloured in by Trinity. At that time, the wicked Archbishop McQuaid [the Roman Catholic Archbishop of Dublin] preached that it was a mortal sin for Catholics to go to this bastion of Protestantism. You realised you were in a slightly strange institution. And then my wife, whom I met at Trinity, was the daughter of a very distinguished mathematician called Stanislaus Broderick. He became Professor of Pure Mathematics at Trinity when Edna and I were there. He'd been brought up a Catholic in West Cork, so he had to choose, in the shadow of McQuaid's nonsense, between his church and his intellectual discipline – and he chose the latter.

And how much was your sense of identity shaped by your time at RBAI, do you think?

I went to Trinity because of the Classics master there, an extraordinary monster called Charlie Fay, whose ghost still intimidates me. Inst had a very rich culture. Being in the centre of town, it drew pupils from all parts of Belfast. I can remember one maths class in which I was sitting close to a lad in Pirrie House, and that meant East Belfast, and his Dad worked in the shipyard. And then in the same row of desks was a boy from Dill, whose father was a lawyer and he lived in South Belfast off the Malone Road. So the fact that the school was classless just by practice was tremendously important; it was also non-sectarian. Most of the schools were strictly speaking non-sectarian but Inst was, in quite insouciant practice non-sectarian, in as much as there were Catholic teachers there and the man who really had the profoundest effect on me after Charlie Fay was Joe Cowan, an English teacher who was a Catholic. Fay was a very powerful teacher through bullying really, while Joe was a beguiler and charmer. He had a non-unionist slant and slipped into lessons poems which weren't on the course, because the unionist hegemony in its education programme made sure that there was no Irish literature. So we didn't do Yeats or O'Casey or Wilde. I remember the first time I read MacNeice – thanks to Joe. It was a poem called *Sunday Morning*. There was in Inst just enough to remind you that one of the school's founders, William Drennan, was a United Irishman.

When it comes to your own poetry, whether it's been about nature or the First World War or the Troubles, what has motivated you to write?

They're very mysterious, the pressures which produce poems. As what you might call an œuvre – a body of work – accumulates, you realise retrospectively that there are in fact themes, pre-occupations, and you've named them. You didn't mention love poetry. I'm proud to have written some love poems which I think are good. They're written for obvious reasons. Then in 1969, Northern Ireland erupted. Things got steadily worse. I think all the poets that I knew were flabbergasted by the ferocity of it all. It seemed important not to latch onto it, not to take an opportunistic attitude to the suffering of the community – not to, as somebody said, 'Latch onto the headlines'. It was John Hume who coined the phrase, 'The politics of the latest headline'. You could adapt that and talk about the 'poetry of the latest headline'. We were all aware of the fact that that would produce bad art.

So you approached it in an indirect way – because you have dealt with those issues. You have talked about some of the terrible things that happened in the Troubles.

But I said somewhere else that a bad poem is a bad enough offence, but a bad poem about the suffering of one's fellow citizens is a sin against the light. There've been plenty of those, plenty of what my friends and I call 'Troubles Trash'. The good poets approach the subject obliquely. Many of the good poets realise that 'the raw material of experience', to use an awful phrase, needs to settle to an imaginative depth where it can be transformed and then emerge as art. But I thoroughly dislike the notion that the Troubles might be a fruitful topic. I don't like that.

The idea of rich pickings?

Well, indeed. Nor do I like the notion that art can be a solace. It may be, inadvertently. Just today I got a card from George Larmour whose brother John was murdered on the Lisburn Road in an ice-cream shop. My poem's called *The Ice-Cream Man*. We keep in touch and the fact that he values my poem does mean a lot to me.

It's a very beautiful poem, very simple – and yet it's incredibly powerful.

Well, I'm glad you think so. I had to remove any artistic guile from it. It was important for me that it should be as simple as possible. In fact, generally speaking, I feel that more and more. Anyone can be complicated and smart. It requires a certain amount of bravery to be simple.

Your poem *Ceasefire* is another deceptively simple piece which, despite its classical setting, is in fact about the end of the Troubles and the need for reconciliation.

Well, the beginning of the end to use Churchill's phrase: 'This is not the end. This is the beginning of the end.' I sensed I was onto something. It was August 1994 and there were rumours of an IRA ceasefire. I was on the train down to Dublin. I had been reading that passage in *The Iliad* and I thought it would be marvellous if I could write a short poem. I'd been reading that passage in *The Iliad* where Priam goes to visit Achilles to ask for the body of Hector. I had also in my mind Gordon Wilson's face, the draper who spoke so movingly after his daughter died in the Enniskillen blast. I got home and I realised that the beginning moment of the episode when Priam grasps the knees of Achilles in supplication, if it came last, if I put the rhyming couplet at the end... I thought, if I can squeeze the whole episode, which was quite long, into three quatrains, I have a sonnet. I was, almost for the first time in my life, thinking in terms of the wider public and I think I knew I had struck gold. I showed it to Edna and I sent it down to the Literary Editor [at the *Irish Times*], the great novelist, John Banville, a friend of mine, and he called, 'Stop press!' And it appeared the same week as the IRA did in fact declare their ceasefire, so it had quite an impact. It's probably my best-known poem and because it's my best-known poem, I get a bit fed up with it, you know. Like *The Lake Isle of Innisfree* when Yeats had written all those other extraordinary poems – but wherever he went, everyone said, 'Ah, give us *The Lake Isle of Innisfree*, Willie'.

But the final two lines are very powerful.

Yes, they are. Oh no, I'm not denigrating the poem. They're kind of wearily iambic: 'I *get* down on my *knees* and *do* what must be *done* / And *kiss* Achilles *hand*, the *killer* of my *son*'. Strong stuff.

And, of course, you were an eyewitness to that other much talked about act of reconciliation when the Queen and Martin McGuinness met and shook hands in Belfast in July 2012.

Yes, I was there right close to them. Martin McGuinness has done an enormous amount for the Peace Process as a politician. I think it began a long, long way back. It began with those early ceasefires, you know. My poem may have made a small contribution but there were Methodists and Quakers and priests all working behind the scenes – and brilliant folk like Maurice Hayes, George Quigley and Ken Bloomfield. Women in the various ghettoes were peace-making; there were many, many hands behind it and one of them very early on was McGuinness – and he'd a very wild crew to bring with him. One of the things that was introduced by him, and by others, was a mannerliness. Our politicians began to stop shouting and to have conversations. We need more and more and more of that.

So are you broadly optimistic about this place as somewhere to live and to bring up children . . . because some people remain pessimistic?
Yes, I know. But even in the darkest days, I chose to talk up notions of reconciliation and the long-term possibility of peace. It seemed important not to despair. The North of Ireland is a place where you have to be on your toes, you have to be alert. Definitely through the Troubles you'd be reading people's eyes and their tones of voice just to know where you were – at a very shallow level, to avoid embarrassment. At a more crucial level, to avoid being beaten up or murdered. Part of me needs that edginess. I find life in other places really rather two-dimensional compared to here. That means accepting to some extent the darkness. It was an important part of my education getting to know Catholics because when I went to school, the Catholic Church made sure that Catholics didn't go to Inst. When I went to Trinity, McQuaid and the Irish bishops made sure that Catholics didn't go to Trinity. You might call it a kind of apartheid operating, invisibly. I didn't know. I wasn't aware of the fact, really. I wasn't aware of the fact until I came back to Belfast and Seamus Heaney and his wife to be, Marie Devlin, were the first Catholics who became close friends. That's very strange to be twenty-one or twenty-two and live in Ireland and never to have had a close friend who was an Irish Catholic.

And now, of course, you and Seamus and many other distinguished poets are thought of as part of the 'Ulster School'. Is that an idea you embrace warmly?
I don't altogether like the idea of the 'Ulster School'. I'm quite sure that the

poets and writers from the North of Ireland got more attention than they would've got if they'd lived in Blackpool or Wolverhampton. The Troubles did tragically, I suppose, focus journalistic attention. But when I think of poetry, I think not just of my close friends and earliest colleagues – [Derek] Mahon and [Seamus] Heaney and [James] Simmons – I think of [Paul] Durcan and [Brendan] Kennelly, for instance, in the South. I like the notion of a coincidence of talent, that we all came from the same small part of a very small island and started to write at roughly the same time and became friends – a bit like the French Impressionists. I think each one knowing about the others acts as a kind of inspiration and one supports the efforts of one's friends, but one's also in competition and that creates a convection current – everyone floats upwards.

For a long time you have escaped for family holidays to County Mayo in the West of Ireland. Does the time you spend there shape how you think of your identity?

No. I don't go there in an escapist spirit. It was all part of the same thing for me. It was all part of being Irish, discovering the West of Ireland through this exquisitely located cottage which belongs to a friend and discovering another preoccupation which had been there since boyhood – the wildflowers and the wild birds and learning about them. It was just another way of growing and discovering myself. It was never an escape from home. It was, if you like, a home from home and much and all as I love Mayo – and feel bereaved leaving it when I do leave it – I'm always pleased to get back home to Belfast. In the early days it was two different worlds. They didn't collide, they gradually coalesced and my Ireland – my own personal Ireland – is Belfast and the western seaboard of Mayo and to a lesser extent, because I visited it less, County Clare.

So your sense of Ulster identity is important to you as is your sense of being Irish. You also have a keen interest in the British war poets and I know your father's involvement in the First World War, and the fact that he was awarded a Military Cross in 1918, means a great deal to you.

My twin died in September [2012] and I'd given him my father's Military Cross. When he died I brought it home to Belfast. I've been a few times with my wife to the battlefields and cemeteries of Northern France. That's a huge wound which I think we're still coming to terms with. We were up in the Highlands of Scotland a few weeks ago and there was a war memorial by the road. I had to stop and look at it. I thank my lucky stars that I didn't have to fight in such a maelström and that my son doesn't have to fight in a war. Wars are planned by old men and fought by young men. It's important not to forget the victims. In the case of war, that means the soldiers who died in battle or were wounded. It's crucial that we remember them, otherwise we lose our souls and we lose our reason and our powers to forgive. I don't like commemoration being used as a political tool. My friend Michael Viney [the artist, author, broadcaster and journalist] says this beautiful thing – that poetry gives things a second chance. I think that poetry is useful in that it has the power to commemorate and to dignify the memory of the dead.

MARY McALEESE

Born in Belfast in 1951, Mary McAleese became the first person from Ulster to be elected President of Ireland. She studied law at Queen's University Belfast and went on to pursue a career as a barrister, a journalist and an academic. After fighting an election campaign during which her theme had been 'Building Bridges', she became President in November 1997. She was returned unopposed for a second term in 2004 and during her fourteen years in office she was widely credited with successfully reaching out to Northern unionists. In May 2011, President McAleese hosted a four day state visit to the Republic of Ireland by the Queen.

Mary McAleese:

For me, Ulster is a series of images. It's a geographic identity, it's nine counties of the country that I was born into. It's that geographic place and that historic place. It's a series of places and memories. It's the team you cheer for when Ulster meets Connacht or Munster or Leinster in the rugby.

Mark Carruthers:

Would you call yourself an Ulsterwoman?

It probably wouldn't be the first label I would think of myself as, to be honest. I've often done it, depending on what way a conversation went. For example, when my daughter met the man who has become her husband, I pointed out to him that he and his father, two good Kerry men, had to go to Ulster for their wives. One had to go to County Down and one had to go to Cavan to get their wives – so in those contexts it might come up. But would I think of it as my primary identity? Probably not. Certainly it's meshed into my identity, there's no doubt about that – but is it the first thing I would think of? No.

Does it help, do you think, to define your sense of Irishness, though? For instance, do you think of yourself as *Northern* Irish in any sense?

I would find that more difficult to say because I think the poles of identity differ from person to person. You could be born in the same street as someone and still have different poles of identity that pull you. For example, I was born in Belfast but my father is from the West of Ireland and we would go down to the West every month, to my grandparents, so you have the gravitational pull of the West. My father was educated through Irish, sending his children to schools outside the parish so that they would get access to the Irish language, so the Irish language means something. Ulster-Irish would mean something to me, funnily enough, even though my grandparents spoke Connacht-Irish. So, the poles of identity for me are quite mixed. When I think of myself, I think of myself essentially as a woman certainly of the North, of that there is no doubt, and partly of Belfast where I was born and grew up – and so you have the gravitational pull of Belfast. Also Antrim, the county you're born into. But much stronger than that, ironically, was the pull of County Down because that's where my mother was from.

Do you remember, as a teenager growing up in the early '60s, how what was happening around you in North Belfast shaped your sense of self?

My sense of self was fairly well established by then because that's the nature of Northern Ireland. It produces strong identities. That's what people put a lot of effort into creating. I was born and reared as a person with a very strong sense of Irish consciousness and I think that would probably have been much stronger in many ways than any sense of being an Ulster person. It would have been woven into being an Ulster person, an Ulster person who was quintessentially Irish, with a very, very strong sense of Irish identity and a strong interest in Irish history and Irish politics. And then woven in through that was the issue of religion, coming as I did, from the Catholic tradition which had a very strong sense of Irish identity but, of course, was a universal church.

Was it an issue that despite that strong sense of Irishness, you were living in a part of the island that was administered politically in Belfast rather than in Dublin?

Yes, but growing up, funnily enough, that didn't bother me so much. I lived in a Protestant area when I was growing up; my friends were all Protestants, I went to their churches, my two sisters were bridesmaids at two Protestant weddings of neighbours and friends. We were actually quite political kids. I remember having great debates in school, and indeed in the street, about the arrest and trial during the 1960s of a Nazi who had been captured and brought to trial in Israel. It was a great *cause célèbre* at the time. I wasn't particularly exercised about the fact that I went to a different church from the friends that I played in the street with – actually if the truth be told, in those days, they came to my church and I went to their churches. I was a frequent visitor in churches on the Shankill Road. The Reverend Sydney Callaghan [a former Moderator of the Methodist Church in Ireland] knew me as well and probably better than some of his own parishioners and he told that [story] at a wedding that took place where one of my best friends married a British soldier. My sister was her bridesmaid and the wedding took place in Thiepval Barracks [in Lisburn], right in the middle of the Troubles. These are things that some people would say couldn't happen among Catholics and Protestants but they were normal in our household anyway.

Do you think that kind of contact has too often been overlooked?

Well, that's what happens. We saw it with the First World War with those who took part and died from the island of Ireland. That whole story became skewed and twisted because it didn't suit anybody's edited version of history. It didn't suit Catholics and nationalists to admit that 250,000 people from Ireland took part in that war, of whom the vast majority were Irish nationalists. It didn't eventually suit the Protestant story to acknowledge that Irish nationalists took part in that – so yes, we play games with history. Actually we play games, remarkably, with immediate history and we seem to get away with it because of the capacity of the human person for amnesia and a willingness to not remember. Growing up for me, I had my identity and others had theirs. It became a lot harder to sustain those relationships through the Troubles, but they lay easily on us during quieter times.

You spent several periods of time living and working in Dublin. Do you think those experiences of living outside Northern Ireland shaped your sense of identity?

Working in RTÉ certainly made me realise how quick people are to put others in boxes. I was in my early twenties and expected something a little bit more than being put in a very simplified box that wrote you off as a Northerner and as a woman. I'm pretty used to being written off as a woman and pretty used to being written off from time to time in the North, as well, as a Catholic. You're used to those kinds of things, but probably it helped my understanding of the country I lived in and its complexities. I certainly found living in Dublin very challenging from that perspective because you were dealing with people who, just like at home in Belfast, thought they knew each other, but didn't. I discovered that, of course, to my cost, living in Dublin and working in RTÉ particularly. People made assumptions about who you were, what your politics were, what your beliefs were, what your values were and that really made me realise that these problems are not peculiar to Belfast or Northern Ireland. These are very much human problems around identity.

There is a view, of course, that there's more of a partitionist mentality in parts of the South than there is in much of the North. I don't know if you subscribe to that or not?

I wouldn't say that. I think it undoubtedly exists, but the extent to which it exists is arguable. The extent to which it existed in my day in RTÉ was very evident but I don't think that it's as widespread now. There is no doubt that when people don't have the chance to interact with one another – when they don't get to know each other, human being to human being – it is easier to live buried inside your own sense of identity which excludes the otherness of the other. One of the great things about living through the peace process is that now there's a greater sense of opportunity for people to get to know each other and to break down those unnecessary narrow vanities of identity that exclude one from the other. Going back to the First World War, a lot of people thought that their identity was wrapped up in a particular view of history that turned out not to be true. It's been a great liberation for people to discover that actually there are people who can stand on the same platform with you now and who you can be friends with. We had our Taoiseach laying a wreath for the first time at Enniskillen last year [2012] on the 11th of November – so we can do things now when we start to break down what I might call 'the building blocks of identity', that were fictitious. I think we always have to be very careful about constructing fictions with identity and we've invested a lot of effort in Ireland in the course of the peace process in trying not to dismantle all that is who we are and what we are.

Given the not entirely positive experience you had at one stage in Southern society – and you've mentioned your time with RTÉ – is it fair to say you didn't feel completely part of that society?

I didn't feel particularly part of that institution; I was very comfortable always in the South. My father's from the West of Ireland and I have chosen in later years to go back and live there; that's where my home is now. Why? Because I'm completely, utterly and absolutely at home there, in a way I'm probably not anywhere else in the entire world.

So was the decision you made in the late 1990s to run for the Irish Presidency in any way influenced by wanting to be the first Northerner to attain that office?

It never even occurred to me, no. It was nothing to do with being a Northerner and yet, in some ways, it had everything to do with that in the sense that I loved the island that I was born on. I loved the place I was born – Belfast. I loved Northern Ireland and I loved the Republic of Ireland. It was a disaster for me to grow up in a place where there was so much communal hatred and communal ignorance across the border. I had lived in the North and I had lived in the South. I knew them both reasonably well, probably as well as anybody and better than an awful lot of people that I knew, and my husband's the same. We also knew Northern Ireland with a degree of intimacy that frankly we didn't meet very much in Dublin, even among people who were supposedly experts on the subject of politics in Northern Ireland. They would not have had our experience and so I felt that I had a synthesis from my lived experience and, from the value that I placed on reconciliation, I felt I could do something useful. So, to that extent being a Northerner was absolutely essential and it proved to be essential to the job – but it was more than wanting to be the first person from the North. That to me would be a very trite reason for doing anything.

But it was specifically about trying to bring both parts of the island closer together?
Absolutely. That's what 'Building Bridges' was always about. It was also about helping a country that was in a very serious time of transition, as the Republic was. Given the role of the President is essentially a pastoral role, a leadership role and not an everyday political role, it was a perfect place to be in.

And how aware were you of the view in certain quarters in the South that was frankly uncomfortable with the idea of a young woman from the North wanting to come down to Dublin to be President?
Well, there was a tiny bit of that. I was aware of that from the first days that I ever set foot in Trinity College. There's a constituency of that view, but they are tiny and they never bothered me because they were so utterly insignificant. What really overwhelmed me from the day I was elected was the opposite. The choice of me [as President] was a deliberate choice and it was a very significant win. The numbers who voted for me were very, very significant. Also, bear in mind that by the time my seven-year term was over and I ran for election a second time, nobody stood against me. Nobody – and what does that tell you? What that tells you is the level of interest and the level of approval of where we were going and what we were doing. You get the odd crib, but that's life. I'll put it like this: I never lost a minute's sleep over thinking that people questioned my identity as an Irish person. It never occurred to me.

And when you made it to the Áras [*Áras an Uachtaráin*, the official residence of the President of Ireland], how quickly did you feel comfortable about establishing those new North-South links?

From day one. In fact, it was a leitmotif of the election campaign all the way through. We started from day one with all the phone calls and the drawing of groups into the house and talking to people who we knew would be helpful to us. We started with a bunch of friends and acquaintances, people who had offered their help, and we started to work our way through the plan from day one. That plan was to try and peel away the onion layers and invite to the house, initially, people who were willing to come – and then keep going back and back until we penetrated right through to the people who were saying, 'over their dead body would they ever stand in our house!' We knew they were the people we had to get to. We were prepared to put the effort in and even people who would rebuff us, we would go back to over a period of time and say, 'Have you changed your mind? We'd still like to have you down for that cup of tea and a chat'. It was about befriending and I think, in many ways, it was a very simple and a very sustainable way of doing it – though it was very labour intensive.

How big a diplomatic challenge was it for you as a Northern-born President of Ireland to visit Northern Ireland in your capacity as head of state in a different jurisdiction?

Well, Northern Ireland was home. I got into the car and I went up home and I obviously observed the niceties and the diplomatic protocols because that was demanded by the job and I honoured those one hundred per cent. But it would never have occurred to me that I was anything other than right to go and to be part of life there.

But you must have been aware of those people in the North who were uncomfortable with that and who wouldn't meet you?

Yes, sure that's fine. They're perfectly entitled to do that. I'm not stupid about Northern politics. Nothing would have stopped me and I thought it was a very worthwhile thing to do to keep making the point that we in the

Republic – me as President of the Republic – wanted in every way possible to be friends and I was prepared to put the effort into doing that.

And part of that, presumably, was the relationship that you developed over time with the Queen?

Well, I had really begun to develop that before I ever became President. I had met her twice before I became President, once in a large group of people when I was taking her around Queen's University. The second was when she asked me to come and talk to her and we had a private lunch about Northern politics and about what I might call the disenchantment or the disengagement of Northern nationalists from this thing that we call British identity. So I knew her mind on Northern Ireland and I knew her mind on Ireland generally, and I knew from that moment that one of the great regrets in her life was that she was unable to come to the Republic. I formed a view from that meeting that she was fundamentally a very good person, a terribly knowledgeable person about the politics and the intricacies and the difficulties involved and that she, like me, was committed to reconciliation. So when I became President I had it in the forefront of my mind that one of the tests of us in the long run – of how far we had all advanced and how far our relationships had matured, how far the vanities of identity had given way to a more authentic identity – would be whether we could sustain a visit from Her Majesty the Queen, and I think that proved the point when she came. First of all, we were able to host a four-day visit. There were some people who didn't want her to come, or who thought [it best] just to have the Queen for a day. Then there were others like me who said Ireland and Britain are in a relationship now of trust and collegiality and this will be a measure of that.

It was regarded as a hugely successful visit for both of you. Did it exceed your expectations?

In every way. It was crowned for me when she got the biggest postbag that she ever received after the visit. I also received quite a sizeable postbag and one letter was from a very elderly lady in her nineties who said that she was an Irish republican through and through. She said she had no time for monarchs and, in particular, she had no time for the monarch 'next door', so she didn't approve of me asking her. But she said out of deference to me, she watched the first five minutes on television and then she couldn't turn the television off; it became compelling and she said she cried for four days and at the end of it she said she was convinced that it was choreographed by the angels. I felt that was a very beautiful way of putting it because I think that those really were four extraordinary, blessed days for the two islands – for Great Britain and for all of Ireland, North and South. They were very, very blessed days.

And as well as being successful on the political stage, it was successful for the two principals concerned because of the personal relationship between both of you?

I think so, absolutely. I'm sure people will analyse that over the years to come – two women of faith, two women of determination and two women who set that goal a very long time before and were determined to work towards it and to bring it about in whatever way they could. I think that part of it was that over the years too, we had all stood back from this issue that we call identity and we had begun to see that identity is something that can run on parallel tracks. It doesn't necessarily need to run on one track; you don't need to see yourself just as an Antrim person. You can be an Antrim person, you can be an Ulster person, you can be an Irish person, and you can be an Irish person who's also got a very strong British identity – and I think we started to give ourselves permission over the intervening years to think of ourselves as people who could carry elements of different identities within us. For instance, I'm accused here in Rome of constantly being a very 'Protestant' Catholic. I regard that as a badge of honour. It mightn't be a badge of honour by those who say it but I regard it as a badge of honour. I think my great, great grandfather, who was a good Scottish Presbyterian, might possibly have approved. Most of us are a mixture of identities anyway. This search for a purity of identity is ultimately a fallacious way and place to go because for most of us, identity is a patchwork. That's not in any sense to denigrate it because I think there are days when your identity is strong – the days when you're in Cardiff and Ireland has just won the Triple Crown and the Grand Slam and you know you're Irish. But you also remember on that day that you're standing with people who regard themselves as Ulster-Irish,

Ulster-British and British-Irish. They're cheering for Ireland and if we were to put all the pieces of our patchwork quilt of identity together, they'll have squares that are the very same, but they'll have squares that are different – but there's enough in that patchwork quilt to cover all of us. I like that. We are not clones and we must constantly challenge the push to make clones of us and to be people who are obedient to an image of pure identity. I think that has not served us terribly well. I've always taken the view that it's a dreadful invasion of a person's human and civil rights to dare to think that the only way you can resolve a problem is by robbing them of their identity. I think acknowledgement of identity is a very important thing.

And identity is not fixed in your view? It's multi-layered and it's constantly evolving.

Identity is always something that has the capacity to be enriched. I've lived now for a year and a bit in Rome and I'll be here for another year at least. I'm never going to become an Italian or a Roman, but elements of this place will rub off and friendships that I make here and understandings that I have here have really introduced me to my sense of European-ness. It's impossible not to become completely aware that this is the cradle of European civilisation. I think if we approach identity in a way that it should be something that enriches us, then it really opens us up to the world. I grew up in a place of conflict where people retreated into identity, where people wanted to pull the blanket over their heads and not face the world of other people's identities because it was too complex. The best way for us to approach identity is with a real curiosity about other people's identities. A welcoming, respectful curiosity is by far the healthier way for human beings to live. In places where you don't get that, you get misery. A lot of people's lives could be lost or damaged where identity becomes too rigid a coffin.

BERNADETTE McALISKEY

Born in County Tyrone in 1947, Bernadette Devlin served as the MP for Mid-Ulster from 1969 to 1974. She was the youngest MP at the time and remains the youngest woman elected to Westminster. She became involved in politics while studying psychology at Queen's University Belfast and was a prominent figure in the student-led civil rights organisation, People's Democracy. A committed socialist and republican, she witnessed the events of Bloody Sunday in January 1972 and famously struck the then Home Secretary, Reginald Maudling, when she was subsequently prevented from speaking on the matter in the House of Commons. In January 1981 she and her husband, Michael McAliskey, were shot and seriously wounded by loyalist paramilitaries in their home. She now runs a Tyrone-based community development organisation.

We meet over coffee in her office in Dungannon.

Bernadette McAliskey:

I think Ulster, very clearly to me, is a very old idea. Ulster and Cúchulainn go together for me, so Ulster comes out of mythology and it has nine counties. It's one of the four provinces of Ireland. I have never thought of it in my core identity as a modern, political idea.

Mark Carruthers:
So it's always had a historical dimension to it?
It's always had an almost mythical, historical dimension, and because it's like that I quite often forget that Louth isn't in it, because, to me, Ulster goes down to the Boyne and that's where Cúchulainn stood and got hammered. It's a kind of mythical place that is one of the ancient provinces of Ireland.

Would you ever have identified yourself at any stage in your life as an Ulsterwoman?

Not in any modern sense. I know that's where I'm from, but I don't think of myself as an Ulster person. I don't think I have any modern concept of belonging to Ulster as opposed to Munster, Connacht or Leinster. I know I belong to Ulster when it comes to the Ulster finals of football. That's the context of Ulster for me, I suppose. It's cultural. Where does Ulster come into my reasoned thinking? The *Ulster Fleadh* and the Ulster football finals, rather than anything else.

For a long time, of course, the political establishment here regarded Ulster as being synonymous with Northern Ireland.

They've always done that and I suppose that's not something that I feel part of. I'm not hung up about it. Unionists talk about Ulster as Northern Ireland, but Ulster has nine counties. They think of Ulster as six counties and they also talk about 'our wee province of six counties' and it registers in my mind, 'God love you. Do you not know Ulster has nine counties?' This political entity, whatever it is, is not a province in the context of Ulster. But it doesn't cause me any sleepless nights. It's just something I don't buy into, but it has never entered my consciousness that they're right and I'm wrong. Ulster is a very ancient delineation, if you like, and historically its boundaries, like many other boundaries, have been fought over from mythology to now.

But interestingly you never seem to have had any problem with the concept of Northern Ireland. In your autobiography, which was published back in the early 1970s, you use 'Northern Ireland' throughout the book, though there are some people who never let that phrase cross their lips.

I'm not one of them. I don't know where people got the sensitivities around how you name the place, but it's never been a problem for me. I have always, I think, lived in Northern Ireland. The phrase 'the North of Ireland' doesn't come easily to me. It's not ever something that is in my common, everyday vocabulary, and never was.

So, in a more general sense, do you regard yourself as Irish? Or do you think of yourself as Northern Irish?

I suppose I have a well-honed sense of my own identity. I'm not in any doubt that my nationality is Irish, always has been and always will be. I am an Irish citizen. I have an Irish passport. I am also, whether I like it or not, a citizen of the UK. I would then raise a political concept that has nothing to do with identity. It's a political argument that you can't use the same definition of citizenship where you have a monarchy as you can where you have none. To be a citizen in a constitutional republic is a different thing from being a citizen in a monarchy – where you're a subject. I don't identify myself as a subject to anybody. That's why identity is interesting to me: identity is subjective. It is kinship and it is culture. Culturally, my identity is of this place. My nationality is Irish, but many different things tie me to this place. James Connolly said that Ireland without its people was nothing to him. I know what he was saying, but I would have an attachment to this place if nobody lived on it but me. I have an attachment to this place and to me that's where identity comes from. What is it that makes the landscape of this place sit in my comfort zone? What is it that makes me love Donegal or Connemara?

Then you have other identities that are about your social and economic framework. All kinds of things come to make me the person I am – my own development of self, which is where identity comes from. My strongest identity in the context of Ireland was mythology, because my father read us all those stories. I grew up on it. I developed a cultural confidence and competence through my family in that I knew who I was. I think my first consciousness of identity was within that family circle. My father died when I was nine, but he told us things that we never questioned. I was a smart child. I never doubted that *Tír na nÓg*[12] existed, to the extent that when my father died, despite the fact we were devout Catholics, I firmly believed that he'd actually gone to *Tír na nÓg*. We used to go up to Portrush on our holidays and I firmly believed if I kept an eye out on that shore, there was a distinct possibility that he could come riding out of that water on a big white horse. I was probably in my teens when I figured out there was as much truth in the white horse as there was in life everlasting and angels. When I went to grammar school, the notion of history, as opposed to mythology, was very exciting for me.

12 *Tír na nÓg* is a mythical Irish land, literally 'Land of the Young'.

What about later, when you moved in the late 1960s to Queen's and became involved with the civil rights movement and People's Democracy? To what extent do you think that helped to shape your sense of your own identity?

I think when the civil rights and PD came along, what it gave was, in an odd way, a theoretical basis reaffirming who I already thought I was. When you get past that which you acquire from parents and kinship and background, what is it in real, everyday life that is forging your identity? My clearest identity was class. I had no ideological concept of working-class as opposed to any other class. That also, I suppose, was absorbed. I think my first anger was around class and poverty. Religion never featured again. My mother was probably a charismatic Catholic before they were invented and fundamentally a Presbyterian. She made up the rules. When she didn't agree with the Pope, she just ignored him. I grew up on a mixed estate and I was protected from the harsh realities of the sectarianism of the state I grew up in until I went to university.

And what motivated you to get involved politically at university?

It was class. It was equality.

But presumably part of what was wrong, in your view, was the British nature of the state?

It was very clear, but to me that's not about identity. Those two things get mixed up. It's very popular now to talk about minority ethnicity because we have new immigrants and migrant workers in the context of Northern Ireland, but there has never been a discussion on the ethnicity narrative over the whole history of Northern Ireland. That was discounted and yet it was fundamental when the state was formed. You had, if you like, a minority ethnic group which was the Irish group with the Catholic marker. Catholic and Protestant became handy markers for a whole lot of other things and I think that part of the problem has been that many people have now almost created an identity around that. I think we have confused that issue of citizenship and rights and equality which is a whole different narrative from kinship. If you go down the citizenship narrative, then you set out checks and balances and people know what the rules are and they're the same rules for everybody. People know what their rights are and they're the same rights for everybody and you recognise that some people may be able to exercise those with a lot more ease than others because issues of power and privilege come in. But if you go down the ethnicity and identity route, then how do people get into the club and how do they get out? It lends itself to privilege and hierarchy. So identity fascinates me – all kinds of identity: gender identity, national identity – and I belong to all of these groups. I'm a woman, I'm Irish and I'm working-class. I'm not poor. I've been poor. It fascinates me that I'm not poor. I spent a long time being poor and sometimes people still want to belong to that club because they were poor and they still talk to themselves as if they understand poverty because they used to be poor. You know, you don't really understand poverty if you're not poor – and thankfully I'm not.

It's interesting to listen to how you define yourself. Do you think people misunderstand who Bernadette Devlin was?

I think maybe some people do and maybe some people don't. Maybe some people see clearer who she was, and is, than I do because I'm talking about myself. I really cannot control and cannot take responsibility for how other people interpret me.

And it doesn't bother you any more?

No.

Did it?

I think there were times when it frustrated me because people keep putting you in a box in which you don't belong. It's not a big problem for me because I can take it or leave it and maybe as I've got older, I've learned that. I have a sense of who I am. I am a person and I am a human being and that gives me basic rights and responsibilities. I'm always revisiting that and learning more about it. No matter where I was, I would always take part of this place with me and in that sense I belong to it and it belongs to me. I could live anywhere on the face of this earth and become part of that place – and in that place, I'd still be me. I would still be minding other people's business and still be poking with a stick at something to see what was underneath it. I'd still be saying, 'I don't think that's a very good way of doing that. You'd be better doing it this way'. But the core identity of me, the only way this works, is around those principles that all come together to have made me a socialist. That's probably what I am when I'm cut to my core and asked which of these are you prepared to trade?

You wouldn't trade the socialism?
No. That's my core identity.

So where was the line in the sand that you wouldn't cross in terms of protecting your sense of identity?
In terms of identity, I don't think there is a line. I think identity is always evolving. You don't draw the line in accordance with your identity. How far would I go to protect my Irishness? What would I do to protect my sense of Irishness? Keep breathing, because that's all it takes. How far would I go to get what I want? That's the honest question. Again, that's where my self-identity would merge into something else. I don't want anything that badly. I would say the fundamental question, particularly in the context of Northern Ireland, would be: for what would you kill somebody? I think that's the fundamental question. I have no hesitation in saying that I would not kill to protect an idea. The issue of carrying a protection weapon came up after I had been shot. I had a protection weapon, but I didn't want it and I never carried it. I enjoy life and I enjoy being alive, but at some point I'm not going to be alive and I knew that I would not kill somebody to protect my own life. Would I have killed to have saved my children? Yeah. If the people had come to my house to kill my children, I'd have killed them to stop them doing that. There's no doubt in my mind that I'd have done that. Would I have taken up armed struggle? No.

What about the people who did? Were they mistaken?
That's not my judgement. That's a different conversation. That's a whole political conversation. But did they have the fundamental right to take up arms? I believe they did. That doesn't mean it was a good idea. It doesn't mean it helped to solve the problem. I have a right of freedom of expression, but if I have any wit, I'll not run down into the middle of a flags

demonstration outside [Belfast] City Hall shouting 'God save Ireland and down with the Queen!' Having a right to do something doesn't mean that you have an absolute, irrevocable right to do it right now, in this place, in this way, at this time. That's where I think people get those things wrong – where you have the concept of rights and responsibilities. Did the fact that people took up arms – whether they were republicans or loyalists – entitle the government to deny them certain rights like the right to a fair trial and humane treatment? Does the violation of a right excuse the other person for the violation? No. And are we all equals in this? No. The state has the mechanism to hold the citizen to account, but there has to be a mechanism by which the citizen can hold the state to account for its duties of equality and protection of rights. If it doesn't have a mechanism, society falls apart. So, many people would say, 'Oh, she's an apologist for the IRA. She supports the IRA because she supported the rights of IRA prisoners in the prison. She supported the rights of people to a fair trial'. You get put in that box because if the narrative is simply about Catholics and Protestants, nationalists and unionists, them and us, then there are only two boxes and you have to go into one.

And how do you feel now about the people who made up their minds about you to the point that they tried to kill you for it?
I can understand how they got there and I hold them less culpable than I hold the people who create the circumstances in which that's how people see their way forward. The people I hold least culpable in that whole event were Smallwoods, Watson and Graham, who were the three people who came and shot me. One of the things that angered, frustrated and saddened me was the number of people who, when Smallwoods was killed himself, thought I should be pleased about that.

And you didn't feel that?
No.

Did you feel anything?
No. I didn't feel that I'd lost a great friend. I didn't know that man. I never saw him in my life until the day he came to my house. They're not people to

me, because I don't know them; they are three names: Watson, Smallwoods and Graham. Nor do I know the soldiers who were lying outside my house before they came. Nor do I know who facilitated all of that to happen – but I hold the state responsible for it. The paratroopers who were lying outside my door knew something was going to happen and I always remembered saying to the young para who finally came in, 'Why did you not arrest those people before they came into my house?' He said, 'Our orders were to arrest them coming out'. Now he didn't know, but the person who told him to arrest the people coming out of my house knew what they were coming in for. I had spoken to the soldiers on the way in the night before. They were lying not the length of this room from my back door. There were three or four of them that I could see, their wee faces looking up and them all camouflaged, and I said to them, 'Goodnight gentlemen. Cold night to be lying out and no homes of your own to go to'. In my smartass remark, I didn't know that they were lying out there because these other guys were coming. I'd never seen them lie that close to my house, along my lane. If they were lying outside my house to arrest people coming out of my house at that time of the morning, then somebody somewhere knew Watson, Smallwoods and Graham were coming. Now, if we had died that day we would have been in the historical review along with Pat Finucane [the Belfast solicitor murdered by loyalist paramilitaries in February 1989] and everyone else, but because we didn't die, that was the end of that. But that was a diversion from identity.

What did the young twenty-one-year-old Bernadette Devlin from rural mid-Ulster make of the Palace of Westminster in 1969?
Well, it kind of happened, is all I can say. Looking back on it, to have gone into Westminster at twenty-one and be unfazed by it has two explanations: youthful arrogance or youthful idiocy. I'd prefer to go for the former. Sometimes young women ask me about speaking. They ask how I learned to speak like that. I didn't. It was as if all the things that I knew fitted together. Part of not being fazed by Westminster was about knowing who I was. It was no part of a career move. It was like being in the belly of the beast. It was a club. It was archaic. It was male-dominated. There was a perception to me that more time was spent drinking tea and alcohol and shuffling

about than actually doing anything. My memory of my time at Westminster is the things that happened outside – making those links with Dagenham workers and Indian workers, battling up and down the length and breadth of England and Scotland around the Industrial Relations Act and building grassroots movements around Troops Out. I very much saw my period at Westminster as activism in England, which also included having to go and 'entertain the troops' in Westminster every now and again by scolding them.

And, of course, famously slapping one member in the face as well.

Well, hitting. I won't say he asked for it, but I was right. There was a tradition in the House of Commons that after the government spokesperson and the opposition spokesperson, I should have been called to speak. I was the only Member of Parliament who witnessed the event that was being spoken of [Bloody Sunday] and I wasn't allowed to speak. I kept getting up on a Point of Order but I wasn't allowed to speak and then the debate was closed. I think I was going to walk out, but even though I was in a bad temper I had absorbed the culture and practice that you don't go without stopping at the table and nodding your head. It was when I stopped at the table that two thoughts crossed my mind. One was that I could lift this big mace, which would be quite historic, though I had no idea what weight it was. Then I saw your man [the Conservative MP and Home Secretary, Reginald Maudling] sitting, in the corner of my eye, smirking. Actually, he didn't come to much harm when I hit him, and I always remember that I kind of caught him by the tie and I was sorry afterwards that, if I'd been thinking straight, I should have actually caught him by the tie and turned the tie around. He only got slapped; it was nothing. But [the Conservative MP Sir John] Biggs-Davison jumped up from the lower bench and hit me quite hard, which caused Frank McManus [the Nationalist MP for Fermanagh and South Tyrone], who was sitting two rows back, to come bounding down and hit him. Frank was a boxer and he nearly knocked him out. My abiding memory is not of hitting Maudling, but of Hugh Delargy [the Labour MP], who was quite an elderly and large man, kicking Biggs-Davison on the ankles and saying, 'Call yourself a Catholic?!' That was the funniest part of that whole debacle. The House was suspended – but he [Maudling] was lying through his teeth and it took thirty years and the Saville Inquiry [to get to the truth].

'Lying' in that he said the paratroopers had fired in self-defence?

Yes. That whole government front bench knew. They were covering up a scandal on that day and they knew that I knew – which is why I wasn't allowed to speak.

You spent time in Westminster and in England. You obviously got to know British politicians you didn't like – but you must have got to know some you did like. Was there ever any point at which you felt any sense of Britishness?

No.

Never?

Don't know what that is. I'm not saying there's anything wrong with it. I've no idea what it is.

Because for other people, obviously, it's a treasured concept.

I know. That development of cultural identity into geographical areas of nations actually comes with the formation of nation states. It's not a natural, organic development of peoples as clans or kinships or nations. It's much easier to retain that concept of identity within the concept of the nation state, in what might be described as oppressed nations – so it's easier for the underdog because the sense of Irishness is reinforced. Of course a lot of the Irish identity is interesting because you filter out all the bits that you don't like, so a core part of the Irish identity is oppression. It is problematic for erstwhile empires to really claim a coherent cultural identity that is coterminous with its imperial boundaries. It's just very difficult, because you get the 'British National Party' Britishness and then you get the 'sense of tolerance' Britishness and they don't go together. They don't go together and one is born of empire and the other one is born of international exposure to difference. They're not the same thing. To be kind to the concept of Britishness, and to paraphrase my father's words, it's not easy to have raped and plundered an entire universe and then try to put together a shared family identity around that. Not easy. I have no idea what it is, but I appreciate that it's not something that can be put together as easily as Irish identity.

EAMONN McCANN

The journalist and political activist Eamonn McCann was born in Derry in 1943. He attended St Columb's College and became politically active when he went on to study at Queen's University Belfast. He quickly became a prominent civil rights activist and was involved in several key events in the early Troubles, including the Battle of the Bogside in 1969 and Bloody Sunday in 1972. His outspoken leftwing views and campaigning zeal have led to him becoming well-known as a political and cultural commentator on both sides of the border.

We meet in a café on Guildhall Square in the centre of Derry.

Eamonn McCann:

Ulster used to mean to me the nine counties of historic Ulster and to some extent it still does. The fact that Northern Ireland was also called Ulster was an issue, a conversational issue anyway. And then more recently – and I suppose I'm jumping ahead forty years – it doesn't worry me any more and I don't even think about it. I've now taken to calling Northern Ireland 'Northern Ireland'. That's gradually come about almost without me noticing, so I suppose now I would say Northern Ireland about the six counties, and Ulster will be, now that I think about it, more reserved for the nine counties, back as it was in the beginning. I hadn't actually thought about that, but that's true. I suppose the use of 'Ulster' to refer to the six counties was a very unionist thing. I think the unionist people have an affection for [the term] Ulster – 'Ulster Says No'. And when you see the old flickering film and the black and white photographs of events from 1912 through partition and so forth, the word Ulster was used over and over again. So I suppose in the early stages I imagine when people refer to Ulster, they have in mind Protestant Ulster.

Mark Carruthers:

Would you ever have called yourself an Ulsterman?

No. I can't remember. I suppose in terms of Gaelic football, it would
have been the Ulster Championship and so forth. Gaelic football had no
following in the Bogside. It's got a little bit of a following now, but Derry was
a soccer city and still is. Gaelic football has never been the major game of
nationalist Catholics in Derry.

'What does Ulster mean?' has never been a big issue with me. I did have
a reluctance for many years – it was just instinctive – about calling the
six counties 'Northern Ireland'. You grew up in an atmosphere where,
for example, in the Derry when I was growing up, you'd never have said
'Northern Ireland'. It was always in inverted commas. I mean, I commented
somewhere that in Northern Ireland even the punctuation is patriotic.
Even though Martin McGuinness has learned to say Derry/Londonderry
– which I don't like – he still hasn't learned to say Northern Ireland; it's still
the North. He just can't bring himself to say it. You watch the statements
coming out from their [Sinn Fein's] departments. At the top of it, it says NIA
– Northern Ireland Assembly – but it's all 'the North', so it is still a sensitive
issue for some. I have to say that I'm a bit cloudy about what I thought
in the past about this, [but] I've got no problem with it any more. I now
think that it's just ridiculous to have a problem about the United Kingdom,
for example. It's the simplest and shortest way to refer to Great Britain
and Northern Ireland as the UK. So I use it and I use interchangeably –
Northern Ireland, the North – and I throw in the six counties sometimes in
the *Telegraph* just to annoy people. I regularly throw in Free State about the
South. It really upsets them. I was speaking to Garrett Fitzgerald [the former
Taoiseach] a few years back. We were in the Mansion House [in Dublin]. I
forget what it was about and I knew he hated it and I deliberately threw in
about six 'Free States' – 'Free State people' and 'here in the Free State' – and
sure enough, about the sixth time, he literally began quivering and stood
up shaking: 'It's politically wrong. It's morally wrong. It's constitutionally
wrong!' People do get very upset about these things and it's harmless fun
sometimes to just annoy them with it. But when I write in the *Derry Journal*,
as I sometimes do, or in the *Telegraph*,

I refer to the UK and Northern Ireland. I do get people bringing it up to me in the street. We've got very strong nationalists and traditional republicans around our way. They don't like it. It's not all that angry or anything but they do feel called upon to make the point. I can remember an occasion signing a hotel register. I know exactly where it was – it was at Trinity Lodge [on] the King's Cross Road in London and I was with my partner, Goretti, and I was signing in and I wrote down Northern Irish. And Goretti said, 'You just wrote Northern Irish'. 'Oh, so I did. Yeah!' And in a funny away, I felt liberated. I really did.

Well, is that an admission of a degree of Britishness then?
No, it's not. I'll tell you what it is – it's an acceptance of Northern Irishness. It's an acceptance of the fact that I think that we in Northern Ireland have shared an experience. We shared an experience which we're well aware people in the South did not share with us and don't understand and one of the things that unionists have said for many, many years is, 'The people in the South are different. They don't understand us. They certainly don't understand Northern unionism'. I think nationalists from the North, as well, are aware that the people in the South don't understand. It's not that they don't care in some cynical way, but they're not as engaged – and why would they be? – with Northern Ireland politics as we are. There's a resentment even among Northern nationalists about the South. I remember during the hunger strike there was a constant thing with some republicans anyway – 'Those bastards down there' and 'the Free State fucking government blah blah blah'. So we in the North, I think we like 'our Troubles' in a strange way. People in Northern Ireland are aware that it's the violent division and the violence of the republicans and loyalists and all the whole shebang of it that makes Northern Ireland special. It's what makes us known in the world – and in a funny way we're really proud of the violence and the whole process by which it came to an end, or may have come to an end. I think the people in Northern Ireland were always proud of the Troubles, you know. Now, that's not to belittle the suffering and the grief and the pain which is terrible and still goes on. We're exporting our peace process. It's our biggest export industry, the way it's a model for South Africa and the Middle East. No it's not! They are totally different – there's no connection, no resemblance

whatever to the Middle Eastern conflict. But there's people saying, 'Aren't we great? We're a model for the whole world. The whole world, boy, look at us'. The Sinn Féiners say this all the time. I remember Martin McGuinness saying that all over the world people admire our peace process. He was standing outside Mitchell McLaughlin's house which had just been paint-bombed, and Martin's saying, 'All around the world, people's admiring our peace process'. I can hear him say it, 'Aren't we great?' So now Martin calls it the Irish peace process, but he knows really it's the Northern Ireland peace process. This is where it all happened, you know. We all take pride in Northern Ireland in curious and contradictory ways because this is a curious and contradictory place. It's an oddball place, this.

Do you think that the whole notion of identity and cultural identity in particular has been given too much prominence here?
Well, I think that for a start, one of the things that really irks me is the thing of the professional peace process. What is it? The PUL community – Protestant Unionist Loyalist. What's the other one? Catholic Nationalist Republican – CNR – and they talk as if it's become a mantra, defining these two communities by reference to religion, to politics and to culture all in three little letters. I think far too much emphasis is placed upon them because it's the only thing that's emphasised when we come to talk about the conflict and in particular, the end of the conflict. The most sectarian events that I have ever attended have been events to do with reconciliation in the last five or six years, absolutely; where you have to identify yourself as Catholic or Protestant. You have to. There's no point in you being there if you don't because that's what's being reconciled. I can remember in the Europa Hotel – five or six years ago – there was a lot of academics and 'experts' from around the world. Nearly all the audience was people who came to Northern Ireland for this three or four day conference. And the highpoint of this was Spike Murray and Billy Hutchinson [a former UVF prisoner, now leader of the Progressive Unionist Party] standing at the same microphone. Not two mikes, one mike and the two of them standing very close together talking about, 'I'm a Loyalist and blah blah blah. Ten years ago, I would have blown this man's head off'. Ho! Ho! Ho! And everybody laughed and applauded. And then they both emphasised, 'I have not given

up one inch of my identity or my aspiration and neither has he. But we can stand here and discuss it now!' You know? 'We don't fight over it, we talk over it!' Great rounds of applause from all these people and afterwards, it's absolutely true, this, I went up and made a little speech which just a few people listened to politely and I remember coming down and there was a lunch served. I sat down and an American woman said to me – a professor of something – 'You know, you must regret not being able to take part in the peace process'. And what she meant was I was neither – I must regret that I didn't fit into this fucking sectarian model of Northern Ireland!

Which, of course, is not how you felt about it at all.
I'll never go back to one of those peace-mongering gatherings of 'community activists'. And what's more, there is a layer of people who have now emerged who are running all this and they're all bilingual and they go to fucking conferences in Oslo or wherever they are to discuss the Northern Ireland experience and if people in Northern Ireland stop thinking of themselves as Catholics and Protestants in the morning, there's about five or six thousand people in decent, well-paid jobs who will be unemployed – the peace-mongers. It really gets on my wick when you hear about people who emerged from Northern Ireland and who dabbled around here and who are now wherever they are representing the fucking United Nations!

But is the experience here a mechanism you can use to understand and unlock other conflicts?
Yeah, that is the argument. They got peace in Northern Ireland because neither side wanted to fight on. I mean the mass of Catholics did not want a war for a United Ireland if that meant a war against your Protestant neighbours or your Protestant community which is what it was shaping up to continue to be. The genius of people like Adams is that they understood that from a very early stage. From the early 1980s they got that. At the same time, if you look at the history of it, even going back to John McMichael [the late UDA leader] and so on, the mass of Protestant working-class people did not want a war to keep Catholics out of government. I remember standing in the Guildhall Square out there. I was chairman of the Trades Council immediately after the Enniskillen bomb, or was it Greysteel? I was closing

the meeting and I was giving a sort of peroration, whatever you would call it, and I looked down. The square was packed with people. That was the most significant thing about it – about six or seven thousand people and the people out there would be Catholics. Martin [McGuinness] and Mitchel [McLaughlin] – both of them are friends and neighbours of mine – were standing about six or seven rows back. I remember I made eye contact with both of them. I remember Martin giving me an almost imperceptible nod as I was speaking and I was thinking after, 'That's really, really interesting. He knows. He's looking around him. These are our people. These are people from the Lecky Road, from the Creggan estate and so on, standing there in dead silence, listening'. I think that had far more influence than it's given credit for. 'Jesus Christ, Martin, what the fuck was that about?' – after Enniskillen, there were loads of people saying that. 'What the fuck are yous at?' These were people who would not criticise them in public and yet the key factor in the Provo ceasefire was the Catholic working-class. It wasn't Bill Clinton. It wasn't Tony Blair. It wasn't Bertie Ahern. They were also around, because it had to be finessed, of course. It had to be codified in political terms but that was the key element.

So the problems here were always more to do with civil rights and class warfare than they ever were about national identity?
It had to do with a national identity to an extent that I either simply didn't realise or didn't acknowledge at the time. I think a major mistake played by the Left in that period, and by myself and other people of the Left, was not to have a sharp enough critique of nationalism and not really to hammer away at that as we should have been doing. I was in the Northern Ireland Labour Party when I was at Queen's. My father, a trade unionist all his life, used to boast, 'There never was a nationalist vote going out of this house'. He hated all that. At the same time, in some ways, he *was* a nationalist. He had great pride in the South. He had great pride in things like Aer Lingus, but at the same time he hated Eamonn DeValera. He was a Labour man. There was that phrase at that time, someone who's just a 'Labour man'. My father was always a 'Labour man'.

In the darkest days of the Troubles, when you were walking about this city, did you feel that your identity was being shaped by the Provisional IRA on the one hand and the RUC and army on the other?

I think it did. I think it's pushed everybody. What it did to me really was disorientate me. I'd do everything bloody different if I could go back to 1968 in a way. I think it's dreadful, the incompetence and blindness and confusion that characterised the Left, right throughout this period. There was a theory coming out of the 1960s that it was the duty of socialists to support anti-imperialist movements while supporting your own socialist party at the same time. Now, this is all very well in some places – in fact, maybe it's not, but anyway – in Northern Ireland I think that this was never an anti-imperialist struggle. If this was an anti-imperialist struggle, there's a difficulty in understanding the Peace Process in the sense that if, for example, the Provos were really fighting for a United Ireland, how come they're stopping so far short of that? I mean, how come you've those scenes on the Falls Road when Gerry Adams announces that, in effect, we've given up the armed struggle? That's what was meant really, you know? We didn't get a United Ireland. All those lives were lost in pursuit of the inevitable failure. I heard Martin [McGuinness] saying in a speech [previously], 'We won't stop until the last British soldier…' How come the supporters were out giving Adams bunches of flowers? How come there was champagne? They were dancing down the fucking street! There's really only one explanation for that, only one possible explanation for that behaviour: that it wasn't about a United Ireland, that it had never been about a United Ireland. It was about equality within Northern Ireland. It was about reforming the Northern state. That's what it's about and there wasn't all that much opposition to it.

So at this stage in your life how would you describe your identity?

I'd say I'm Northern Irish. That's what I am. I'm Ulster-Irish, which means you're Irish as well. Northern Irish and Irish. I don't feel even to an infinitesimal degree, British. I don't feel British at all and that's just the way I was brought up. I couldn't feel British. I mean, I spent years working in England. I've always resented this place as being [about] reconciliation between Ireland and England. I don't need any fucking person to reconcile me with the English people – I was never unreconciled. I've no animosity against them and I had a great time in London, a terrific time working in England; I never had any animosity. Best people in the world, Cockneys. I mean Cockneys are just like you read about in books – they are funny, they are witty, they are chirpy. If I had to rank myself, I'm Northern Irish and I'm Irish and I don't get upset if people call me other things. I mean I call Derry 'Derry'. I'll never call it anything else. I've got no time for Derry 'stroke' Londonderry. I have no time for Derry/Londonderry. Nobody calls it that in ordinary conversation. I call it Derry, but if other people call it Londonderry, I don't feel marginalised. I don't feel humiliated. I don't feel hostility towards them. Call it what you like, you know? There's far too much attention paid to all this here, but Northern Irish I've got no problem with. I actually like to sign myself in a hotel, 'Northern Irish'. I'll nod to myself with satisfaction afterwards. Stupid, isn't it? They don't have these problems in France, I can tell you . . .

JACKIE McDONALD

Jackie McDonald is a leading loyalist who is widely believed to be the Ulster Defence Association's so-called 'brigadier' for South Belfast. Born in 1947, he joined the UDA in the early 1970s and quickly rose through its ranks. He was arrested in 1989 and sentenced to ten years' imprisonment for extortion, blackmail and intimidation. He was released from the Maze Prison in 1994 and played an important role in the downfall of his fellow loyalist Johnny Adair and his faction. In recent years Jackie McDonald was known to be an admirer and confidant of the former Irish President, Mary McAleese, and her husband, Martin.

We meet in the Taughmonagh Social Club near his South Belfast home.

Jackie McDonald:

I've had different views on what Ulster is over the years. Obviously, as a young lad, Ulster is red, white and blue, and the Red Hand, and defending and fighting and what have you. Now, sometimes I call myself British and sometimes I call myself an Ulsterman. I'm not sure what Ulster is to a whole lot of people now, but to me it is an identity and something I want to be respected, something I want to be seen as a shared space and something that's for everybody that wants to be part of it. John McMichae had a term for it: 'Ulsterism' – anybody who wanted to live in Ulster, didn't matter whether they were Protestant or Catholic, as long as we're prepared to live together and share the space. I believed in that, though it's been difficult for many years.

Mark Carruthers:

A lot of people see the notion of Ulster – and particularly your background in it – as a negative thing.

A whole lot of people are just thinking about the six counties – and 'six into twenty-six' doesn't go and all that. They feel under threat and they feel as if people are trying to take it from us and I believed that myself for a long,

long time. But now I see that the only way we're going to have peace on this island is if we live together and I don't mean uniting Ireland, you know. We need a united *notion*, never mind a united nation. We need to understand that if you don't live together, you die together, and we can't go back to ripping each other apart the way we used to.

But if I'd been doing this interview with you twenty years ago, you very probably wouldn't have been saying that, would you?

No, but I was starting to turn then. Twenty years ago I was in the Maze Prison, but when I came out and I saw the way things were, I realised that all the problems in this country weren't republicans, you know. There's young people – and even not-so-young people – in this country [who] think if you're a Prod you must be all right and if you're a Taig you're all wrong. But some people from within loyalism have [also] been the villains of the piece. They've done as much damage, and more damage, in some areas to loyalism and the loyalist community than the republicans ever did. Not everything loyalism did, or loyalists did, was right. People are talking about truth, you know? They want Gerry Adams to tell the truth. They want Martin McGuinness to tell the truth. And I realise, looking at the whole thing, loyalists won't want to tell the truth either and the security forces won't want to tell the truth. The British government certainly won't want to tell the truth.

Do you think you were good for loyalism? You said yourself you were in the Maze twenty years ago for extortion, blackmail and intimidation.

And threats to kill. The worst thing that ever happened to me was Jim Craig [the late UDA 'fundraiser' and racketeer]. That's what I'm saying about the villains within loyalism.

And Jim Craig was fundamentally corrupt?

No doubt. Absolutely no doubt. John McMichael was the complete opposite. John McMichael believed in defending Ulster, but he knew the killing couldn't go on. He was involved in it. He was part of it and he was part of the operations against the Provisional IRA or the INLA but, at the same time, he was one of the main authors of *Common Sense* [a loyalist discussion paper published in 1987 and widely regarded as a thoughtful contribution to the current political debate]. He knew that we had to share this space in the future. The violence and the killing and the war against the Provies or the republicans was the here and now, but we had to get over there. We had to get to where we could share the space and the good people could live together.

So what was the line in the sand for you? Was Ulster, for you personally, something worth killing for?

Oh well, it was worth killing for. It's the twenty-fifth anniversary of John McMichael's death and John would not have believed in 'trick or treat' [the 1993 Greysteel massacre], or the Ormeau Road bookies [massacre in 1992] or Loughinisland [1994 loyalist killings]. John took the war to the IRA or the INLA – to known activists – and a lot of this information was coming from people within the republican community who did not like the IRA. Maybe they had a son who'd been knee-capped. For some reason or other there was information coming from the republican, nationalist community to us about who were the villains and who was a likely target, and John believed, and we had to show, that the IRA weren't this invincible organisation. So it was directed at known republicans, not just a Catholic in a Celtic top.

And that kind of purely sectarian attack was wrong?

That was wrong. I would never have supported that, but I was in prison when this was all starting to happen, so the train of thought was 'Do unto them as they do unto us'. You know, when you think about some of the atrocities that republicans carried out on the loyalist community, you could see that there were people there who said, 'Well, if it's good enough for them, we'll do it back on them'. And that was the logic at the time. Although I didn't agree with it, I could understand why it happened.

Do you think if somebody had given you a gun and told you Gerry Adams was going to be in a certain place at a certain time twenty or thirty years ago, you would have killed him?

I would. You know, we targeted many leading republicans, and Gerry Adams was obviously very high on our agenda at that particular time.

People used to say to me, 'What does the UDA do?' and I said, 'Anything from helping an old woman across the road to killing Gerry Adams'. That's what we'd do and that was the remit. That's exactly what we did – from community work, looking after the community the best way we could, to eliminating leading republicans, and Gerry Adams certainly was seen to be the main character at that time. People I would know in Londonderry no doubt would have been looking at Martin McGuinness, but from the Belfast side of things Gerry Adams would probably have been the leading target for people I would know.

But that wouldn't be the case now?

No. As far as I'm concerned, whether people believe the IRA or not, or believe Sinn Féin or not, I would rather Martin McGuinness and Gerry Adams are doing what they're doing today than what they were doing twenty-five or thirty years ago. Whether they're ever going to be believed is a problem for themselves because they brought this upon themselves. Blackmail, intimidation, threats to kill – that's something I have to live with. I regret that part – that's the part I got caught for, but I was a good loyalist. We did what we had to do and it wasn't for financial gains or for any personal gains. It was money for the war chest, but targeting republicans was the main agenda for people like myself and John McMichael.

And you made no apology for that whatsoever?

No, because that was the there and then.

You just said you got caught for extortion and blackmail, intimidation and threats to kill. There may have been other things, of course, which you weren't caught for. Do you still have to deal with that on your conscience?

Oh yes. Funny, we're having problems with ex-prisoners, ex-combatants who can't live with their pasts sometimes. They have their own demons. They've lost their kids, they go home to an empty flat at night. And speaking to leading republicans, they're telling me the exact same thing happens with their prisoners. They'll go and watch Manchester United playing on TV, have a couple of pints in the pub or the club and they'll laugh and smile and everybody thinks it's great, but then they go home to an empty flat and they get a tin of beer out, or whatever, and they're depressed. I have this thing – well, I'm working on it and trying to bring it together – called 'Shoulder to Shoulder'. We can all appreciate the background we came from. It doesn't matter whether it's red, white and blue, or green, white and gold. We've all got the same problems and it's actually worse for the people who were never caught, or weren't caught for certain things, because they can't tell anybody.

Do you think that loyalists, and loyalist paramilitaries in particular, just don't really fully understand where they fit on this island? They don't know who they are or who they belong to…

Yes, I agree with that a hundred percent. That's part of the problem of loyalism, you know. When I got stopped by police or was at the airport and was asked, 'What's your nationality?' I'd say, 'British, Northern Irish'. But there's a lack of confidence within loyalism and that is a major problem. That is why we have so many problems with people integrating with the other side. People from Sandy Row or other parts of Belfast would have great problems talking to somebody from the Short Strand because there is a lack of confidence.

So does that come down to a lack of leadership? Did middle-class politicians let them down?

They let them down in the past and I think they're still letting them down. People like myself and others in the loyalist working-class areas were cannon fodder. I've a great lot of respect for Paisley now because he eventually said, 'Yes' – but going back, an awful lot of friends of mine and other people within the loyalist paramilitary organisations ended up in prison because of his blood-and-thunder speeches.

He denies that, of course. He's absolutely clear that that's not the case.

No, but obviously he's going to say that. There was a survey done in the Maze Prison and an awful lot of the people, when they were asked, said partly it was because of Paisley's blood-and-thunder speeches. He was getting them all hyped up and wound up and they were going out and doing things about it.

So the charge that's being laid is that, down the years, leading unionist political figures made the snowballs and you threw them?

Exactly. It was all about getting people on the streets.

You now support the Good Friday Agreement, but in 1974 you were very involved in the Ulster Workers' Council strike that brought Northern Ireland to its knees. Did you get it wrong in 1974?

No. We actually ran the country for a couple of weeks and it was an awful lot to be proud of. Some people were saying, 'Yous are doing a great job'. Other people were saying, 'Why can't I go to work?' Business people were saying, 'You're going to put me out of business'. We tried to accommodate them, you know, and it was a good time. There's always these different points of view and everybody's entitled to them. This was protesting the proper way. This was a peaceful protest. People were coming out of work and standing up and saying, 'We don't want this. We are Ulster people, we're British and we are not having this'.

But you've got to accept it was anti-democratic. The levers of power were grabbed by paramilitary organisations and that's not a democratic resolution to a problem.

But democracy wasn't in everybody's mind at that time. That was our way of standing up and saying, 'We're not having this' – without bombing anywhere, without shooting anybody.

And that was for Ulster?

That was for Ulster. Everybody was united. On the morning that the strike started, I stopped the first bus coming down the road from Lisburn. The driver opened the door. I says, 'Go back where you came from and just tell them not to send any more buses out', and that was the start of it. I worked in Balmoral Furniture, where Bobby Sands was caught, and I was the dispatch manager. I had the keys to the lorries and the car park, and the night before it started, I went in, opened the car park and took three or four lorries out. I had drivers with me and we blocked Taughmonagh off. There was people there to slash the tyres, make sure the lorries couldn't be moved and that was the start of it. Taughmonagh was a community. It was mostly a Protestant community at that time, right enough. But everybody stuck together.

But how do you imagine your Catholic, nationalist neighbours must have felt seeing masked men running about slashing lorry tyres and blocking roads? Do you accept it must have been a pretty frightening experience?

There's no doubt about it. I grew up in Finaghy and it would have been ninety-five percent Protestant, but there was maybe ten decent Catholic families there and we played cricket and football together on the local green. We knocked about with each other all year round. Maybe at the Twelfth we'll mess them about a bit, but a couple of days later we're back playing cricket or football again or running about together, so I knew Catholics were decent people. It was the IRA and their violence [that] changed that whole dynamic, and that was forty-odd years ago. The Catholics had to move out of Finaghy. Well, they didn't all move and they didn't all move out of Taughmonagh where I was living at that time either, but they felt threatened, or they were threatened, so they moved to Twinbrook and they moved to wherever else they moved to. Even today I will see some of those people. We're obviously forty years older and we would never mention the Troubles. It wasn't their fault that the Troubles started, and it wasn't mine – so we can relate to each other as the friends we once were.

And how do you regard those people? Is your identity of Ulster exclusively Protestant or exclusively unionist?

No, it can't be.

So where do they fit within your notion of Ulster identity, do you think?

It should be if you want to live in Ulster and you want to be British, or you don't mind being British, and you're not going to try to shove anything down anybody's throat. I think we should all live together. There are members of the IRA or the INLA who I speak to through 'Prison to Peace' and I believe they're genuine enough and we trust each other up to a point. We go into each other's areas, which is potentially very dangerous, but we trust each other enough for me to go to Strabane or the Falls Road or Short Strand or Dundalk, or wherever. So there has to be a certain amount of trust there, but there are decent people who murdered on the loyalist side and it will be the same, I'm sure, on the republican side.

And what about those people who live in the other three counties of Ulster that aren't in Northern Ireland? Clearly if you're an Ulsterman or woman in Donegal, Cavan or Monaghan you're not British. It gets quite complicated around the edges, doesn't it?

It does, certainly. There's actually Orangemen in Donegal who are offended when the tricolour's burnt on the Eleventh night on the bonfire. They've said to us, you know, 'That's my national flag you're burning'. Although they still feel part of Ulster, they mightn't feel so much British. They would be Protestants, but they wouldn't be loyalists. It used to be we decided if we were going to be a loyalist or not. The press decide who's a loyalist now. If you do right, if you're good, you're a unionist; if you do wrong, you're a loyalist. I don't think the people in the other three counties would see themselves so much as loyalists. They'd be Protestant and proud of it by birth and conviction, but they mightn't see themselves as loyalists.

How close was your relationship, then, with the former President of Ireland, Mary McAleese, and her husband Martin?

Martin and I met through a mutual friend of ours, my solicitor, Denis Moloney, who used to go to Queen's with Mary. I was actually with Denis in Belfast outside the court one day and he said to me that he was talking to somebody who wanted to have lunch with me – a lady. 'Who's that, Denis?' 'Mary McAleese'. 'Aye', says I. 'Dead on, Denis'.

And she was the President at this point?

Yep. So he says, 'Give us your phone', and he phoned the Áras and the Irish Army answered of course. 'Is Mary there?' 'No.' 'Is Martin about?' 'Hold on.' Next thing, Martin's on the phone and he says, 'Do you remember that fella we were talking about the other day? He's with me now. Here he is'. And he just handed me the phone and Martin and I started talking as if we'd known each other all our lives – a real gentleman. He says, 'Would you come down? Bring a busload down?' I asked about and I ended up bringing sixty people down from Sandy Row and Holywood, East Belfast, Lisburn, Dromore, Banbridge. We're going down and they were saying to me, 'We're getting some stick going down to Dublin', because nobody had been, certainly nobody from the DUP or anybody in the political circles had been. Mary and Martin were there and Martin just says, 'This is Mary. She's not the President, she's Mary'. So we had a meal and were shown round the place and Mary and Martin were doing a bit of networking and talking to people and later on we're having a cup of coffee and Martin and I were sitting talking and he says, 'Jackie, if we look back in ten years' time and things haven't changed or things get worse, we can look back at this moment and wonder what would have happened if we'd done something'. So we agreed that day to do it, that we'd work together and extend the hand of friendship. Ten years on I think we've done all right and Mary played an essential role in all that. There were two people from Northern Ireland in the Áras. Now when will that ever happen again? What's the likelihood of that ever being the case again?

Interestingly, you told me in an interview in this very room when Martin McGuinness was running for the Irish Presidency that you were relaxed about the possibility of him becoming President.

It wouldn't have bothered me. It's not our country. It's none of our business. I think I said that at the time too. We're the hypocrites, you know, criticising what was happening down there when we've told them for forty years that Northern Ireland's none of their business. But Mary was a fantastic lady. She still is and she invited me down in her second term. So I went down and it was a great day. I was talking to all sorts of people. We went to Dublin Castle, sat with the great and the good, did the whole business, came back to the Áras, and Martin, on the way back, says to me, 'Have you any preference to where you sit?' And I says, 'Martin, I'm your guest. I'll sit wherever you want me to. I'm not going to tell you where to put me'. So I ended up at a table with Dermot Ahern [Ireland's Minister for Foreign Affairs] and Dermot was leaving after the meal to go to Yasser Arafat's funeral. I was sitting beside Dermot and they had Martin McGuinness there and we're talking away. Mary got up and made a great speech, talking about 'People in the room, without naming any names, who've shown a great lot of courage to be here'. That was all very well received, but [another guest] was getting my hand and he had Martin McGuinness' hand and he was trying to pull the two hands together and everybody's watching and he [Martin McGuinness] says, 'You can't do things like that. If we want to shake hands

then we'll just shake hands'. So Martin McGuinness and myself shook hands
and this applause went up because I suppose it was very significant. And
I have known him since then and I could talk to him almost anytime. I've
spoken to him and Peter Robinson together as First Minister and Deputy
First Minister and there's not too many from my background who could
say that. I've told them both that I support them because they've both taken
risks and they've taken chances and they're trying to move on – but all that
came about through Mary.

**But not so very long ago, you would have looked at things very
differently.**
But when you get to know people . . . You see, that's part of the problem in
our province and I was as bad. Now don't get me wrong, when I worked
in Balmoral Furniture, or when I was working in some other places that I
worked, there was Catholics worked in them. I lived with them and they
were decent people. They were really decent people, but when the Troubles
really started and friends of mine were being killed and going to prison, I
hated every Catholic I didn't know. Because of what I was involved in I had
to just scrub all the emotion and become cold-hearted and hard-hearted
and a different sort of a person altogether. That's what the thing does to you,
and any Catholic I didn't know was a potential threat because they would
have been the eyes and the ears of the IRA, or an activist himself.

**But do you now accept that you can have a different worldview as far as
Catholics and republicans are concerned – and still be a loyal Ulsterman?**
Oh yes. You see, you have to be honest with yourself. All the bad boys aren't
green and all the good guys aren't orange. There was going to be good and
bad on both sides and I think the republicans realise that too. They'll never
forgive the IRA for what they did, but loyalists did it too. The British Army
did it too. The RUC did it too. The republicans killed more republicans
or Catholics than they did loyalists. Loyalists are responsible for killing
multitudes of their own people – so there was bad and wrong done by both.
They did bad and wrong to each other but they did bad and wrong within
their own communities, so we're all guilty of something and it's not right to
just say Martin McGuinness has to tell the truth or Gerry Adams has to tell

the truth. We would have to tell the truth too. Everybody would have to tell the truth. There are decent people out there who got involved in the whole thing and nobody was entirely right and nobody was entirely wrong. We all got it wrong, or certainly parts of it wrong.

MARTIN McGINLEY

Originally from Raphoe in County Donegal, Martin McGinley is the editor of the *Derry Journal* newspaper and a renowned Irish traditional fiddle player. In the 1990s he worked as a journalist for BBC Northern Ireland in Belfast and subsequently ran the Sail Inn pub in Killybegs in Donegal. He has presented many music programmes on radio and television for both the BBC and RTÉ.

We meet in the editor's office of the *Derry Journal*.

Martin McGinley:

I suppose I probably primarily think of myself as being somebody from Donegal but then, after that, I would definitely consider myself an Ulster person as well. I suppose it's part of what's happened in my own life. I've lived in Donegal, I've lived in Derry and in Belfast, and most of my working life has been spent across the nine counties of Ulster. I've visited and worked in most of them doing one thing or another, and I socialise there as well. So I'd say, although I obviously have links with the rest of the country and I'm comfortable anywhere on the island, I think I'm probably most at home in Ulster.

Mark Carruthers:

So you've a very joined-up idea of the nine counties of Ulster?

Yes. I suppose it's partly because I was brought up in East Donegal, which certainly would've looked – perhaps more than other areas in Donegal – across the border and would've had a lot of links. Donegal was looking towards that land border with Derry, Tyrone and Fermanagh because it really is only linked by a few miles to Leitrim and the rest of the Republic, so for me, it would be very much part of a nine-county Ulster.

When you were growing up in the town of Raphoe in Donegal, would your family have looked towards Belfast or Dublin?

Neither, because Belfast and Dublin were faraway places. My father worked for the Irish Potato Marketing Board, so he would have been up and down to Dublin for meetings, but generally our ambit was Derry and Strabane and I took my holidays in Plumbridge with my aunt and uncle, who had a farm up there. Derry and Strabane, and maybe as far as Plumbridge over the hill, which is about ten miles from Strabane, was our area. We obviously were very aware of Belfast. When I was about eight, the Troubles started, so we were probably glued to our TV sets as much as anybody across the North following what was happening. We knew all about what was happening in Belfast, who was rowing with who and all the developments, but we wouldn't have looked to Belfast as having any sort of pull for us in Donegal.

So was it strange when you went to live and work in Belfast?
Well there was a transition period when I moved to Derry, which was in the '80s and the Troubles were still very much happening there. This city-side area of Derry is broadly Catholic and I suppose in some ways it was one of the first areas to emerge from the Troubles because it seemed to be post-Troubles before the actual peace happened. Bloody Sunday was still very much in people's minds, along with all the things that happened since then like the hunger strikes and the funerals here. There was lots of tension, lots of division, and I think it really shocked me at first, the level of the division that existed. I don't think I was prepared for it because although I grew up in a Plantation town, as they call it, where Catholics and Protestants lived side by side, we went to different schools. I went to St Eunan's College. Some other people went to the Royal and Prior which didn't have Gaelic, so that's what drew me to St Eunan's. So I was aware, obviously, of difference and maybe not mixing as much as you might have done with people who lived in your own town – but to come here to the North, it's taken to another extreme. The one incident that really brought it home to me, I think, was when I was up in a bar in Waterloo Street and news came in that a policeman had been shot and a cheer went up and – I mean, you know about 'physical force nationalism', but when you see people actually rejoicing at somebody else getting hurt or killed, it's still a shock.

And was that then amplified when you went to Belfast?
I suppose Derry was more an extension of Donegal with the added element

of the Troubles, and there was a bit of a learning curve about what was happening. The city side of Derry was ninety-seven percent Catholic, so it's like a little enclave, whereas Belfast was much more mixed. I was there for about seven or eight years. I was very, very comfortable. I'd lots of friends there and, of course, I was interested in music. That's one of the things that gives you an entrée into a whole network of people, so in terms of the social life, I would have spent a lot of time socialising in the music fraternity, playing the fiddle around various places at weekends. Working in the BBC, there's a big community there as well, and you get to know a lot of people, so I found it an easy move for me into Belfast, and an interesting one as well.

And to what extent would you say Irish traditional music has shaped your identity?

In terms of identity, the music's quite catholic in the sense that it's a universal thing. I would see it as that anyway. There are no real barriers. We have Catholics playing traditional music, Protestants playing traditional music, and nobody really cares. It was more about what you could play, how well you could play and what sort of tunes you had, and the musicians were drawing tunes from all traditions. It could have been the Orange Hall set-dancing traditions; it could have been the music of County Down – Scottish music and Irish music. If it was good music, it was good music – and again if there was a good company and good tunes, nobody really cared who was playing them or what their political affiliation was. I suppose people might expect that if you play traditional music it's a statement, maybe something to do with your political affiliation, but for me it was just an extension of doing violin lessons when I was young. It was never part of a nationalist project or anything like that.

Do you think some people misunderstand that?

Maybe. It's the same as playing music in any part of the world. The good musicians tend to be focused on the music and focused on who's playing what, where, when. If you're talking about the notion of Ulster, there definitely are connections there right across Ulster of a particular type of approach to traditional Irish music, and there's a lot made of the Scottish link in particular, which would be strong right across Ulster.

So traditional music in this part of the world is discernibly different from, for example, what it would be like the further south you go on this island?

Yes. Donegal has a particular fiddle tradition. It has certain hallmarks. It's a more vigorous style, it draws on the bagpipe tradition and on the Scottish repertoire. A lot of the top players would have been influenced by Scottish masters like Scott Skinner or people like that, and would have learned the tunes off the old seventy-eights and maybe also from travelling to work in Scotland. There's a lot of seasonal traffic between Donegal and Scotland, so that led some people to describe Donegal music as Scottish music played badly. Down South there would have been an attitude that Donegal music wasn't really Irish traditional music. In other words, it wasn't sufficiently purely Irish to be regarded as Irish music because there was a Scottish influence in it and I suppose, by extension, you get that right across the North as well, because Scotland's our nearest neighbour really and you can get to Scotland quicker than you can get to Monaghan probably, and certainly quicker than you can get to Dublin. There was a lot of traffic to and fro and, of course, a lot of Scottish immigration into the North as well, so a big Scottish influence on the music is one of the distinguishing marks.

That connection is very striking when you visit Donegal, especially during the holiday season.

Practically everybody's got Scottish connections. I mean Ramelton, where I'm living now, had a Scotch fair at one time where they invited all their relations over from Scotland. There's still a bus [that] leaves every morning from Gweedore to Glasgow – the 'Glasgow bus'. We're well past the heyday of Irish emigration to Glasgow, but there are still massive connections. And then you had, of course, the Scotch boat here in Derry, which was a sort of an institution.

How do you think people in Donegal feel about that whole British connection as far as Ulster is concerned?

Donegal is a big county. There's a hundred miles from Malin to Glencolmcille, if not a bit more. That's further than it is from here to Belfast, so obviously people from East Donegal would be much more familiar with that tradition than maybe people on the western seaboard. In East Donegal people are familiar with the Protestant/unionist tradition and in Raphoe I used to march behind both the Orange band and the AOH [Ancient Order of Hibernians] band on their various days out when they came back to Raphoe and marched around the Diamond. I love music so I was marching behind the two bands. You're familiar with the two traditions. Donegal is part of the Republic so maybe we naturally look towards the Irish government and would be reading the *Irish Independent*, the *Irish Star* or the *Irish Daily Mirror*, whereas once you cross the border you're talking with people who are interested in what's happening in Stormont or what's happening in London.

You've said you would regard yourself primarily as a Donegal man and then an Ulsterman. And then do you put Irish third?
I don't know. I suppose I'm Irish in an international context. I just came across this book here, *Ulster for Your Holiday*, and I would get annoyed when people try to write Donegal out of Ulster because clearly it doesn't hold water at all, because if you look at it geographically, Donegal is the most northerly county. It's the biggest county in Ulster and its land border is with three other counties in Ulster and a little bit of Leitrim. The Derry Journal is based here in Derry, but one of our biggest circulation areas is Inishowen, and at one time the *Derry Journal* was *the* paper for Donegal, so to try and write Donegal out of the equation is nonsense. But aside from that, I just think we have more in common with people elsewhere in the North and I suppose what doesn't help then is the attitude in Dublin towards 'Nordies'. They lump everybody in together and they don't really care whether you're from Donegal, Tyrone, Down or Antrim. There are some people down there seem to have something against Northerners and there's very little interest down there in stuff that's happening up here in the North. They're not addressing Northerners' stories. The *Irish Times*, to be fair, does make an effort and so does RTÉ, but in general terms if you're looking at newspapers and the media from a commercial point of view, they're not interested.

MARTIN McGUINNESS

Born in Derry in 1950, Martin McGuinness is a former leading member of the Provisional IRA and is now Deputy First Minister of Northern Ireland. By 1972, when he was twenty-one, he was second-in-command of the IRA in his home city. He claims he left the organisation in 1974, though that has been contested by many commentators and political opponents. He negotiated alongside Gerry Adams with the British government in London in 1972, and the following year he was convicted of IRA membership in the Republic and was sentenced to six months imprisonment. After his release he became increasingly involved in Sinn Féin politics. He was first elected to the Northern Ireland Assembly in 1982 and to Westminster in 1997. In May 2007, Ian Paisley and he were elected Northern Ireland's First Minister and Deputy First Minister respectively. He ran unsuccessfully for the Presidency of Ireland in 2011.

We meet in his office in Parliament Buildings at Stormont.

Martin McGuinness:

I come from the North-West, from Derry, adjacent to Donegal. My mother came from Donegal, my father came from Derry – so to me, Ulster is about nine counties, not six counties. It's one of the four great provinces of Ireland.

Mark Carruthers:

Would you ever call yourself an Ulsterman?

I have absolutely no difficulty calling myself an Ulsterman, none at all. I'm a Derryman, I'm an Ulsterman and I'm an Irishman.

In that order?

Yes. I've always seen the landmass of Ulster as being very much part of the island of Ireland, but I've also been very conscious that after Ireland was partitioned, the name 'Ulster' was seized by those people who believed in a six-county entity as something to identify them with a partitioned Ireland. The people that I associate with, like Gerry Adams and all our leading figures in Sinn Féin, never have any difficulty in describing themselves as Ulstermen and Irishmen.

Quite a few unionist leaders in the past referred to Northern Ireland as Ulster, of course.
It was used as a weapon against those who believed in a thirty-two-county Ireland. It was an attempt by them to make it clear to the world that Ulster/Northern Ireland is a six-county entity and bears no relationship whatsoever to the other twenty-six counties on the island of Ireland. So, in many ways, the name was seized upon to politically express an ideology.

When do you think you first became aware of the notion of identity?
My grandparents had a farm five miles outside Buncrana in County Donegal. It was a thatched cottage, a smallholding with a few cows and sheep, and from I was no age, as soon as school was out in the summer, the only place I wanted to go was Donegal. I used to spend weeks there with my grandparents and I was always conscious that they were living in Donegal, but they were living in a different political entity from the one I was living in. I understood that from a very early age, and I hated going back into Derry again because of the lifestyle on the farm. There was a river running across the field, the river where many years later I caught my first salmon. We used to cut turf and we would put it up in little peaks up on the hillside, and it was so idyllic and beautiful. I just couldn't understand the border and I've always felt that the division of Ireland between North and South was wrong. My father came from the Derry city and my mother came from County Donegal which is, in fact, further north than Derry. She was reared in a family which would have been probably more Fianna Fáil-orientated, where my father would have been an Eddie McAteer supporter, the old Nationalist Party. When my mother left Donegal to come into Derry, she came into lodgings in New Street, just off Bishop's Street, and she had to have an identity card to get across the border at Bridgend, which I thought was appalling.

So you had quite a romantic notion of the perfect Ireland?

At an early age my attitude was that I would love to live in a United Ireland and it was because of my experiences in Donegal. Traditionally, in the summer, Derry people just flocked out of the city to the beaches in Donegal; it's our natural hinterland. I think partition has a lot to answer for.

Was your experience of growing up in the urban environment of Derry, with its very real political divide, a different matter, though?

Coming from the part of Derry that I come from, the Bogside, I wasn't conscious of that. I think we lived in our own wee world. We were born in Elmwood Street and we lived in the streets around it and we knew there was such a thing as Protestants, and mostly the Waterside was seen to be Protestant. But our experience with Protestantism was one of the best experiences you can ever imagine. My father worked in a place called Brown's Foundry. He was a foreman in the foundry. He worked with a man called Willie McNeill who lived in the Fountain and they were both in the union. My father used to leave our house in Elmwood Street and he would walk up through the Fountain, and Willie McNeill would step out his front door and they would walk down to work together; they were like two brothers all their lives. Willie was a Protestant, but he was the only Protestant we knew anything about. He was a good person and we looked up to him, hugely admired him, and we knew he was very close to my father. We knew nothing about his political allegiances or how he voted. I would have presumed he was a Labour man, but he could have voted unionist for all I know. We didn't care what he was, he was just such a good human being, and when my father died in 1973 Willie McNeill never left his bedside. My father was a daily mass-goer. He would come home from the foundry as black as your boot. He would always wash himself down, have his dinner and go up to half seven mass in the Long Tower. He did that every day of his life and we would kneel down at nine o'clock and say the Rosary every night. But he went on a civil rights march and that was a big shock to me. It was then I knew that politically there was something very badly wrong.

Was that part of what led you to become politically active?

Yes, although I had an experience prior to that going for a job interview in Derry when I was fifteen. The first question I was asked was, 'What school did you go to?' As soon as I told them it was Christian Brothers, Brow of the Hill, I was out the door. I went home and told my father, but there was no big controversy about it. He didn't try to indoctrinate me or politicise what happened. 'You'll get something else', he said, and I did get something else.

But it was part of that process?

No, even that wasn't part of the process; that didn't politicise me, believe it or not. I just accepted that that's the way life was. When you're fifteen years of age, all you're interested in is playing football. The thing that really politicised me was the killing of Seamus Cusack and Desmond Beattie. Seamus Cusack's aunt and uncle lived on our street. He was shot dead by the Royal Anglian Regiment in the Rossville Street area in July 1971 and the following day Desmond Beattie from the Rosemount area was also shot dead by the same regiment. I was in my own house in Elmwood Street when he was shot dead and we heard a whole sensation happening in the street. We didn't know what was wrong. We came running out the door, down to the bottom of the street, and just about fifty yards across from the bottom of our street was the Celtic Bar, and Desmond Beattie's body was being taken out of a car after he had been shot. They were the things that politicised me. There was no IRA in Derry at the time, but the British Army were shooting people dead.

And was it those two killings that led you to think you needed to do something about it?

Absolutely. I would have been republican in my thinking prior to that, but I would not have been someone who would have said, 'I need to be militarily opposed to what's going on here' – until that happened. My rationale was, who do the British Army think they are, and who do the people who sent the British Army into Derry think they are to send people in here to kill our fellow citizens?

So, it was as much a reaction against something as it was a positive feeling about something?

No, the positive feeling was always there in terms of wanting to see Ireland united, but joining the military organisation was a response to the violence of the state. If you want it in simplistic terms, that's what happened. I think it was October 1971, the first time our house was raided. A huge furniture van came down our street, full of British soldiers, opened up the back doors and went in and raided the house. I wasn't there at that stage; I had left the house, and I was effectively part of the resistance, for want of a better word, in the Free Derry context. Barricades were being set up at different entry points to the area at the Brandywell, the Creggan and the Bogside. I was out and about doing that, sleeping in other people's houses, getting a bit of food here and a bit of food there.

You were on the run, effectively.

Yes. After the house was raided, I was on the run. I was very conscious that our fight was against the British Army and the military forces of the state. You have to examine what happened in Derry; I think people in Derry were very conscious that the fight was against the forces of the state and for us, the greatest manifestation of that was the fact that Derry was occupied by the British Army.

Do you regret the fact that the fight moved on from simply being against the British Army? It also became a battle with fellow Ulstermen.

Well, if people want to be honest about it, we all ended up as victims. We were all victims of what happened – and do you regret it? Absolutely. Of course you have to regret what happened. I'm married to Bernie now almost forty years, but the person who introduced me to Bernie was Colm Keenan. Colm was shot dead by the British Army and he was absolutely unarmed. He would have reminded you of a Bay City Roller the way he dressed. His friend was Eugene McGillen and the two of them were in the IRA. One night they went off into the town dressed up in all their modern gear and when they came back into the Bogside, the Blues and Royals Regiment had come into Stanley's Walk and there was a gun battle. The gun battle ended and about twenty minutes after it ended Eugene and Colm, who had just arrived back into the area, were walking down through Dove Gardens and both of them were shot dead – and both of them were unarmed. That was in 1972, so when people talk about RUC men losing their lives, UDR men losing their lives, British soldiers losing their lives, I couldn't sit here and say that at that time I felt sympathy for them, because I would be dishonest. But when you reflect back on what happened and you reflect on how we all suffered – whether it be on the Bloody Sunday march where fourteen people were shot dead, or other instances of other friends of ours who were absolutely unarmed and were shot by the British Army – you can see how everybody suffered as a result of the conflict. I don't want to be dishonest in what I'm going to say, but I think it's fair to say that during the course of the early days of the conflict, people in the area that I came from had more anger against the RUC than they had against the British Army.

Why do you think that was?

Because I think the RUC were seen as the military wing of unionism and I suppose the imagery of the civil rights marchers being beaten off the streets by these guys with blackthorn sticks had a hugely symbolic effect on people.

So what was the tipping point that persuaded you something needed to be done to bring the violence on the streets to some sort of conclusion?

I was part of a group of people in and around Gerry Adams which was constantly thinking about where things were at. I remember long before the ceasefires, we produced two documents – *Scenario for Peace* (1987) and *Towards a Lasting Peace in Ireland* (1992) – and if people want evidence of the fact that republicans were thinking about how the conflict could be resolved, all they have to do is to look at the content of those documents. Something that I thought was worthy of important discussion in republicanism was when I read a number of theses by leading generals in the British Army in which they admitted they couldn't militarily defeat the IRA. An awful lot of people who I knew were in the IRA were very happy about that, but for me it posed a bigger question: if the 'Brits', for want of a better term, believe they can't defeat the IRA, does the IRA believe it can defeat the British militarily? And if the answer to that on both sides is no, it raises a very serious question about how the conflict is going to be resolved.

And did you reach the conclusion that the IRA wasn't going to beat the British Army?

No, I believed that the IRA was prepared to fight the British Army forever, but I also believed that the British Army would still be there and that British soldiers, IRA volunteers and innocent civilians would die, because in a war situation that's what happens – innocent civilians lose their lives. That raised a big question for me about whether or not we could be part of a process which would see real negotiations dealing with the issues that lay at the heart of the conflict. When the IRA ceasefire came [in September 1994], it was a huge surprise to everybody, and if you're looking for the most critical decision that was taken in the course of the last twenty years, that was the most important decision. That has you sitting here today and me sitting talking to you.

So to what extent do you feel uncomfortable sitting in the Deputy First Minister's office in Stormont? At one stage you were fighting the Establishment, but you're here now, as part of the Establishment.

Not in the least; we've all had to compromise. I'm not the only person who has compromised. The British government had to compromise, the Irish government had to compromise, the unionists had to compromise and we had to compromise, and I don't regard compromise as a dirty word in what is a meaningful process to try and bring conflict to an end. I was elected first as an MP in 1997, and that was an amazing experience for me in the mid-Ulster constituency, because I'm a city boy. People were up for peace, people wanted peace, and they were prepared to vote for somebody who was going to do something to make peace happen.

We've talked about you being on the run back in the early 1970s and now you're the Deputy First Minister. What do you think the young Martin McGuinness who was in the IRA in the early 1970s would make of the Martin McGuinness sitting here today? Do you think he'd feel betrayed?

Well, I don't think it's a fair question because it ignores over twenty years, so the Martin McGuinness of 1972 isn't the same Martin McGuinness of 1990 or 2013. We've had to deal with the tragedy of the conflict, and Ian Paisley isn't the same person today as he was in the 1970s.

But what would you say if that young Martin McGuinness said to you today, 'You've sold out and I feel betrayed'?

Well, what I would say is that in the intervening period there's been a lot of conflict in which a lot of people have lost their lives. It was a conflict that could conceivably have gone on for a very, very long time. It's like I have said to people here presently described as dissidents, 'What are you doing this for? Do you want this to go on forever, because what you're doing isn't going to change anything?' What I have done has changed the political landscape of the North and I am now in a governmental institution alongside unionists on the basis of equality. It's not a United Ireland, but it's a negotiated agreement that we have made. There is a route to Irish reunification, but it's a route that can only be taken by purely peaceful and democratic means.

So now you are working alongside Peter Robinson and, of course, you had a famously warm relationship with his predecessor, Ian Paisley. What has that experience of working in government with unionists taught you?

The first time I ever sat down with Ian Paisley he said to me, 'Martin, you know, we can rule ourselves. We don't need these people coming over from England telling us what to do'. During the peace process, very important things were said at critical times. That was a very important thing for Ian Paisley to say to me. The week of the Good Friday negotiations, Gerry Adams and I met Tony Blair one morning at about 7.30 and Blair told me that he had read a number of books about Irish history and he said, 'You know, we were as responsible for what happened here as anybody else'. That was a hugely important thing for a British Prime Minister to say. And when Ian Paisley said what he did, it was hugely symbolic to me because what it said to me was, at that stage in his life, he wanted to be in government and he wanted his party to be in government. I was in Leeds Castle whenever he came in with Eileen, and the man looked to be at death's door and he had a problem which was corrected. I think he went to see a doctor who sorted out his problem in either Edinburgh or Glasgow on the way back from Leeds Castle, and I think that had a big impact on him and the Paisley family. I think that contributed to the decision to go into government with Sinn Féin. I think they were asking what was Ian's legacy going to be; was he going to be known as the 'no' man of politics, or was he going to be part of something that brought about real change?

There's a lot that divides you from Ian Paisley and Peter Robinson, but the one thing you all have in common is that you're Ulstermen. Does that strike a chord with you?

Well, it certainly struck a chord with me the day Ian Paisley described himself, in front of me, as an Ulsterman and an Irishman. I was sitting right beside him and I couldn't disagree with what he had said because I'm an Ulsterman and I'm an Irishman. Of course, I didn't ask was he a six-county Ulsterman or a nine-county Ulsterman. It didn't matter; he said he was an Ulsterman and he was an Irishman. He put those two descriptions first.

And what about the notion of Britishness – can you, at any level, identify with a sense of that?

No, not at all.

Do you feel a sense of antipathy towards it, or do you feel hostility?

In my younger days I felt hostility. Your experiences, when you're on a journey, shape you. Since the ceasefire in 1994 I have travelled to England many times and, of course, when you end up doing *Question Time* and you're on the news, people spot you in the street – and I've never had a harsh word said against me on the streets of London. I think there's a fair-mindedness about ordinary, working-class British people who didn't like the conflict here and are as happy as we are that it has come to an end. Rather than recriminate about what you were involved in, in the past, they showed great generosity, and I respect people for that, absolutely.

But you could understand the parents of a soldier who lost his life at the hands of the organisation that you were involved in, not taking that view?

Yes, absolutely. I could understand it, surely I could. Hopefully I'm going to go to Warrington later this year [2013]. I was hoping to be there for the twentieth anniversary [of the IRA bomb attack on the town in which two children died], but Peter and I were out of the country. I was in Warrington many years ago and I've been to the Town Hall. I got the warmest reception you've ever seen from the people of the town. The spirit of generosity there is amazing.

Is part of that a need to atone on your part for some of what happened in the past?
No, it's not about atonement. People expect me to put my hands up and say that when I went into the IRA and fought against the British Army, I regret doing it. I couldn't say that. I'd be a liar if I said that.

You won't do that, but you still don't necessarily share the views that you had forty years ago?
Well, we have a peace process now and it has brought about a political agreement. It's an agreement that I am comfortable with, but there's still work to be done. You talk about us being different people, and Peter's allegiance is to the United Kingdom and my allegiance is to Ireland – but I believe he's as committed to the success of the peace process as I am. I'm not sure that everybody in the DUP is as committed as he and I are, but we're in a better place and we have an agreement that can see us move forward on the basis of peace and democracy. I can live with that. I work on the basis that at some stage in the future there is going to be a United Ireland, but it can only happen by purely peaceful and democratic means.

And how difficult was it for you personally to decide to meet the Queen in Belfast in June 2012?
So many things have happened down through the years. Such an encounter would have been impossible without an acceptance by both parties that it was a good thing to do and that it was a gesture that would contribute to the peace process. I saw it as an opportunity to stretch out a hand of friendship to the unionist people who give their allegiance to Queen Elizabeth, but what I was also conscious of was that this was a woman who supported the peace process. I've met British Prime Ministers and I've met former British soldiers, many of whom were involved in the conflict in the North. I don't

know who they were but they came over and identified themselves to me and they shook my hand. So, I said to myself, will this encounter assist the peace process and increase people's understanding of the journey that we all have to travel? I'm travelling on a journey to do this; I've suffered, my friends have suffered, my community has suffered at the hands of the British Army – but Queen Elizabeth has suffered at the hands of the IRA also, and I think it was an important thing to do. I've been criticised for it by a minority within republicanism who didn't like it and didn't agree with what I'd done.

But you don't feel compromised by it?

No. I respect their right to disagree with what I had done, but when you're in the position of political leadership there's only one way to lead, and that's from the front. I've seen countless politicians – and there are countless politicians in this place – who play to the gallery. At the time of the ceasefire I had to go to the IRA and say, 'Gerry Adams and I believe that it would be a good thing to call a ceasefire'. At that time it would have been heresy to an awful lot of Irish republicans, and we had to try to outline for people what we thought would be a process that would see other parties have to respond to what the IRA had done. And, of course, all the parties have responded to what the IRA have done. The DUP wouldn't be in government today were it not that they were convinced that the IRA were serious about the peace process.

You've been clear that you don't feel any sense of Britishness and you do feel a very strong sense of Irishness. Do you have any sense of Northern Irishness?

I thought the census was very interesting. The fact that you had a majority of people identifying themselves as Irish and Northern Irish – and not a majority who identified themselves as British – was very interesting indeed. I'm not one of these people who works on the basis that whenever there's one more of us than there are of them, we're going to have a United Ireland. I think what we need to do is make these institutions work – the institutions of our power-sharing Executive, the North-South institutions, the East-West institutions. The economic argument for an all-Ireland economy, for example, is a very powerful one.

If you departed this earth without having achieved a United Ireland, would you feel you had failed?

No, absolutely not. I don't want to recriminate in the course of this interview about how Catholics were treated, how nationalists or republicans were treated down the years, but of all the politicians from the nationalist/republican tradition that there have been, I'm here on the basis of equality in the most powerful position that any republican or nationalist politician has been in since Ireland was partitioned. I'm quite content to work with these institutions in my firm belief that at some stage in the future it will lead to Irish unity – but it can only happen by purely peaceful and democratic means.

So at the moment what we have is an honourable compromise?

I think it is an honourable compromise. I said recently when Peter and I were asked about our relationship, that every now and again we have a good row. But it's not like the past whenever Seamus Mallon [the former SDLP Deputy First Minister] and David Trimble wouldn't speak to each other for months on end. We sit down and talk to each other the next morning in a calm, sensible atmosphere. There's never been a day when Peter Robinson and I haven't spoken to each other, and I think that bodes well for the future.

DENIS MURRAY

Born in England in 1951 of Northern Irish parents, Denis Murray is best known as the BBC's former Ireland Correspondent, a position he held for two decades until his retirement in 2008. He began his career in journalism at the *Belfast Telegraph* and also worked for the Republic's state broadcaster, RTÉ, between 1977 and 1982. Educated at St Malachy's College in Belfast and at Trinity College Dublin, his time as Ireland Correspondent ensured he had a ringside seat for many of the major highs and lows of the peace process.

We meet in Belfast.

Denis Murray:

I was born in England and my father died when I was quite young. Both he and Mum were from the old 'North of Ireland'. They were born in the early 1900s and married late, so when Dad died, Mum decided to come back to the bosom of the family in Belfast.

Mark Carruthers:

What age were you at that point?

Five, and I found Belfast a terrible shock. We lived in a wee village in the Worcestershire countryside with an orchard and a stream in the back garden, and we arrived in this awfully grey, dour city and it was a terrible shock to my brother and me. We went to call for our friends in the street on a Sunday and we were told they didn't play on a Sunday and that you had to sit in and read your bible. In England, Sunday was a day to play cricket in the back garden with a little beach set and that took some getting used to. I regarded Belfast as a very poor second best to England for many years, but then I went to university in Dublin. I went to Trinity and that really woke up some sort of Irish consciousness in me. A friend of mine from college days said to me quite recently, 'Denis, there's a corner in your head that will always be English', and he's probably right. Despite my best endeavours, I shout for the England cricket team, though I would boo the England soccer team unless they're the only ones in the World Cup finals. I regard myself, I think primarily, as Northern Irish. I like to think of myself as Irish but my wife, who's a Dubliner, and most of my own university friends who come from the Republic, say I'm not. A lot of that's to do with the power of popular culture and the older I get, the more I think that Northern Ireland is much more British than even nationalists would have you believe. For instance, if you talk to somebody of my vintage from the Republic, they'll tell you about the television shows that they grew up on, which were *Wanderly Wagon* and *Forty Coats* and all that kind of thing, whereas we would talk about *Blue Peter* and *Dr. Who*. I always felt that RTÉ should be free to air in the North because it would have led to a greater understanding of what was going on in the Republic. I would probably put myself down as Northern Irish, although if you ask me to narrow it down I would have to say I was Irish first – but there is undoubtedly a part of me that is English.

But your Irishness is a qualified Irishness; it's a *Northern* Irishness?
Yes, though I wouldn't call it 'qualified'. It's just the older I get, the less I'm sure about anything, and also the less I think it matters. When I was working as the BBC's Ireland Correspondent, based mostly in Belfast, but also in Dublin, a fairly complicated situation here had to be simplified for an audience, primarily in England, Scotland and Wales, but also around the rest of the world. But you couldn't simplify it to the point where you were patronising people. It would often be put to me in studio discussions that Northern Ireland's problem was really a sectarian one and there's no doubt that the sectarian thing is very important. But I always used to say that it's much more a matter of identity, in which religion plays a part. It so happens that most Protestants are unionists and most Catholics are nationalists or republicans – but that's incidental. The really big thing is whether you regard yourself as Irish and look towards Dublin, or British and look towards London – and some of the research shows that an increasing slice of the Catholic population now would look to London, rather than Dublin.

And, as well as that, there's perhaps an increasing number of people here who are quite prepared to accept Belfast in its own right?
There's a certain amount of that. I always used to think we greatly

exaggerated how people around the world regarded us: if there's a riot in Belfast, well, what do you expect in Belfast but a riot? I've recently been reading P. G. Wodehouse and there's a punch up at the village fête in one of the Jeeves and Wooster stories and the line in the text says, 'It very quickly began to resemble one of Belfast's livelier nights'. I looked at the publication date: first published in 1923! There's another line in it as well which is, 'What's in the morning papers, Jeeves?' 'Very little, Sir. More trouble in the Balkans, I believe.' Well, you know, *plus ça change*. People don't pay that much attention to us.

On a personal level, what impact did covering some of the most challenging events of the Troubles have on you?

Well, the hunger strikes were appalling. That's the most divisive thing I've ever covered. I had a group of friends I'd been to grammar school with. It was a middle-class group who lived in mixed areas. They stayed friends – and are still friends – all the way through the Troubles. The one thing they couldn't talk about, though, was the hunger strikes. Somebody raised it one night and everybody in the company realised after about ninety seconds that if the conversation went on, it would end the friendships. To the Protestants, the prisoners had no right to wear their own clothes and if they wanted to go on hunger strike that was their problem. To the Catholics, they were young men in difficult circumstances who almost certainly would not have been in jail had it not been for the Troubles and it was only a matter of them wearing their own pullovers and sneakers. There was not going to be a meeting of minds so, in order to retain the friendships, it was never talked about again. The hunger strike was a ghastly period to work through.

The Omagh bomb in 1998 also had a big impact on you, didn't it?

I remember saying to a good colleague at the time, 'Why is this bugging me so much?' He said, 'Because you thought it was over and you weren't expecting that the worst was still going to happen'. He was right. I really did think it was over and I think this happens to blokes – you don't get upset for one reason, you get upset for a whole lot of reasons. I was upset because you could not walk anywhere in Omagh without people stopping you and telling you their story – where they were when they heard about it, how they looked for their mammy or their daddy or their brother, how they went to the hospital. People were desperate to tell you their story; it was like a JFK moment. We got an amazing welcome from the people of Omagh which really surprised me. It was as if people felt better just for telling you what had happened. So, I got a bit upset about it and then I felt guilty for being upset because I hadn't lost anybody. That really, really got to me. Explaining Omagh wasn't the problem; experiencing Omagh was the problem, because people just wanted to tell you their stories and there wasn't a hint of division. To begin with, the police wanted to have an agreement where nobody would go to the funerals and nobody would approach the families, but it turned out very quickly the families were approaching us. The families actually wanted to talk to us. I nearly burst out crying when I saw one thing: exactly a week after the bomb went off, there was a memorial service at the courthouse – on the following Saturday, at the same time in the afternoon – and the local clergy had written a set of prayers and one of the prayers was, 'We thank those who have told our story to the world'. I still get a lump in my throat about that.

In contrast to those challenges, though, you must have derived some considerable pleasure from covering the peace process?
I was thrilled the night of the Good Friday Agreement. I was bouncing around with excitement, not just because it was a huge story – and it's still the biggest story I've ever reported on – but it kind of defied belief that they had done it. It was astounding that these people had actually agreed on something. For all its flaws – and it took a long time to actually get it to work properly – I was very conscious at the time of being an eyewitness to something tremendously significant. And it was hugely significant around the world.

Do you think that process is a model for other conflicts?
Yes and no. One thing I learned was that a lot of these conflicts have similarities but none of them are identical. The recipe has to be changed everywhere. If you think about it, the process here really should have ended maybe two dozen times between 1997 and 2007. There were all sorts of reasons for it to fail but [Tony] Blair and [Bertie] Ahern just kept at it and

they finally did it. I think that's something you can probably take into other conflicts.

Are you personally conscious of having a flexible sense of identity?
On a personal level, I think I'm probably more Northern Irish than anything else because I think there's something in the Ulster thing. I shouldn't be surprised at this, being called Murray, but when I hear the Field Marshall Montgomery Pipe Band, there's something in my collective unconscious that stirs in a very good way. And when I hear Planxty or Altan, something in my collective unconscious stirs. But when I hear the peal of bells for evensong from a Cotswold country church, something in my collective unconscious responds to that too. I'm a Northern Ireland soccer fan but if they're not in the finals I'll cheer for the Republic. If the Republic aren't in the finals, I'll cheer for England because they're familiar names and they all play in the one league anyway. I remember Albert Reynolds [twice Irish Prime Minister between February 1992 and December 1994] who was brilliant at this, whatever else you think of him as a politician or a person. He was brilliant at explaining to the British people why he was doing certain things concerning Northern Ireland. One of the lines he used to connect with 'the man on the Clapham omnibus' was, 'What would Irish football be without Jack Charlton and what would English football be without Roy Keane?' That just struck a chord with people who couldn't have cared less about Northern Ireland but they immediately knew what he meant. On a certain level it's absolute drivel but in terms of reaching out to ordinary people it's an absolute stroke of genius.

LIAM NEESON

Universally regarded as Ireland's most successful film actor, Liam Neeson was born in Ballymena in 1952. A former Ulster amateur boxing champion, he began acting at school and after a period of time studying at Queen's University Belfast and various casual jobs ranging from a forklift operator to a truck driver, he landed his first role as a professional actor at Belfast's Lyric Theatre in 1976. After spells working at the Abbey Theatre in Dublin and in London, he moved to the United States in 1986. His film work ranges from *Star Wars Episode 1: The Phantom Menace* and *Taken* to *Michael Collins* and *Schindler's List*, for which he received an Academy Award nomination for Best Actor in 1993.

We meet in a café in New York's Upper West Side.

Liam Neeson:

I guess, first off, with my upbringing, if somebody asks me about Ulster, I have to think am I going to answer as an Ulsterman or as a Northern Ireland man? That's been confused by the whole political situation, you know. Ulster is an ancient province but images come into my head of tough wee men and women, and a very, very strong work ethic and people who take no prisoners.

Mark Carruthers:

Would you still be comfortable if somebody described you as an Ulsterman?

I'd be comfortable, sure, but I think when I first came here to the States, which was 1986, I would always say Northern Ireland because I didn't want to have to get into a big discussion about what is Ulster or where is Ulster? So I'd say Northern Ireland; it was easier and simpler.

And do you find people mostly tend to refer to you now as an Irish actor?

It's funny but when I first came out to Los Angeles, I was at pains to tell a young, very hip Californian agent, 'If you're calling casting directors, please say I'm a European actor. Say I'm from Ireland – but do not use the expression 'Irish actor''. In London that meant something else – you played bricklayers and Paddies as an Irish actor, rather than an actor from Ireland. It may have changed now but certainly when I was in London in the early eighties it was a kind of stigma.

So, do you agree with the idea that your sense of identity can change depending on where you are and who you're with? Is your sense of identity here in New York different to what it is when you're back in Northern Ireland?

If it's different, I'm certainly not aware of it. I think I'm the same.

You spent some time in your early career living in London. Did you ever think of yourself as a British actor?

No but I remember one episode in 1982. I had done a film at Pinewood Studios and we had got the use of the Queen's Cavalry. It was a medieval sword and sorcery film and those amazing horses were used for a sequence. It was the year the horses were blown up in Hyde Park [in an IRA attack on the Household Cavalry in which four soldiers and seven horses were killed]. I remember the carnage being discussed around the film community. Obviously human beings lost their lives but the people I was with were as concerned about those beautiful horses being killed and that was a little bit confusing. It was around about the same time Prince William was born and I went into my local pub. It happened to be an Irish pub and everybody was drinking and celebrating this birth and I said, as a kind of a joke, 'There's another mouth to feed'. The look I got: how dare you make a joke at Prince William's expense or at the Royal Family's expense! That was quite strange, to put it mildly. I was making a light-hearted comment and I was with a bunch of Paddies. I thought it might get a giggle, that was about it. I wasn't making any staunch, political statement.

So, you never wanted to be seen as a British actor, but still there must have been some acceptance of Britishness on your part when you accepted an OBE?

That was years later. I got it in 2000 but I didn't pick it up for quite a few years. It was a great honour and I thought if I don't accept it, I'll be cursed – and maybe if I do accept it, I'll be cursed as well.

When you were growing up in Ballymena, can you remember becoming conscious of your identity and realising that everybody around you wasn't necessarily the same?

Only on the Twelfth of July, really. That was a time when my Protestant buddies at the top of the street would go off with their dads and dress up differently. I kind of wondered why I couldn't go with them.

Were you envious?

A wee bit, yes. But my grandfather had a pub in one of the main streets in Ballymena, so we used to go there and hang out the windows because the street was a main thoroughfare for the parade.

And you'd watch the parade?

Oh yeah, beginning to end. It was fantastic. We were very young and there was no sense of 'them' and 'us'. That came later when you learned what it was all about.

You were famously quoted several years ago by an American magazine saying you felt you'd grown up like a second-class citizen in Ballymena.

I know. I've been quoted as saying that, but I don't think in my wildest dreams that I would ever have said that, because I wasn't. I probably would have said I was very working-class – but 'second-class citizen'? I just don't know who the fuck I'm supposed to have said it to. All I can assume, without making a meal of it, was that I must have been explaining the rise of the Troubles to a foreign journo during the promotion of some movie and I said something about Catholics in the North, in general, feeling like second-class citizens when it came to things like jobs and housing and gerrymandering – hence the civil rights marches in the late '60s, in tandem with the civil rights marches in America around that time as well. I know that I would never have said that I *personally* felt like a second-class citizen, because that just wasn't the case.

So you yourself never felt like that?

I never did because there were never any real doors closed to me. I went to Catholic schools and then I went to a mixed school, Ballymena Tech, where I became a prefect and then head boy. I was never aware of any doors that weren't open for me.

You went to Queen's University in 1971, just as the Troubles were beginning to really change things in Northern Ireland. Do you remember what that was like at the time?

I certainly remember getting a big awakening in January 1972 when Bloody Sunday happened in Derry and I was off to a lecture the following Monday morning. I remember coming back up the Malone Road and being surrounded by all these students shouting 'Scab!' and I hadn't a fucking clue what they were talking about. It made me feel deeply embarrassed. I hadn't heard any news; I didn't have a radio, the TV certainly wasn't on. Then I found out what had happened and I felt shame at my own ignorance.

And they were shouting abuse at you because you had gone to a lecture on that Monday morning?

They had spread the word for all students to boycott lectures because of the atrocity that had happened in Derry. I didn't hear about a boycott and the lecture was held. There weren't too many students there as far as I remember.

Those were dark and challenging times. Did that really bring home to you what was happening?

It did. I started reading the papers a bit more, doing my own bits of study on Irish history and British history on a very basic level, just to get over my own feeling of ignorance. I went to a good secondary school and a good technical school but we didn't learn that immediate history.

So, you hadn't grown up in a political household?

Not really, no. I can't say it was. When the news was on, I remember my mum and dad would be listening to it with deep concentration but there were no real discussions when anything like that went on.

And, interestingly, until your involvement in the film *Five Minutes of Heaven* with James Nesbitt in 2009, you hadn't really done much work at all about the politics of Northern Ireland. Why was that?

It just wasn't an issue for me at all. I remember I did a little television play in 1981 with Colin Blakely, God rest him, called *Nailed*, where he was an undercover policeman and I was a suspect in a bombing and he was interrogating me; it was just a two-hander. That kind of opened my eyes a little bit to police procedures over in Ireland. God knows, I've been offered many, many potential scripts down the years and I never wanted to touch them because they were flagrant commercial projects trying to use the background of the Troubles as thrillers. That's fair enough but I just didn't want to be involved.

So what was it about *Five Minutes of Heaven* that attracted you?

For me it's always about the written word and it was a fantastic script. My English agent said, 'I'm sending you this script. I don't think you'll be able to put it down'. Sure enough, I read it and I wasn't able to put it down. I thought this is really fantastic writing for a start, and it was based on real events and two real people. This was a very relevant little story but it was also a huge fucking story about two people trying to get their lives together in the wake of horrible violence.

That whole notion of dealing with the past remains very difficult; it's not resolved for many people. Did it make you think about the whole situation in Northern Ireland at a deeper level?

Absolutely and in a very emphatic way. These were two individuals and we were telling their story. Thousands of people have lost loved ones or lost limbs – and how do you get over that? I guess you have to; life goes on. That's one of the great gifts we're given as actors: you can be put in a situation and you can let your imagination go. What would you do in that situation? These incredible little acts of heroism that these victims of violence are doing every day – just waking up in the morning and deciding to get out of bed is a fucking act of heroism, I think.

You've talked before about slipping into the back of Ian Paisley's church in Ballymena when you were a boy to hear him preach. He attended the event in Ballymena [in January 2013] when you were awarded the Freedom of the Borough and there was an obvious warmth between the two of you.

Yes, I met him before with Martin McGuinness at an event in New York a few years ago. He was in a room talking to businessmen and I was eventually brought in and he was very, very warm and very affectionate. I said, 'You're responsible for me being here Dr Paisley, for this silly profession of mine'. 'What are you talking about?' he says. 'I went and heard you preach. You inspired me to be an actor.' 'Eileen, come here 'til you hear this. Tell her what you just told me.'

Because he was an actor?

Oh yeah. He was a great actor. He was in the moment quite a few times. He was preaching hellfire and damnation.

And did that make you feel uncomfortable?

It didn't, because I was watching a great performer. I just thought that guy is giving it the bollocks, you know. I didn't think: I am going to die in hell; I'd better leave.

A lot of people might say that, like Ian Paisley, Northern Ireland has been on quite a journey in recent years. When you go back there now, does it feel like a 'normal' place?

Certainly when I was there doing *Five Minutes* with Jimmy [Nesbitt], Belfast felt youthful; there was an energy. Just walking around the streets and going into some hostelries and restaurants, there was a kind of exuberance. It was a real positive vibe of potential.

When you came to the States and decided to stay here, were you consciously determined not to let your Irishness go altogether?

I knew I could have dual citizenship. I didn't want to give up my Irish passport because that's what I am: I'm Irish. I didn't want to give that up but that being said, I'm equally proud of being an American citizen. I've worked here, I've been reasonably successful and America has been good to me.

A lot of people still cling to the identity of their birth in those circumstances, though.

No, I don't have the cascading shamrock on the 17th of March. I keep well away from that stuff. Because I've a certain celebrity status, I just don't want to be manhandled into this faux Irishness. You can easily go back to a mythical Ireland that doesn't exist. America's still kind of searching for an identity. In the age of the world, it's an adolescent. That's been my experience: America's still looking for an identity because it's a very young country – and that's what I love about it too, because you do sense potential. Ireland? It's a little country three thousand miles to the east of New York!

How much of a challenge is it for you to be seen today as something of a global ambassador for Northern Ireland? Are you aware of that?

Yes, to a certain extent, but I don't go about waving a flag. I'm pretty private and I keep myself to myself. But I guess I am. It's funny – later this morning I'm going to do another session on this animated movie. It's called *The Lego Movie*. The movie's all animated Lego pieces and I did my first session about two or three weeks ago. I'm playing this bad cop; Will Ferrell's a dastardly baddie and I'm his first lieutenant. In passing I thought, 'I'm going to play it Northern Irish'. So, I told the director, I said, 'Listen, you know, I'm just going to play this in my own accent'. 'Of course, that's what we want'. 'Oh, really?' 'Yeah, just be Irish'. I said, 'Well, I'm going to be Northern Irish'. 'Is there a difference?' And then I play my character's father in the film, so I thought I'd make him Southern – and I'd play my own character very strong 'Ian Paisley Northern Ireland'.

And does it work?

We have this Californian director who said, 'Oh yeah. I think I can hear the difference'. And I said, 'Well, you know, there is a difference!' They can just hear a slight difference. I'm also doing a Western with Charlize Theron in New Mexico soon and I was reading through this classic gunslinger script and I thought, 'Oh fuck it, he's from Northern Ireland!' So I told the director, Seth MacFarlane, 'Listen, this gunslinger – he's from Northern Ireland'. 'Ok, that's good.' So, dispense with the dialogue coach; we don't need that! It's partly laziness, because I don't want to have somebody coming up to me every ten minutes saying, 'Sorry, that diphthong sounded wrong there!'

So, ironically, you're back doing the Northern Ireland accent after a lifetime of not really doing it.

I suppose so, yes.

And if you had to choose a label for your sense of identity now, what would it be? Would you still settle for Northern Irish?

Certainly Irish-American; that's what I am. And then, if I have to be specific, Northern Irish-American.

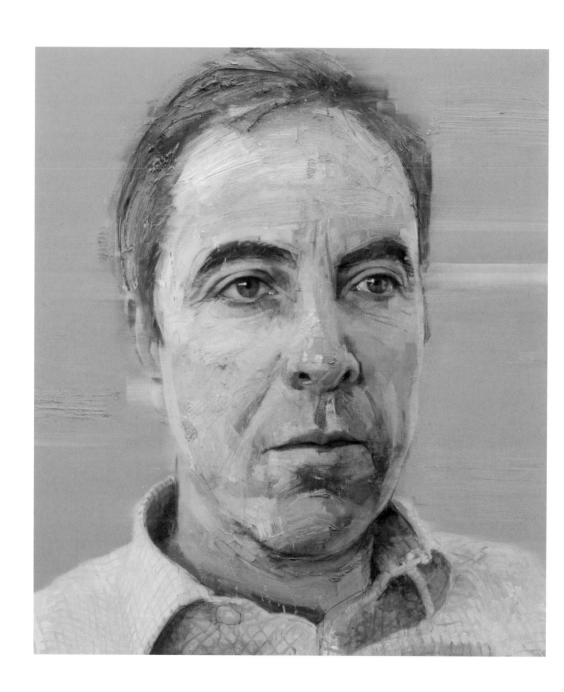

JAMES NESBITT

Born in Ballymena in County Antrim in 1965, James Nesbitt is one of the leading actors of his generation. The star of countless UK television dramas in a career spanning over twenty years, his big break came in 1996 when he was cast as Adam Williams in *Cold Feet*. Since then, his TV credits have included *Murphy's Law*, *Jekyll*, *Occupation* and *Monroe*. His film credits include *Bloody Sunday*, *Five Minutes of Heaven* co-starring Liam Neeson, *Welcome to Sarajevo* and *The Hobbit*. In 2010, he accepted the ceremonial position of Chancellor of the University of Ulster.

We meet in Belfast's Merchant Hotel on one of his frequent visits back to Northern Ireland.

James Nesbitt:

I think Ulster is a massive contradiction. I think it's a place of anomalies and contradictions. When I think of my childhood, I think of an idyllic, rural existence against which there was the backdrop of conflict which never really impacted on my life. I felt, and continue to feel, very proud of where I come from. I think it has a distinct voice. I think that even though it was at times riven, when I leave Ulster I feel that people from Ulster are very, very united. Funnily enough, it's not dissimilar in a way to the dwarves in *The Hobbit*, now that I think of it – that slightly tribal sense of great in-fighting and huge bickering but when challenged as a unit, very loyal and together. I think that Ulster's a great secret. I'm very proud to come from it because I think it is very different from anywhere else I've been. You can feel isolated as an Ulster person, but you can also feel that you can walk anywhere in the world as an Ulster person.

Mark Carruthers:

And would you choose to describe yourself as an Ulsterman?

Well, I suppose I marry Ulster and Northern Ireland really. I never once in my life said I was British, I don't think, even though I've a British passport. I grew up in a Protestant background. I very much was part of the Protestant culture in terms of its bands and the music, but I've always considered myself an Irishman. I've always, all my life, said, 'I'm from Northern Ireland'. I consider myself very much an Ulsterman.

But you extend that to Irishness rather than Britishness?

Yes, I really would. Maybe when I was younger, maybe when my own thoughts weren't fully formed or were still evolving I would, have been persuaded that loyalty was to the Crown, but very quickly that went, because the Crown had very little impact on my life. It was the environment that really shaped me, I think, and to me that was the countryside at first and that was the Northern Irish, Ulster countryside. The accent was Ulster, my culture was Protestant/Ulster and certainly when I moved away I considered myself very much a Northern Irishman.

What about your early days as a bandsman when you were growing up?

First of all, there was the Ballygelly Accordion Band near Lisnamurrican in the Braid. We actually did an album. Someone brought me in a photo of it today, *The Pride of the Braid*. I was ten and I played with them for a while, but I remember I went to Scotland to march with them and it was the first time I think I questioned the notion of loyalism. I think I saw the fanaticism on the streets of Glasgow, which I think I found overpowering and I couldn't quite connect the two, even though my family originally comes from the Borders. Music was part of my childhood and it was just an extension of that that I would join the band, but when I went to Glasgow and marched, I began to see what I felt was the rather ugly political/violent associations – tribalism at its worst, I felt. And I remember coming back and saying that to my father; I didn't like it, and that's when I left the Ballygelly Accordion Band and joined his flute band, the Ballymena Young Conquerors, which was a concert C flute band that wasn't attached to an Orange lodge.

So it wasn't a marching band?

No, we marched, but it wasn't attached to a lodge necessarily. It wasn't like a 'kick the Pope' band that just had the little E flat flutes. This was a band with many different parts. We played classical music and we used to play concerts. They were world champions in 1958. Now, they were staunch unionists that made up that band and, of course, my childhood was peppered with strong unionism, with 'official unionism', which I suppose would have been my father's take, maybe stretching to Alliance at times. But, of course, in Broughshane there was a huge Free Presbyterianism. There was a DUP influence, but also, as I may have told you before, my father sent me and my three sisters to the convent to learn the piano. Now whether or not that was a conscious or subconscious balancing act on his part, I don't know. I tend to think that it was probably a deliberate act of his to find some sort of balance.

So it was a very traditional Presbyterian upbringing where Sunday was Sunday?

Oh absolutely, but my parents I would always have described as God-loving rather than God-fearing. My father, I think, has kind of moved away a lot from religion in the last number of years, but we were churchgoers. I did go to Sunday school. I was part of the Boys' Brigade, but it never felt staunch. Sunday was a day of church and then you were able to go out and play football, but the TV wouldn't be on and in the evening we would sit round the piano and sing hymns. But as boring as it could be at times, once we got to an age where we just said, 'Listen, we don't want to do this any more', we weren't forced to. It was actually celebratory and it was a way of playing music together and singing together and it felt quite normal at the time. Of course, in retrospect, it seems very, very odd.

But it would not have been untypical of the time.

Oh, absolutely. I think the change in the last, say, thirty-five years is astonishing. I mean if my children had a window into what my childhood was like, they would find things like that just completely alien to them, but there was a simplicity to it which I bought and understood. There was also something to eventually rebel against. As children we absolutely need that. I mean the notion of parents nowadays having to be best mates with their kids is something I challenge at times because I think that your kids have to rebel. You have to give them something to rebel against. They have to so that they can separate, so that we can let them separate. It was not untypical at all, but it was a simple, rural, happy life.

So what was it that opened the window then to the wider world for you?

Well I think the wider world was probably opened up by my father. If you look at the teaching methods my father had in Lisnamurrican Primary School, a school of maybe under forty children with two classrooms. Dad taught me in Primary four, five, six and seven and this was a very relaxed education which I think the government would do well to be mindful of now. These were farmers' children, most of whom would go into farming, but my father certainly opened windows. He was doing that for me anyway at home but for the pupils, he would spend days just reading to us at times. He'd read Dickens to us. He taught music – he was a self-taught musician. He taught all these kids how to play recorder. We would travel round the country for recorder concerts and it's a part of Ulster that I have always cherished – and something that has angered me is that notion of the dour Presbyterians, you know, the fun-sucking, immovable, very serious people. That was not my experience at all! It was Dad that opened those windows at first. I was always known as the master's son. All my life, 'There's the master's son'. It was a farming community and my dad would close down the school for potato-gathering holidays, that was just a way of life. So for one week every year the school would close down. We'd be picked up at half five in the morning on the back of a trailer attached to a tractor and we'd go off and gather spuds. So you were also meeting people of all ages at a very young age. You were listening to people who'd spent all their lives in the fields. I would go to Carnlough to where my great-aunts ran the Bridge Dining Rooms. I'd work in the kitchens there. You'd have the clatter of the cutlery and the sound of women laughing and talking and sharing stories, so Ulster to me was an identity that I was loving at that age because I was hearing stories, I was hearing tales, I was finding things out. I was understanding and appreciating humour for the first time. I think it prepared me very well for when I eventually moved away.

When you moved to London to go to drama school in 1985, did you feel a bit lost at first?

I was quite defensive. I think one of the things about being a Protestant Ulsterman was [that] I felt quite defensive. I felt misunderstood on behalf of my race, you know, on behalf of the Protestants. I felt we were misunderstood. I felt that we weren't allowed to be the ones that were cultured. I felt that we were tired with this notion of being dour, whereas the Catholics got away with having a copy of Yeats in one hand and a rifle slung over the other shoulder, you know, marching off into this kind of cultural utopia where they had right on their side. So I felt quite angry about that when I first went to England, particularly when I arrived at drama school and everyone hearing my accent automatically thought I was very much a republican. They'd be like, 'Brits out!' and I'd be like, 'No it's not like that. You don't understand'. It was interesting being an Ulsterman, being an Ulster Protestant, at that stage. I've never once flirted with the notion of rejecting my Protestantism. I never did that. It was the attachment to the Union that I didn't really get because I just couldn't understand. I felt there was more than a body of water separating me from central government. It felt a totally different place to me. I could never understand why I was supposed to toe the sovereign line. It was complicated when I first went to drama school, trying to navigate the opinions I was forming – but I also felt a little bit trapped by my Protestantism, or my unionism, at times.

So did that experience help shape your sense of identity? Did you find yourself challenging your background or was it reconfirmed for you?
Oh I think it did both. I think that's a great question. I think that's the ultimate question. I mean that's the question that I suppose I've spent years trying to articulate as well – and form an answer. I think, as I said at the beginning, it's a country of anomalies and contradictions and I think out of that it has shaped me and created this character full of anomalies and contradictions. I never once lost the notion of home being Ulster. I've never lost it. It is embedded in me in the same way that John B. Keane [the celebrated Irish playwright] used to write about paganism on the West coast of Ireland – the earth being the connection, the land being the connection. I always felt that very strongly, but I also felt at times hampered by it. I felt at times it was hard to shake off, but that was at a time when the accent was sometimes difficult.

Being cast as Adam in *Cold Feet* was your first big break. Was the decision to play him as a Northern Irishman your decision?

My decision. It was written for someone from the North of England and in fact the writer was, I think, vehemently against that notion. Andy Harries [the Granada TV producer], I think, had to soothe quite a lot of dissenting voices within the hierarchy of ITV. It was only a pilot at that stage but I think they knew that it had great potential. I walked into the interview and I said, 'I've got to do this Northern Irish'. And that time was when there was a crossover period, a very significant time in television and in the arts about how Ulster was being perceived. It was vital because the only Ulster voices you heard, apart from maybe Jimmy Ellis in *Z-Cars*, were either reading the news, imparting usually pretty difficult and troubled stories, or actors with Northern Irish accents in dramas about the conflict. Certainly with *Cold Feet* I absolutely knew it had a chance. I read it and it was just of its time. I just knew that the characters could really develop and I thought this is the opportunity to get the accent out there, and I think it made a significant contribution. And as the series progressed I began to write a lot of my own character and in fact some other characters, but once I had found the voice of Adam – which was a lot of my voice – I was then able to put a lot in. I remember there's a scene where Adam gets good news and I do a wee march, I think, in the kitchen with Rachel [Adam's wife in the series] where I sing 'The Sash'. I got into terrible trouble about it, but I love the idea that you could get that out there. Of course that was bringing it back to the Troubles, but you actually saw where he came from. And then, of course, we had the opportunity to bring *Cold Feet* to film in the Causeway and Belfast. I was really proud of where I came from at that point and so many of our contemporaries were living in England – yet in terms of that voice being heard, it just wasn't.

And then the other big seminal point in your career was, of course, very much connected to the Troubles. Playing Ivan Cooper in *Bloody Sunday* was about as far removed as you could get from playing Adam in *Cold Feet*.

I was talking to my father about this recently actually. I think people have a misconception of me. As gregarious as I was at that time, I come from a very small place. I spent a lot of time as a child as an isolated Ulster boy, loving where he was, loving kicking the ball against a wall but pretty green, I suppose.

You mean green behind the ears, not green politically, of course.
Yes, green behind the ears. But I had a father who would open windows into literature and the arts. I had a mother who had an incredible sense of humour, was a wonderful storyteller and had a great sense of balance. When *Bloody Sunday* came along, again I knew. Paul Greengrass [the director] came to see me in Manchester. I was shooting the third series of *Cold Feet* and he talked for a very long time about why he wanted me to do it, why he felt I was the only person. He said, 'You're the only person who can play this part'. He said, 'I've put Ivan Cooper at the centre of it. I'm going to get a lot of flak about that, but he's got to be at the centre of it because he was a Protestant leading a nationalist cause, or what was essentially a nationalist cause. You're the only actor who can do it.' It really was something that I thought long and hard about for a while but I also knew, having read the script and having spoken to him, that it was clearly something I had to do for me as an actor. It had a big impact, that movie. Certainly, in terms of my own identity, it threw up all sorts of things.

Did you in fact uncover a story that you had never really taken the time to discover before, or which you had never really been exposed to?
I had been exposed to it.

So did you choose to disbelieve or disregard it?
Oh no, I think I believed it but I think I disregarded it. I think that's what we did and I think that's an important component of my life, actually.

So as part of preparing to play Ivan Cooper you went to Derry and met the families – and you forensically examined what happened?
Forensically, absolutely.

And how much of a revelation was it then to suddenly be exposed to people who had also grown up in the same place that you'd grown up in, but who had such an enormously different experience of life?

Well, I think that's what's incredible about Ulster, that just up the road from me, people my age had served time. Raymond McCartney, who I met, who himself had been the first hunger striker was a similar age to me, maybe a little bit older. As Paul Greengrass said, I'd probably listened to the same music as a lot of those boys in Derry, probably followed the same football team. What divides people in Ulster cannot actually be outweighed by what unites them. When I went to see the families they, of course, were at first suspicious.

And were they suspicious of you because they knew you to be an Ulster Protestant?

I think they were, yes. I think so.

Except, of course, that Ivan Cooper was also an Ulster Protestant.

Yes, but I think even though Ivan had a ninety-nine percent Catholic electorate, there were probably people that were a bit suspicious throughout of Ivan. I'm not saying they made Ivan a scapegoat, but Ivan called the people out to march. John Hume didn't march that day and that was what was so brave about what Paul did in putting Ivan at the centre of it. Yes, I think they were very suspicious that not only was I a Protestant, but I was a successful Protestant actor, swanning into Derry to tell their story. So the only way to do that was, of course, to go in and forensically, as you say, study what had happened. I read everything before I went to meet them and then – without telling Paul or the producers – I went to Derry by myself. I met with Ivan and then I went into Derry, booked myself into the Strand Hotel and ordered a pint of Guinness in the Strand Bar. I sat down and just before I was about to take a sip, this guy tapped me on the shoulder and there was a kind of a porthole in the bar and I looked through and there was a guy there and he said, 'Who am I?' And I said, 'You're Bubbles Donaghy. You were the first guy shot in Bloody Sunday. You were shot in the thigh but you survived'. And he leaped across and he hugged me and he said, 'Ok, you'll be all right'. It was an astonishing moment. It was like fate. I often think, and

I shudder to think, if I had looked around and said, 'I don't know'. Because that's what Ulster is. We are prepared to love and we are prepared to trust but it has to be reciprocated. I don't think we suffer fools here. People talk about the great welcome, but the welcome has to be earned, in a sense.

But you also had to win over 'your own' community. You received death threats, your parents' house was attacked – there were a lot of people who were very unhappy that you had, in their eyes, sold out.

You know, I disagree with some other Ulster actors who say they're just actors. I think absolutely, as a Northern Irish actor, we have a responsibility to tackle the Troubles, I really do. I mean there are some who'd disagree with that. I felt it was absolutely incumbent upon me for so many reasons, but the Protestant people were thinking, 'Well, what the hell is he doing that for?' I can understand that, but I think that's born out of fear. So much of what happened here is born out of ignorance and ignorance is born out of fear; prejudice is born out of fear. The most important person I had to persuade really was my father. Dad had probably never really taught Bloody Sunday in primary school. I think transparency is absolutely the key. Dad went into Eason's one day and he read everything about it. He said, 'Well of course, you've got to do it' – and in terms of my Ulster identity, what's interesting about the end-game of Bloody Sunday for me was that because it was essentially an act of murder against the 'other side' by, supposedly, the side that my culture would support, it didn't turn me against Ulster and everything it stood for. If anything, it made me hang on to my Ulster identity even more because I felt it was an Ulster that belonged to everyone. I'm very glad I did it.

You subsequently became involved as a campaigner in support of victims of the Troubles – and, of course, that's an issue you tackled in the drama *Five Minutes of Heaven* which is a film about the legacy of the conflict and which co-starred Liam Neeson.

It was very interesting that Liam took that on. Funnily enough I sort of hold you responsible, because you brought me together with Liam – and Liam and I should have met bloody years ago. Liam grew up in Corlea Gardens, opposite my granny. It could only happen in Ulster – the biggest star we've ever had and when I met him, the first words he said to me were, 'Here, was your granny, Granny Nesbitt?' I mean it's magnificent, that. I mean it's truly magnificent on so many levels. He remembered her well. That's another thing about Ulster, you know – there was Liam, remembering my granny well. He may not have remembered what he did yesterday, but he remembered Granny and her garden – her never wanting to throw the ball back. He remembered Granda Nesbitt tending the roses, very clearly – and Ulster does really do that. We met at that event in London and he said we should work together, and then this script came up and he phoned and he said, 'Right, this is the one we should do'. An extraordinary act of courage, I think, as an actor because the older you get, the more successful you get, the more fear you get of being found out – and Liam often says that. For Liam and me that was a journey for both of us, going back to Ulster through different ways and we did it very much together and it was a glorious experience. If ever you wanted to see what distinguishes Ulster people from almost anywhere else, watch what Liam and I were like in that movie. We were playing people from opposite sides. We were playing people that had huge connections through where he grew up and through my family – like his sister, I think, courted my uncle Bertie in Ballymena for a while. They all knew each other and yet we had somehow managed to avoid each other – and yet we were united professionally and personally and we had wonderful times working together and playing together. We had a lot of tears and a lot of laughter and it was definitively Ulster, the way we were.

And, of course, your new role as Chancellor of the University of Ulster is one which brings you back here on a regular basis now.
Well, I love 'Ulster'. I call the university 'Ulster', and sometimes it's funny when I come back to do press and I say I'm very keen on promoting 'Ulster' and people think I'm talking about the province, but I'm talking about the university – but essentially it is a university that is very much of Ulster. There are so many ironies about it. That's the university I dropped out of, then I got my honorary doctorate and now to be Chancellor with my education background is very exciting because what I feel passionately about is that tertiary education should be available to everyone and 'Ulster' firmly believes that.

You spent a lot of time in New Zealand recently filming *The Hobbit*, but you do come back here a lot and you've now got business interests here as well. Could you envisage ever not being within easy striking distance?

Oh God no! I'd live here. I mean, it would be difficult. Ulster is absolutely embedded in my children. They're privileged children but they absolutely know where their father comes from. They know the importance of a pound, they know that their granny sang to them as children and they can still remember the words. They can't remember Granny teaching them the songs but they still have the words. They can both speak with perfect Northern Irish accents. I've a production company called 'Brown Cow Films' because it was the first thing Peggy said in a Northern Irish accent – 'How Now Brown Cow'. They know what 'oxters' are. That's what's so important to me about my Ulster identity – that it lives, that my children are conscious of it and that it is somehow embedded in them because they are half-Ulster, Peggy and Mary, and they know that and they love it and actually it's something that they are remarkably proud of. That's identity, you know. That's lasting identity, I think.

FRANK ORMSBY

Born in Enniskillen in 1947, Frank Ormsby is a poet and anthologist. He edited The *Honest Ulsterman* for two decades – from 1969 to 1989 – and his anthologies include *Poets from the North of Ireland* (1979 & 1990), *The Long Embrace: Twentieth Century Irish Love Poems* (1989), *The Collected Poems of John Hewitt* (1991) and *A Rage for Order: Poetry of the Northern Ireland Troubles* (1992). His most recent collection *Fireflies* (2009) features poems set in rural Fermanagh, Belfast and America. From 1976 until his retirement in 2010, Frank Ormsby was Head of English at the Royal Belfast Academical Institution.

We meet in South Belfast.

Frank Ormsby:

I think that in the days before I thought about issues like identity, I thought of Ulster as one of the original provinces of Ireland. I thought of it as the six counties plus the three other counties from the South of Ireland. I'm not sure when I would first have heard the term 'Ulster', but I suspect that it was probably not until my first year at grammar school where we covered basic Irish history and touched on the *Ulster Saga*, the cycle of mythological tales in which, of course, Ulster figures very prominently. I have a feeling that at that stage I didn't think of the term Ulster as problematical in any way and it was only later that I began to think of it in those terms and to realise that it meant certain things to some people and different things to others.

Mark Carruthers:

So are there two Ulsters for you? Is one that ancient, mythological province of Ulster and alongside it the contemporary Troubles-ridden Ulster of more recent times?

Yes, I suppose that's true. Although I say that I wasn't aware of the term Ulster for quite a long time, I was aware of the entity that was called Ulster because I was brought up in a border county, which in fact bordered

Donegal, Cavan and Monaghan, so there was some sort of sense of being in the state called 'Northern Ireland' but also being attached, as it were, along a border with these other three lost counties of Ulster – although I don't think we would have thought of them in those terms.

Do you remember any sense of being peripheral when you were growing up in Fermanagh?

Well, you're right in suggesting that the geographical position of Fermanagh – and this is maybe an experience that all people who live in the so-called border counties have – is more or less equidistant from the two main centres of power, which are Belfast and Dublin. And there's something quite isolated about the whole notion of living in a border county. I grew up in a working-class, Catholic, rural background and we would've been broadly nationalistic. I remember that in the obituary for my father which appeared in the *Fermanagh Herald*, the Catholic newspaper, he was described as 'an enthusiastic Gael' and I think that is a very good description of him, in that he had this almost sentimental kind of Irishness. He listened to Radio Éireann, followed Gaelic football and that was very much the background against which I grew up.

So did your family feel manacled to the North, while looking towards the South? Was it ever as pronounced as that?

I don't think it was as pronounced as that, although, interestingly, the South of Ireland was generally referred to as the 'Free State', which, when you look back at it, is quite a loaded kind of term. I was never quite able to work out – and I still don't know – what the attitude of my parents would have been to the IRA campaign in the 1950s. I was born in 1947 and there was this campaign in the '50s in which the border counties in the North were particularly hard hit. I suppose they were very vulnerable to attack from the South and there were a couple of IRA men killed, for example, on an attack on Brookeborough RUC Barracks which must have been in the '50s at some point. There was an attack on Rosslea Barracks. The village that was closest to us was Irvinestown and the RUC station there was like a kind of fortress. There were sandbags around the windows, high wire in front and traffic-bumps on the road outside. Protestants who lived in places like Fermanagh must have felt particularly beleaguered at that time. I suspect that my mother didn't take much interest in these things. I think my father's interest was probably that of the sentimental nationalist. I certainly never heard any expression of support for violence, for example, in our household. I suppose it was the nationalism that is devoted to Irish music and Irish sport, particularly Gaelic football.

So, cultural nationalism.

I think so, yes. Until my father went to bed at night we listened to Radio Éireann and as soon as he went next door to the bedroom, we, the children, switched over to Radio Luxembourg, so already at that stage the mixture of cultures was coming at you. I've often thought as well, that it was kind of ironic that although I definitely don't think of myself as English in any way, nevertheless the literature that has meant most to me is English literature. The literature that brought me to poetry was English literature and I remember at a conference in the '80s, the Southern poet Paul Durcan saying vehemently, 'I will not let Margaret Thatcher come between me and John Dryden'.

You've talked about the influence of your family on your sense of identity. When you came up to Queen's, though, and began a new life in Belfast, did that alter your sense of self at all?

Well, I think it did. First of all, as a Catholic I lapsed during my first or second year at Queen's which I suppose obviously my family would have regarded as a retrograde step, but I thought of it as progress and a step forward. I think I began to get more of a perspective on some of the prejudices that I'd brought with me. When I look back on some of the attitudes I had when I was growing up, I realise how prejudiced and bigoted they actually were. I can remember, for example, listening to the World Cup Final in 1966 and being very unhappy when England went ahead and absolutely delighted when Germany equalised. It was as basic as that – some kind of in-grown, difficult to shift, anti-Englishness. But I think that I grew well clear of that.

And did poetry help you move away from that, do you think?

Yes. There's no doubt about that at all. I mean, I just think it's one of the civilising consequences of being a writer and of studying literature. I think that it extends your tolerance in all kinds of ways. I think it leads you towards self-interrogation of your own attitudes to things. I think it's something that opens up the possibility for development and progress in your outlook and in your attitudes, and I think that it probably therefore helps your sense of identity to become something more complicated. When I think of identity, I think of something that's unquantifiable, something that's constantly changing and constantly complicating itself. I mean, my God, I think if you felt you had arrived at some kind of fixed sense of your own identity, it would be time to think again. There's something seriously wrong then.

So your notion of identity has changed as you have grown and matured?

Well I think so and I suppose the whole issue of identity became an issue when the Troubles broke out. I'm not saying it wasn't an issue before that, but it was the Troubles that kind of brought it to the forefront of people's awareness and one of the poets, of course, that I would have read for the first time in the 1960s was John Hewitt for whom the whole issue of identity became one of the central themes in his poetry.

Did you get to grips with the English canon first and did that then lead you to Hewitt and his fellow Ulster poets?

The schools' anthologies were anthologies of English poetry. They were in fact anthologies which had been put together for the use of English schoolchildren and very few Irish poets ever made it into the schools' anthologies. I mean, you could expect to find Yeats there. You might or might not find Louis MacNeice. If you did find Louis MacNeice, I suspect it was because the anthologists thought of him as a 1930s English poet rather than as an Irish poet. And there were others like James Stephens and Pádraic Colum. There was a kind of smattering of Irish poets, but the material that you studied tended to be Shakespeare, Wordsworth and the figures from the main canon of English literature. There are episodes that come to mind when I think about how I first began to get a sense of poetry from the North of Ireland and one was coming across the work of Patrick Kavanagh. I was taught mainly by priests at St Michael's College in Enniskillen. Many of the priests were from Monaghan and Cavan. For them Kavanagh, at least Kavanagh's poetry, was important and Kavanagh was a kind of hero. Also I remember an occasion – I'm not sure whether this coincided with the Arts Council tour that John Montague and John Hewitt did of the province called 'The Planter and the Gael' – but certainly, at some point, one of the priests who taught us English photocopied certain poems by Hewitt and John Montague. And that was really the first time that I had any sense at all that there were poets writing about County Tyrone in Montague's case and County Monaghan in Kavanagh's case, and that my own rural background was a fit subject for poetry. There was a sense that these people were writing about a world that was particularly familiar to me. I didn't start imitating those poets right away. I think I went through the kind of imitation process that most young poets do. You find yourself writing pastiche of T.S. Eliot and Gerard Manley Hopkins, you know, two mainstream figures from the English literature canon.

But then when you've done that, you eventually find your own voice?
I think so, and I suppose it's also partly to do with discovering, say, American poetry. I always thought that a major influence here was the emergence of the paperback – the paperback revolution of the '60s. There was a series called 'Penguin Modern Poets', for example – over two dozen little anthologies, each one giving a selection of three contemporary poets. There were also anthologies of American poetry and so I must say that, when I think of identity, I think of it as cumulative. I think of it as rippling out all the time and everything that you come in contact with – and especially the things that you absorb – obviously have the effect of refining and changing your sense of identity all the time.

And is John Hewitt, in your view, the key to understanding this place?
No. I think he's probably *one* of the keys to understanding it. I suppose he comes at the question of identity from a particular kind of background, different from that of the Catholic poets, for example. I think that Hewitt was the one who brought to the forefront all these issues of identity which

we're familiar with now. They have been in the air and in the water for quite a long time now, but when you look back at the essays and the poems that Hewitt was writing in the '50s and '60s about European regionalism and so on, there's no doubt that he was the one who was thinking about all that and articulating it. When the poets of the 1960s emerged – like Heaney, Longley, Mahon and company – these essays were already there. They were part of the literary traditions that the newly emerging poets began to absorb.

People seem drawn to his ranking of identity – Ulster, Ireland, Britain and Europe. Does that concept make sense to you?

I sympathise with the attempt to get at the heart of this issue of identity, that orderly and disciplined attempt to define it, but, of course, Hewitt's poetry in a way runs counter to that. It strikes me as the poetry of somebody who is constantly searching for his identity, you know, the fact that he tried to pin it down in an interview in the *Irish Times*. It's useful and it's interesting, but I'm sure he didn't think of it as the last word either. I think it was interesting to see him trying to include what he thought of as all the main strands. It's a bit like Stephen Dedalus [the literary alter ego of the novelist James Joyce] writing his address inside the front of his geography book at Clongowes, and it extends beyond County Kildare to Ireland, the World and the Universe.

Is part of the difficulty with identity in this part of the world, that for many people they want to be defined by what they are not, rather than what they are?

Well, it's a very exclusive approach and a negative approach in the sense that it's shutting out so much that could contribute positively to the breadth of your identity. I suppose, by and large, it's generally easier to say what you're not. I mean, I said a while ago, 'I know I'm not English', for example. I know that I don't feel British. Why I don't feel British, I'm less sure about. I do feel Irish, but more and more I would think of myself – when I think about this at all – as Northern Irish.

So it's a qualified Irishness?

Yes, and I suppose, on some broad level, the idea of a United Ireland appeals to me strongly, but I think that both halves or both parts of Ireland would have to change considerably before that became viable or became a kind of possibility.

So it's not something that you're itching to see happen?
No, absolutely not.

How did that sense of Irishness square itself with your lifetime teaching at the Royal Belfast Academical Institution? It's a liberal school that traces its early days back to the United Irishmen but today it's probably seen as being more British than Irish in its outlook.
Well, the school is very public about being non-denominational and I think that has always been one of the strengths of the place. I suppose I arrived at RBAI just by good luck. It was the second job that I applied for and I got it. In retrospect, I think it was a valuable experience for me because – it's very tricky to talk about this really – I suppose for the first time in my life I was dealing on a daily basis with people – staff and pupils – most of whom were from a very different kind of background, religiously and politically, to me. In that respect, when we were growing up in Fermanagh, we were very isolated. It's the old story from Northern Ireland that we had very, very few Protestant friends. We would hardly have mixed at all with people of other religions. I think it helped to broaden my horizons and I don't want to give the impression that I arrived there intolerant and somehow became tolerant overnight, but I think that there is a way in which dealing with people from a whole range of backgrounds on a daily basis – and I suppose also teaching a civilising subject like English – is bound to impinge on your own identity. I think it was a very fruitful and enriching experience. On the other hand, of course, I don't know what it might have meant for me if I had spent my entire professional life teaching in a Catholic school because I haven't had that experience. I can't really make comparisons.

Two of the best poets in the English language, Seamus Heaney and Michael Longley, come from this place. They're from very different trad-itions and backgrounds, though they have long been very close friends. There are many others like them too – so why has this place produced such a remarkable depth of successful, popular, challenging poets?

I think there's probably a variety of reasons. The much maligned Eleven Plus probably played its part because the Education Act of 1947 meant that a lot of people from both Protestant and Catholic working-class backgrounds were able to win scholarships to grammar schools and go on to the next levels of education, something they probably couldn't otherwise have afforded to do, by and large. I suppose people like Heaney and Longley represent the first group through into university education as a result of the Eleven Plus examination. And I suppose you could say that the civil rights movement probably owed a lot to that as well, as would the SDLP. I think the same might be said of the Belfast Festival at Queen's which was starting up in the early '60s and, of course, one of the things that the Festival organisers did was to produce a series of poetry pamphlets. The first series they produced represent the first little pamphlet collections of people like Heaney, Longley, [James] Simmons and so on. When the Troubles then broke out in the late 1960s, the media latched onto the fact that in a province where there was so much violence on the streets and so much turbulence, there was also a counter-movement, if you like, and that all sorts of creative energies were being let loose as well. I'm not suggesting that the outbreak of the Troubles was a matter of good luck for the writers, but there's certainly a sense in which it drew attention to them in a way that might not otherwise have been the case. There was a famous article by Mary Holland, I think, in the *Observer* which must have brought this new blossoming of poetry to a wider audience.

But they were good too, of course. That's the other thing.
Oh yes, that's the other thing. I mean, the sheer quality and the recognition of Heaney, in particular. The sort of acclaim that he got from the beginning gave 'provincial' writers a greater degree of confidence.

Journalism is sometimes referred to as the first draft of history, but what were the poets doing? Were they and their fellow writers helping a wider audience to understand better what was happening here at the time?
I think that writing was just one of the forces for good. I suppose what the writers had to offer was an exploration of the place where they'd grown up, which in itself was illuminating. While it reflected the differing backgrounds

of the writers in various ways, it nevertheless wasn't propagandist in any sense. It got beyond the divisions and it reflected the horror and outrage. In the '70s, you sometimes heard poetry from the North of Ireland being criticised on the grounds that the poets all lived in leafy, university shelter belts, that they had no direct experience of the areas which were hardest hit by the Troubles. I must say I always thought that idea was nonsense because in a sense the poets were in exactly the same position as the vast majority of the population. You could say that about most of the population, that they didn't have direct experience of the worst of the Troubles.

And they just wanted to get on with their lives.
Yes.

Like most people.
Well, that's right. I suppose, in a way, you could say that they kept the values of peacetime alive. Any good poetry written during a period of turbulence or of war does that, in a sense. The best of the poetry from the North kept alive the values of peacetime which, in itself, is a useful and necessary function.

Are you happy to describe yourself today as an Ulsterman?
I wouldn't object to it.

Would you prefer Northern Irish?
No. I don't think I would worry much one way or the other. I'm happy enough with Ulsterman. I'm happy enough with Northern Irish, and I think probably quite a number of people move back and forth between those two terms without much agonising. I started the interview with a sense that issues of identity are, by their very nature, fugitive and elusive. I expected to come out at the end of the interview without having clarified anything at all really – and, in fact, I think that has probably happened. I'm perfectly happy with that. I think in a way that's how things should be. As I said before, identity is something that continues to ripple out all your life and your identity next year might not be – probably won't be – the same as your identity this year.

GLENN PATTERSON

Glenn Patterson is a Belfast-born novelist and screenwriter. Born in 1961, he attended Methodist College Belfast and later the University of East Anglia where he studied creative writing. His novels – among them *Burning Your Own, Fat Lad, The International, Number 5* and *The Mill for Grinding Old People Young* – often reassess events of the recent past. His articles and essays have appeared in the *Irish Times, Guardian, Observer, Sunday Times* and *Independent*. He co-wrote the screenplay for the film *Good Vibrations* which was released to much popular and critical acclaim in 2013.

We meet in his room in Queen's University where he teaches creative writing.

Glenn Patterson:

Ulster doesn't have any kind of useful meaning for me. It exists purely in the symbols – hands and flags. That's it. It's not a concept that can help me in any way say anything about who I am. Of all the things by which I would choose to identify myself, Ulster would never feature. I don't have a provincial identity.

Mark Carruthers:

So you would never describe yourself as an Ulsterman?
No.

Never have done?
No. A Northern Irish man yes, but Ulster? I'm trying to think myself back to my teens and at what point you become aware of yourself and your place in the world and your place's place in the world. Ulster was the first word in all the paramilitary organisations around where I lived, you know? I didn't see me in the 'U', if you like. It was the 1970s. The UDA were parading on our playing fields up in Finaghy. It was very easy to be caught up in it at the time – and to think that the UDA and the UVF actually did claim to represent you in some way!

So, from the very outset, it had a negative connotation?

No, I'm not saying it had a negative connotation, but it never was anything that I remember thinking of myself as being 'Ulsterish'. I mean what even is the adjective? I am – 'Ulsterish'? I don't know. I am 'of Ulster'? So in terms of the extent to which it actually is accurate in its description of the place that I live – first of all, it's not. I live in the province of Ulster but the administration here is a Northern Irish administration. It's not an Ulster administration. I support the Northern Ireland football team.

And what about the Ulster rugby team?

You see, that's rugby. I have no interest. I went to a rugby playing school, but I was a footballer, a soccer player. It really doesn't represent me. It never has done.

Some people, of course, use the notion of Ulster as a way into their Britishness. Some people use it as a way into their Irishness. Some use it entirely interchangeably with the idea of Northern Ireland.

I would never use it interchangeably with the sense of Northern Ireland. I have a real sense of Northern Irishness which has got greater as the years have gone on. I will always have a sense of Northern Irishness, I think, no matter what happens. It's not something that is dependent on the political future – whatever the realignments will be. I would still think that putting 'Northern' before 'Irish' is helpful in understanding, for me, who I am – but it doesn't diminish the Irishness of it. But it does actually tell you the variety of it, so Northern Irish – Northern Ireland – makes a kind of a sense to me when talking about my identity. But Ulster never really did.

Do you shy away then from that whole bigger notion of identity? Do you try to avoid the British versus Irish debate?

No. My mother always described herself as Irish. My father always described himself as British. She was Irish because she was born on the island of Ireland. He was British because his passport was British.

And were they both from this place?

Yes. He's from Lisburn [in County Antrim], she's from the Woodvale [near the Shankill Road in Belfast]. That was how they described themselves. That was how they dealt with that. Their parents had been born in an Ireland that was not divided, so my grandparents lived through partition and therefore that question of identity was complicated within their lifetimes. When I was growing up, I felt that it was a choice of that or that. You had to choose one or the other. That identity was divisive.

So, did that affect your parents' political outlook? Did it make your mother nationalist in outlook and your father unionist in outlook?

Well, I think that Dad was a Labour man but I think they probably were unionist, both of them. But unionism itself shouldn't have precluded a sense of Irishness. But growing up as a teenager in the 1970s you could not embrace or even recognise a sense of Irishness at all. It was either that or that. But at a certain point was the idea that you actually take on more identities, as many as you possibly can, so I'm Irish, I'm British, I am European and I am greater for all of those things, and I think that's been the change here. It's possible to hold several identities at the same time and they're not mutually exclusive.

Do you think you were shaped in that bigger vision, then, by the move to live outside Northern Ireland?

I went to East Anglia when I was twenty. I'd finished school and I went to work in Crane's Bookshop on Rosemary Street in Belfast. So I started there and then I went from Norwich to Manchester in my mid twenties. The highlights of my year when I was growing up were New Year's Eve and the Eleventh of July. Those were the big nights. I built bonfires. I was still in my mid teens. I was going to Methody and come the summer months after Easter, we were out building bonfires. We all had hatchets we would buy from the hardware shop in Finaghy Crossroads. I don't think we ever cut anything down, but we'd be collecting stuff. I was doing that until I was sixteen. If I say it was what you did, that's not to say that I'm washing my hands of it and it looks strange to me now. It was only a handful of years before I was at the University of East Anglia studying for an MA in creative writing.

Were you horrified then, do you think, when you looked back? Were you very keen to escape that part of your past?

Well, you see, this is the thing. I thought that the only thing you could do would be go the other way. You had to go right over to the other side. So you had to reject everything to do with that and, if you rejected that, then in Northern Irish terms, what was there? I remember going to a 'Troops Out' stand at my university and getting into an argument with them there. I think whoever was sitting at the stand had a Labour Party badge on as well and there might have been plastic bullets sitting on the table in front of them and I got into an argument about the Labour government's record in Northern Ireland. I was conscious of the fact that I was seen as a Protestant from Northern Ireland and actually – do you know what? I was just about to say as an Ulster Protestant and that's probably the only time I would use the word 'Ulster' because that's how it felt. 'You're an Ulster Protestant.' So it always had slightly negative connotations when it was used of you. That's how I felt. I felt, here I am and they think they know me straight away because, 'You're an Ulster Protestant'. You know, we don't need to take this seriously; we can't have an argument with you because you're speaking as one of that unattractive tribe.

So, has part of your experience over the last twenty-five or thirty years been to try to redefine that notion of Ulster Protestantism? To say, effectively, I can hold to those ideals but actually it's a lot more complicated than you might think?

I remember being in a house in Norwich at the signing of the Anglo-Irish Agreement in 1985. There was a huge demonstration and I was living with four other people – my girlfriend at the time who was English, from the Channel Islands, and three other people – and I remember walking into the front room. The TV was on and somebody said, 'Who the fuck are they?' And I thought, 'Actually, I *know* who the fuck they are'. You know, probably if not members of my own family, then, quite a lot of people I know are in front of the City Hall at this moment and while I didn't agree with them, I just thought, you can't ignore that. You can't look at that and say, 'Who the fuck are those people?' I think I started at that point. I think that was my moment of thinking, 'Well, what I want to know is, who the fuck *are* they? How's it got to *here*?' And I think I probably started then. Up until that point, I can't remember what I was writing, whether it was set in Northern Ireland or not, but within two months of that I had started writing my first novel, *Burning Your Own*, which was set in Belfast in 1969. It was set on a housing estate. I remember, when I was younger, the Border Poll. I remember being terrified of the Border Poll which was 1973. I think I was in P7. I remember being terrified of what would happen if the result of that was to get rid of the border. I was petrified! It did actually feel as though the bottom would fall out of my world. So I think I remembered that in 1985. I think I remembered that feeling that you were vulnerable, that your identity, that who you were, could be written out of existence. I think by the 1980s I no longer believed that to be so, but I was interested in writing about people for whom that did seem to be so.

And did you set out to be a chronicler and an explainer? Or were you reinterpreting or maybe even apologising?

Re-examining. I don't know how to talk about what I did when I was young and building bonfires, except I did it. You bought a hatchet, you all lay around the bonfire, you made huts, you got off with girls, you tried to get drink. You stayed up as late as possible. I mean it was such a big, big thing for me. That was the rhythm of the year and so many of the rituals of adolescence were bound up in it for me. And, as I say, New Year's Eve was very similar. New Year's Eve was street parties, going in and out of people's houses. Everybody's parents had parties, doors were open. I feel no affinity with it at all now, you know?

And do you ever see any of those people you were friendly with in those days?

The thing is I was living in so many different places at the same time and I think we all often do. I was going to school at Methody – I did the qualifying exam and, like a number of people in the estate where I grew up, we all went. There was, I don't know, maybe half a dozen of us. I went to Methody in September 1973. All I wanted to do at the end of the day was get home because I was scared. I had to get on the bus. It was a real terror when the bell rang. I ran through the school to get on the first bus going up the road. If you think what the place was like in those days for people getting home. Getting home was a big thing but once you were back, that was pretty much it. Out of school hours were spent entirely around Finaghy. You've got a couple of lives there going on at the same time so, you know, you're doing one thing when you're at home, you're doing maybe something else when you're at school. [The singer-songwriter] Andy White was in my class in school. We were firm friends from quite early on. I can't remember, to be honest, if I ever felt there were things that were in conflict. That was just it. You went here in the daytime – and the evenings and the weekends, you spent there.

You've come on a long journey since those early days in terms of your writing. The critic and academic Ian Sansom describes you as a 'national treasure'. Were you conscious of being part of an Ulster school of writers?
I knew very little about them. John Hewitt came into the bookshop that I worked in. When I was at school I read very, very little. I saw Frank Ormsby read at the Ulster Museum. I think I may have seen Seamus Heaney in the early 1970s. I was taught by Sheila Smith whose husband, Denis, was involved in the theatre. Sheila and Denis were neighbours of the Longleys. I wasn't aware of an Ulster tradition in poetry or in prose or in drama at all. Stewart Parker would have been writing plays when I was at school. I knew none of it. The curriculum was largely an English curriculum, so I had no sense of it. I had to seek it out when I went away. I don't actually have a good grasp of countries. The writer who was most important to me was Salman Rushdie and I've said this quite a lot in the past, but I think it might bear saying again, that *Midnight's Children* and *Shame* were the two most important works of fiction for me at the time when I was starting to write. They were also the most important works of fiction for me trying to come at Ireland and its twentieth century history in particular. Rushdie's idea of countries as 'willed fictions', writing about the partition of India, all of that really resonated with me and, when I met [the writer] Robert McLiam Wilson in early 1989 at the launch of his first novel, I discovered that he was also a huge fan. I remember thinking to myself that I don't have a good understanding of countries. I don't believe in nation, whereas cities,

I thought, I can understand – so I started using as my primary identity, Belfast.

So you'd rather be seen as a Belfast writer than an Ulster writer or a Northern Irish writer?

Yes. But if something is used descriptively, that's fair enough. If you're trying to think of writers who've come from the nine counties of Ulster, I would certainly be one. If you're looking for Northern Irish writers, then I would certainly be one. If you're looking at Irish writers, I would certainly be one. But the one that I think actually says something useful about who I am is Belfast. I feel myself to be somebody who is at home in the city. This city. I think that's the one thing that actually means something to me.

DAME MARY PETERS

Universally respected in Northern Ireland, Mary Peters was born in England in 1939 and moved to Ballymena at the age of eleven. Later, as a pupil at Portadown College, she developed an interest in athletics. She represented Northern Ireland at several Commonwealth Games and competed for Great Britain and Northern Ireland in the women's pentathlon at the Olympic Games in 1964 and 1968, finishing fourth and ninth respectively. In 1972 she famously won the gold medal at the Munich Olympics. Since then she has remained a prominent Olympian on both the national and international stages. In April 2009 she was named the Lord Lieutenant of the City of Belfast.

We meet in her home near Lisburn in County Antrim.

Mary Peters:

I get a warm glow when I think about Ulster as a province. I came here from Liverpool as an eleven-year-old and went to live in Ballymena and that was a culture shock, as you can imagine. The people of Ulster opened their hearts to me. They wore different clothes and they had different accents, but I had an idyllic time growing up in Ballymena and then moving to Portadown where, again, there was a lot of love and friendship. The headmaster was English and welcomed me with open arms into his school and made my life very happy, despite the fact that my mum died when I was at that school. He embraced me whereas my father couldn't because I was so like my mum that he found it very difficult – and he married again within six months of my mum's death because he couldn't be without her. So I was embraced into the family of Ulster folk through sport. That became my new family because my brother emigrated to Australia. My father and stepmother moved back to England and I was left alone here.

Mark Carruthers:

And was that a conscious choice on your part to stay here?

Yes. I had started at training college to be a teacher of domestic science and if I had gone to England I would have lost that year and then had to start again in a new college in England and I had settled in after three months and become very friendly with all the girls in my year. There were only fifteen of us and they used to take me home for weekends – so Ulster did embrace me.

And once you had made that decision to stay, did you ever contemplate moving to live anywhere else?

No. I was offered many opportunities to go and work in America and Canada and Australia where my family emigrated to, but here has a special warmth – despite the years of the Troubles. There's humour and there's friendship that I don't think you'd get anywhere else in the world.

What about the other side of Ulster which was the backdrop to your early athletics career when you were training? In 1972 when you won the gold medal, Northern Ireland was on fire.

I know. When I look back at the number of people who died that year, it passed me by in a strange sort of way. I just got on with my life. I had never any hesitation of saying proudly that I come from Ulster or Northern Ireland and people used to cringe and say, 'Oh, poor you'. And I used say, 'No, you don't see the side of Northern Ireland – Ulster – that I live in'. It has beautiful countryside, a lovely coast road – the finest in the world – a beautiful lake district, the Mountains of Mourne. But it's the people that make this wee province what it is. It's the genuine love of people – and that sounds ridiculous when you're talking about the Troubles but I could never see that bad side of people.

But yet that was what you were being confronted with when you turned on the TV or the radio. Did that not frustrate you?

Oh, obviously – but that's why it was all the more important for me to bring some good news back here, to create a more normalised situation in Northern Ireland, that people didn't think just of the Troubles, that they thought of good things happening. There was so much good in sport going on and cross-community projects that the terrorism seemed to be less important to me as it was to many others, because I wasn't born here. I was English and therefore couldn't be seen as one or the other; I was different anyway.

So if you are asked for your nationality now do you still say you're English?

I say I'm from Northern Ireland; I'm an Ulsterwoman. I genuinely say that – and believe it. I'm not 'unproud' that I was born in England but I feel very much a part of this community and all that it stands for.

And on the bigger picture, you've competed for Great Britain and Northern Ireland; you've been involved in the British Olympic Association for a long of time, and you've been a global ambassador for British sport. So while you may have lost the English badge, the British badge has nonetheless remained important.

Yes. I couldn't compete for Ireland because I wasn't born here and I couldn't carry an Irish passport and therefore I hadn't a choice when I was competing. My first Commonwealth Games was in Cardiff in 1958. I was representing Northern Ireland at those games and then it was a natural progression to compete for Great Britain and Northern Ireland. Now people do have a choice; they can choose between going for Ireland or going for Great Britain – but I didn't have that choice.

But are you saying that if you'd had that choice you might have chosen to compete for Ireland?

No. I was good enough to compete for Britain – and I don't mean that cynically – but sometimes people take the easier option of going for Ireland because it's easier to get on an Irish Olympic team than it would be to get on a British team. But I was the best in Britain anyway – though I did compete for Ireland once.

You did?

Yes I did, in Belgium. It was a selection of a small team and they asked me would I like to go – and I went and wore the Irish vest. That would have been probably in the mid-sixties.

Before you'd really made your name as a British athlete.

Yes.

How have you managed to stay out of the cut and thrust of the political debate in this part of the world?

Well I'm a non-political animal anyway. I have my own views, but I don't express them widely. I've been approached on a number of occasions to stand for political parties and I've said, 'No; definitely not'. I feel I can do more good being down the middle. I can go to any school or any part of the community and be accepted as a sportsperson and that can perhaps help a new generation get involved.

And when you came back in 1972 from the Munich Games, you were met with that huge presence at the airport and then you were paraded through the centre of Belfast. Were you thinking everybody was out to greet you, or did you think it was just one side of the community?

No, I never thought about that. Very soon after that lovely parade through the streets when I came home, I was collecting for the [Mary Peters] track and I went up the Shankill and down the Falls with tin cans and buckets collecting money. It never occurred to me not to go to both communities because the track was going to serve both communities.

And were you welcomed equally in both communities?

Absolutely. People ran out of their houses with their aprons on putting money into the bucket from both sides.

When you got back to Belfast you famously said, 'I went for gold, I won gold and I brought it home for you'. Who did you mean, precisely?

The people.

Everybody?

Yes, absolutely. And people sometimes say to me, 'You must have thought about what you were going to say'. I didn't. I got to the end of Royal Avenue and there was the Lord Mayor to greet me with all these people thronging about. As I was standing on the lorry I was thinking, 'What am I going to say?' I didn't even know I was going to have to speak. It just came naturally from me. It's like when I said to Princess Anne, 'Hasn't she kept it clean!'

That was when you won the BBC Sports Personality of the Year at the end of 1972.

Yes. I never thought, 'What am I going to say when I get up here?' because I didn't know it was the Princess Royal who was going to present me with the trophy.

And, of course, she'd won it the previous year. It was a funny comment.

Wasn't it? Where did it come from? I don't know. It just was – probably an Ulsterism.

When you got home from Munich someone threatened to kill you on the basis that you were a Protestant and you'd won a medal for Britain. How difficult was that to deal with?

I never honestly, with my hand on my heart, took it too seriously. My father did. He was devastated and wanted me to go home with him to Australia. Why would anybody want to harm me? I hadn't done anything extraordinary except a sporting achievement. I hadn't shown that I was connected to any one side of the community. I just wanted to be successful in sport and put a smile back on people's faces.

But you did stay away from your flat for a few months, didn't you?

Only because the police wouldn't let me go home. I stayed with my coach and his family and was very uneasy at not going home because you like to have your own little space – and when I did go home, there was no problem at all.

And that issue never raised its head again?

Never. There was one occasion when I was collecting money for the track and I went to a hotel and I was challenged to raise a toast to those who were missing that evening – which was obviously people who were in Long Kesh. And I said, 'No, you do that. You know the guys. I don't know them'. There was a bit of drink taken and I had to be very careful, and I left with my money and my bouquet of flowers rather quickly because I didn't want to be left in a position where I was being challenged.

So what about the athletes coming through at the moment? This part of the world had great success at the 2012 Olympics and Paralympics. Do you think it's more difficult for them or do you think it's actually easier for them, given the fact we're living in a new political dispensation?

I think it's much more defined. Boxing is an all-Ireland body as is rugby, as is cycling, as are so many sports. It used to be that our hockey players could play for Ireland and Great Britain at the same time. At Olympic level obviously they have now to make a choice and I think that's right. But both teams benefited from the experience of those international hockey players – people like Violet McBride who had played for Ireland and then became captain of the British team. Both teams benefited from her being on them. It's only the odd occasion when it becomes controversial. People go naturally to one side or the other normally, and it's when somebody picks up on a situation that they feel may be controversial that it makes headlines in the papers.

Some people say sport shouldn't be politicised – but it's hard for sport not to be politicised, isn't it?

It is – and when you look at the British team in 2012, they had a number of Americans and a Cuban girl who had changed their nationalities to compete for Great Britain. I personally feel you should compete for the country of your birth, but then that creates more problems for people like Darren [Clarke] and Rory [McIlroy] because they live on an island and yet the island is divided – and therefore it's difficult. We absorbed Mo Farah into our community from Somalia; he chose to come here and he won medals for us.

As far as identity is concerned, though, it is interesting when you've got people from this part of the world who want to compete for Northern Ireland or Britain – and then you've other people who've grown up in the same jurisdiction who want to compete for Ireland.

I've been to all the Olympics except Beijing. I have been on a bus with a boxer from here wearing his Irish tracksuit and I'm in my British tracksuit and we sit down and talk together. And people say to me, 'How do you know him?' I say, 'He lives down the road!' It is a bit crazy that two people who live in the same village or the same area can be representing different countries – but they are the boxers and they have a choice.

And that doesn't have to be a weakness, does it?

No, I don't think so. We have four Olympic gold medallists here for a population of 1.7 million. It's an amazing result. Where would we be on the list of countries if we were divided, as a separate country? We all happen to have competed for Great Britain – but we have lots of silver and bronze medallists for Ireland and Great Britain. London 2012 was the first time ever that people actually rushed home from work to sit down and watch Paralympians compete. Michael McKillop was outstanding at the Paralympics, as was Jason Smith – both fine young men who have now made a niche for themselves in the world and will inspire a whole new generation.

So when you were involved in the opening ceremony of the 2012 London games, I wonder what you felt. There you were, an Olympic gold medal winner – born in England, raised in Northern Ireland, very involved in the British Olympic movement for many years.

Well, forty years on, that's even more remarkable. I was so proud to stand with Stephen Redgrave and Lynn Davies and Daly Thompson and know that I was one of the chosen few who had had the thrill of being part of the Olympic movement for so many years – and we were almost welded together with pride. In fact, we all linked arms and hugged after we'd passed on the baton to the next generation. When Seb [Coe] rang me to ask me to take part there'd been all the controversy as to whether it would be Sir Stephen Redgrave or Daly Thompson or even David Beckham who would light the cauldron. I thought it was such a genius idea and it kind of recycled me because it brought me back into the public eye which I have remained in, here in Northern Ireland, but perhaps not on the mainland so much. If I can inspire just one young person to get involved in sport, then it's worth it.

And you will forever regard yourself as an Ulsterwoman, will you?

Absolutely and completely. Yes – and proud of it!

PAUL RANKIN

Widely credited with having changed the culinary landscape of Northern Ireland, Paul Rankin was born in Scotland in 1959 and grew up in Ballywalter in County Down. He met his former wife and business partner Jeanne when they were both working in the landmark London restaurant Le Gavroche and in 1989 they opened their restaurant Roscoff in Belfast city centre. It became the first Northern Ireland establishment to win a coveted Michelin star, and the pair quickly established a high public profile with numerous books and television series to their name. Their restaurant empire grew dramatically and shrank again almost as quickly. The couple divorced amicably in 2011.

We meet for dinner in his Belfast restaurant Cayenne, which subsequently closed in March 2013.

Paul Rankin:

I want to answer as honestly as possible and I suppose for me, Ulster – as opposed to Northern Ireland – conjures up an image of an island of trouble and strife. That's how I think of Ulster. It has a negative connotation. That's the first thing it throws up. I suppose if you say, 'I'm proud of our wee Ulster,' it has a different connotation. I came to Belfast in 1969 from Ballywalter as a child of ten. I went to Inst and life just seemed to be full of bombs and killings and road checks – and that to me, was Ulster. Ulster is what we call it. When you're outside it, you say, 'I'm from Northern Ireland'. You don't say, 'I'm from Ulster'. You might say that you're from Ulster if you're down South or you'll say, 'I'm from the North', but Ulster for me has huge connotations of strife and bigotry and death, so, as a teenager the first thing I wanted to do was get the hell out of Ulster.

Mark Carruthers:

And your school was right in the heart of the city, of course.
Absolutely. Crazy stuff. I think half the people didn't know what they were fighting against or what they were fighting for. I went to Queen's for a year

and dropped out in '78. I went travelling in Europe, then came back, worked a bit more and then went off and left for basically twelve years. I think I was proud that I was from Ireland. I'm not sure I was proud that I was from Ulster.

So would you have said you were from Ireland rather than Northern Ireland?

I can't remember, but I suspect so. It was easier for people to understand for a start. It's not something I've thought of very much and, to be honest, my life wasn't incredibly affected by it. I didn't grow up in West or North Belfast. I didn't have any relatives who were killed in it. My father's shop was blown up a couple of times and he was blown from one side of the room to the other. When you're a kid you're sort of protected from that. It was just all those bomb scares in Belfast and the news everyday – the news, the news. It never seemed to make any sense to me, this sort of bigotry. I'd no real concept of what bigotry was, you know? Ours was a very Christian house; evangelically Christian.

But not political?

No. God was supposed to look after the politics. No, my mum and my dad weren't political at all.

So you travelled – and food was your escape?

Food was an accident. I grew up with great food. My Mum's a great, simple cook – that sort of fanatical, simple, great produce type of lady. She wouldn't buy fish unless it was perfect. So I grew up with great food, very well made – lots of good baking, in that sort of Christian environment. There were lots of tea parties and lots of scones and shortbread eaten – good Ulster-Scots tray-bakes. I definitely had that whole Ulster Scots thing going on because my dad was from Scotland. He spoke with a broad Scottish accent. So I kind of ran away, seduced by songs about Texas and *Travelin' Man* and all that stuff. I met Jeanne in Greece and she had worked in restaurants to travel, and so she introduced me to restaurants. I worked as a waiter and I fell in love with the restaurant business.

I'd written to Albert Roux. I'd written him a passionate letter explaining that I was working in the restaurant industry but had discovered food and I wanted to dedicate my life to food and learn how to cook – and he gave me a job as a dishwasher. I understood what he was doing. He wanted to see were you full of shit or did you know how to work? Were you dedicated? Could you hack it? In Gavroche [Roux's signature London restaurant] we used to go through ten new chefs before we'd get one to stay more than a month. That's how tough it was. But if you loved it, which I did, it wasn't that tough. It was tiring, but it was fine.

And then eventually you both ended up back in Belfast, opening Roscoff in 1989 – and you effectively became the driving force of the food revolution in Ulster.

Not blowing my own trumpet, but I think I helped the whole island when I look back on it. It's my background and the international thing combined, you know? I was lucky enough to get that *Gourmet Ireland* series [on BBC Northern Ireland and RTÉ television] which sort of put it out there on a plate. I got the Michelin star and then, on the back of the Michelin star, I got the TV series. I really got lucky because this was a war-zone as far as the broadsheets were concerned and this was like a sign that things were changing, that Northern Ireland had its first Michelin star restaurant – exciting young couple, good looking girl out the front, hairy guy in the back, and so every single broadsheet came over to do an article on us. We got a lot of attention.

I remember being there one night and at the next table was Julia Roberts, who'd come up from Dublin.

You were there that night? Yeah, she was running away from Kiefer Sutherland! And you know I could never go out and say hi to her because I always felt that people came to a restaurant like this to get away from stalkers – and I didn't want to be a stalker! I thought, just say thanks for coming and maybe they'll come back.

And that sort of thing, and the interest it generated, helped put you on the map.

I really learned about local suppliers when I lived in the Napa Valley because there you're working in the Garden of Eden. You're working with some of the greatest soil on planet earth and some of the most intelligent gardeners, and so I really learned about local produce. When I opened Roscoff, what I found was basically some of the best produce on planet earth right here. Absolutely, no question. I think we always knew our beef was great, but there was never any thought about 'Brand Ulster' or 'Brand Ireland', even though we had, at the time, probably the most sophisticated monitoring system – the Quality Farm Assurance system – of any beef being produced in the UK.

So when you look at what the land produces and when you look at what the sea produces, is it stretching it to talk about Irish cuisine?
That's produce; cuisine is different. We just whacked it in the oven or boiled it up. Even world-class produce, we could wreck from a chef's point of view! We haven't produced many world-class dishes. Soda bread is one of them, it's a world-class product – and potato bread. The Ulster fry is the best breakfast in the world when it's cooked properly. I've never had a cooked breakfast anywhere in the world that comes close.

And, of course, there are strong links – including culinary ones – across the Irish Sea with Scotland.
They're so unbelievably strong. I wouldn't say it's frightening, but it's surprising. But the other thing that's strange about it is to learn about how linked it is to the Plantation – how linked that is to all the bigotry that has gone on in Northern Ireland. These were just people who were manipulated to come over and work. They now live in Antrim and Ballymena and County Down and they're just ancestors of these people that came over to do a bit of farming – and it's caused such a bloody war for hundreds and hundreds of years. And the bigotry still exists on both sides, you know? But I still feel a certain resistance when I cross the border – you're not one of us. I was shocked by that. I don't feel it immediately from the man in the street. It's more from a business point of view I feel it – because I'm very obviously a Protestant from Northern Ireland.

So if you had to grab a life belt, would you look to Dublin or London?
I know virtually nothing about Dublin politics. You know what it's like growing up here – it's the BBC, isn't it? I travelled all over the UK, staying

in various cities. I think maybe outside Edinburgh, Belfast is the best provincial city to visit in Britain and in Ireland for a good time – the balance of restaurants, scenery, hospitality, accessibility, all of that. I would say Edinburgh and Belfast are the two top food cities in the UK, no question in my mind. The breadth and scope and quality – it's fantastic!

Do you think enough people in the British Isles realise that?

No. We don't get any attention now that the Troubles are over. We're just a backwater. We're not very good at blowing our own trumpet, are we?

Do you think you sit outside the local community here to some extent?

Because I'm on the media, I've kind of hidden a little bit from community. I feel slightly uncomfortable with the attention I get. Part of me, for example, would love to go live in Italy or Greece or Spain for a while, but then I think there's a certain Judas-type notion about going and living somewhere else when we have such a great place as Ulster. Maybe the lesson or the practice is to be happy in Ulster and play your part in the community and in making it better or in supporting people who maybe aren't as fortunate as we are, because I do feel in life you get much more out of giving than taking. Maybe that's why I became a chef, because you're providing and making people happy. There's a sort of gift of love and nurture with hospitality. It's just the weather here is so shit!

STEPHEN REA

Born in Belfast in 1946, Stephen Rea is an Oscar-nominated film and stage actor. He studied English at Queen's University Belfast and worked extensively at the Abbey Theatre in Dublin and at the National Theatre in London. In 1980, he helped found Field Day Theatre Company along with Brian Friel, Tom Paulin, Seamus Heaney and Seamus Deane. He's been associated professionally with the work of the American playwright and actor, Sam Shephard, and the Irish film maker, Neil Jordan. His film appearances include roles in *V for Vendetta*, *Michael Collins*, *Interview with the Vampire* and *The Crying Game*, for which he received an Academy Award nomination for Best Actor in 1992. In 1983 he married the former Provisional IRA bomber Dolours Price; they divorced in 2003 and she died in January 2013.

We meet in Belfast's Lyric Theatre.

Stephen Rea:

Of course, there are two Ulsters aren't there? There's the six-county Ulster and there's the nine-county, ancient province of Ulster. I feel that I would be identified with Ulster in the same way as Frank McGuinness who's from Donegal, Pat McCabe who's from Monaghan and Shane Connaughton who's from Cavan. I don't feel any identification with the hard-edged loyalist Ulster. I don't feel any connection to that.

Mark Carruthers:

Do you see Ulster and Northern Ireland as being in any way synonymous?
Northern Ireland is not the full province of Ulster, so I don't. Interestingly enough, a unionist said when they were partitioning the country, 'We have to give up our beautiful Donegal'. Why would you give up something that's so dear to you in order to get numerical superiority over another group? It's beyond my understanding. What a self-inflicted wound! What a way of narrowing your own identity to being part of a political process, rather than just living.

So Ulster, as a concept, isn't a term that you would use? Would you ever describe yourself as an Ulsterman?

I'd never say that. I wouldn't even think of it, until you asked me now. I wouldn't say it. I would say I was an Ulsterman in the same way that Pat McCabe would say *he* was an Ulsterman, which is probably never. I'm Irish. My passport's Irish. I'm from the North of Ireland. I'm a Belfast man, that's for sure. I think that identity should be flexible. I don't think it can be fixed. I think that's where danger lies – if you're restricted to a view of yourself which is external to you and not internal to you. I mean, my identity can be as much formed by a poem that I might have read this morning or a piece of music that I might have listened to. It's also interesting, because being an actor, your identity is always potentially malleable. It has to be to live within the work that we do. In fact, maybe part of the process and the tension of living is to constantly adjust your identity. I can't just say, 'I'm an Ulsterman'. I can't just describe myself as that. I feel very comfortable in a lot of different places – in New York and Dublin, and in Belfast too. Your identity is always a work in progress. The Lebanese-born writer, Amin Maalouf, has written about identity – *In the Name of Identity* (1998) – and the danger of having too narrow an identity. So, somebody like Lenny Murphy [the leader of the Shankill Butchers, a loyalist gang which randomly targeted and killed Catholic civilians] may have felt that he wasn't adequately Protestant because his name was Murphy. He may have had some other psychotic condition, but that may also have contributed to it. I'm interested in where people slip through the cracks and the artist always slips through the cracks. I felt when I was growing up I was living in a kind of cultural vacuum. The Orange Order and all of that had nothing to do with me, so the vacuum filled up with a lot of different things: Irish literature, Irish music and a lot of other stuff. What I don't understand about somebody like David Trimble, for instance, who might be around the same age as me, is how come Bob Dylan didn't enter the frame at some point, you know? I'm serious. People can now condemn the '60s, but the great liberation of it was the Rolling Stones, when they were good, and Dylan.

So that international, external influence helped to shape you?

Well, don't forget Dylan was hugely influenced by the McPeakes [Belfast's foremost traditional music family], and interestingly I first saw the

McPeakes in the Ulster Hall and it was mind-blowing. I also saw the Stones in the Ulster Hall in the middle of the '60s So when I say the vacuum was filled with a lot of Irish music and Irish literature, I want to be clear that it wasn't just that. It was also the Stones and Jimi Hendrix; my identity is as much tied up with that.

So, can you remember a sense of political awakening as a young man growing up in Belfast in the 1960s with the rise of People's Democracy and the civil rights movement?

Well, I knew them all: Michael Farrell, Eamonn McCann and Cyril Toman. I was at Queen's with those guys. They had a huge influence on me, I must say, and they were such fun too. When you think of it, they were mild enough requests, weren't they? As Stewart [Parker] says in *Pentecost*, the unionists only had to be marginally generous. I think that's right – but no, they weren't capable of that. I think that people here behave pretty well given the political pressure they've been under. To have to make the twin orthodoxy thing work is an enormous pressure, I feel. The refusal [in late 2012 on the part of some unionists] to accept the ruling of the [Belfast City] Council that you don't have to fly the flag every day is really like refusing 'one man, one vote'. You are allowed to fly the flag, but just not all the time – so take it easy. We're always characterised as being dour and aggressive, but actually I think people are pretty civil when you meet them on a one-to-one basis. It's a constant burden to me to be characterised as something that I'm not.

And do you find that has happened?

All the time.

So people automatically put you in a box?

Of course. The 'Nordy' box in Dublin.

So people in the South see you first and foremost as a Northerner?

Before I open my mouth. I hate to feel my potential being closed down by an image of what I'm supposed to be, because of my accent. I haven't adopted another accent, which I was constantly invited to do as a young actor. In some way, I saw this manner of speech as part of my identity because I like the way people speak here. I like the way we speak Northern

Hiberno-English. There are pockets here where people speak a Scots [dialect] which is actually older than some of what they speak in Scotland, but basically we speak Northern Hiberno, and I like it.

And you've never been tempted to alter the way you speak?
Not apart from when I'm playing a British civil servant, of course. I have done that frequently, but I've always had difficulty with Shakespeare in that I have to try and sound like somebody from Southern England, when in fact Shakespeare wrote in a language which was not in any way amenable to that kind of speech. Shakespeare wrote in what would become Hiberno-English. I also don't see why, in Chekov, I should have to pretend I'm English before I can pretend I'm Russian. That's one of the reasons in Field Day we did productions of plays in a way that local people would speak them.

Are you concerned that a lot of people who share your Protestant heritage aren't sufficiently aware of the historical contribution made in the late eighteenth century by some of their more radical co-religionists?
They were so carefully severed from their old sense of justice. That was done quite systematically and cynically after 1798. The British encouraged and funded the Orange Order, and by a process of bribery and brutality they took the Presbyterians away from any possibility of connection with Catholics. That's how they kept the place going. Identity can't be a fixed thing. There's a line in Terry Eagleton's play *St Oscar* [about the trial of Oscar Wilde] when he's being challenged in the court about the ambiguity of his sexuality and he says, 'Nothing is ever entirely itself and the moment when it becomes so is known as death'. So when people talk about identity as a Protestant, or whatever, it's a form of death if you can only see yourself that way.

And here, people tend to define themselves as much by what they are not, as what they are.

Yes, that's exactly what it is here. 'Them-uns', you know. Stewart [Parker] had read everything. He'd read it all. That's why he didn't write 'balaclava' plays. Stewart could write a play like *Northern Star*, involving pastiche versions of seven or eight great Irish writers. Very few people would actually be able to do that. He approached here with a big world experience, a big world imagination and that's why his work is great, no question about that. Yet he wasn't so divorced from here that he couldn't find a way of inserting that work into this place. He wrote a wonderful radio play about the *Titanic*, a challenging play. I've been accused of going on a journey, and Stewart obviously went on a journey, but nobody could accuse him of the kind of journey that I'm accused of – which is to be a republican. The interesting thing about identity is what people attribute to you. I always used to say that you shouldn't assume my politics are the same as my wife's. I said that frequently, and I also said, by the way, that you shouldn't assume that her politics were the same as they might have been twenty years ago. Anyway, she can't speak for herself. That's what I find most frustrating: what people attribute to you.

Does that sadden you? Is it something that has weighed heavily on you?
Very heavily, yeah. I remember sitting watching the TV with my kid, Danny. He was about nine and there was a news item about a young fellow here who'd been attacked wearing a Celtic jersey. He was obviously attacked because he was a Catholic, and my boy looks at me and he says, 'Am I a Catholic?' I thought, this is a victory – he doesn't know. He didn't have to know. Amin Maalouf says he feels quite happy to be on the cusp of two things: being French and Lebanese, and he now lives in France. I don't know if you remember the French footballer, Patrick Vieira, who was from Senegal but played for France. They said to him, 'Are you Senegalese or are you French?' And he said, 'I'm African. I'm French with a big African heart'. That's refusing all negativity, isn't it? That's saying, these identifying stripes I will use as enabling. You do want to use the Ulster thing as enabling, but it's too often a restrictive thing because someone else's identification of what that is makes it impossible to accept.

Maybe part of the problem is that in a place like Northern Ireland you present a very particular challenge because you appear to have crossed over from one side of the fence to the other. Maybe some people imagine you've gone over to 'the dark side'?
I'm certain that's true, but it isn't very 'dark' over there. I know there have been expressions of it that have been very dark indeed, but I take people as I

find them. It saddens me that I have alienated some of those people, because when I do meet them they're civil enough and I'm civil to them. I didn't consciously leap over a wall, but there was a vacuum and their definition of what it was to be an Ulster unionist was so narrow, it was beyond stifling. You could not live in it. They gave up on the Irish language. It wasn't hijacked by republicans, they gave up on it. There's a famous photograph of some English monarch coming here and it says, '*Céad Míle Fáilte*' at the Belfast docks, because before partition they felt ok about the Irish language. Then partition came along and they said we have to define ourselves as different from an independent Ireland. So they cut away everything, and now they have invented this thing, Ulster-Scots. It's mainly a dialect that all of us have access to. It's not a language. As part of parity of esteem – which I call a 'parody of esteem' – they have to have that included. It's just bricking themselves up all the time. They don't have to do Irish, we all communicate through English. The thing about Irish culture is that it's very inclusive. It includes Yeats and Joyce. It has big literature and I don't see the big literature that's come out of Ulster unionism.

You've mentioned that you feel comfortable living and working in Dublin and in New York. What about your experience of London?

Well, let's *talk* about identity. I did my first professional theatre work in Dublin in the Abbey and then I went to London. Actually, in many senses, I am an English actor because I am a product of English theatre. English theatre is rather restricting in that there is a voice and you have to take on that voice. Because I'm a stubborn 'Ulsterman', I wouldn't. But I'm absolutely a product of the English theatre. Peter Hall [the founder of the Royal Shakespeare Company and former Director of the National Theatre] said at any given time there's about five hundred actors in England doing all the work, and I was one of those. I was fucking happy to be one of those and I share a sense of community with those people and an attitude to work. London theatre absolutely formed me more than Irish theatre did.

So where did the formation of Field Day in 1980 fit into that?

Well, a lot of motives are attributed to us and maybe we acquired motives.

There was money available and I went to Derry and got Brian [Friel] to write a play. It then acquired all kinds of identity, but it was just that we were going to do a play and we decided to do it in Derry. Then obviously the issues of [the play] *Translations* became the issues that informed Field Day: language and identity.

And then the company got the reputation for asking quite difficult questions and starting to push the boundaries.

There was a huge amount of resentment as well. I remember there was an anti-Field Day thing, questioning if there really was some kind of Irish-speaking paradise that had existed before. We were never saying that. I don't think Friel is saying that either. It certainly was Irish-speaking, but nobody's saying it was a paradise. I was reading the other day about the whole stupidity of the identity thing here. Declan Kiberd has a very funny thing in a book called *Irish Classics* (2000). In the Flight of the Earls, when Hugh O'Neill and Rory O'Donnell sailed down the Foyle to escape, it was said you could hear the people on the sides of the shore wailing and crying. Kiberd says they were probably actually laughing! So, identity to me is up in the air. Why do you pin yourself to one thing? It's absolute madness. In some senses I'm an English actor; in some senses I'm an Irish actor. In some senses, because of the movies I've watched and some of the movies I've been in, I'm an American actor. I don't think you should feel uncomfortable with it being ambiguous and flexible, rather than fixed. I hate to be identified. Technically I'm a pagan, by the way, because when I got married in the Catholic Church I had to get a pagan dispensation because I'm not baptised in a religion. It's something I'm glad of, that I'm not baptised, which was probably just laziness rather than anything else.

So, it wasn't a religious household that you came from, though it was identifiably Protestant?

Not in any way religious. I never saw my parents in a church. Actually, I saw them in a Catholic church more often than I saw them in a Protestant church because they would go to funerals and they would go to weddings.

But would you have identified yourself as a Protestant?

I was identified as such.

And there's a difference.

There is a difference. When I went to Queen's first, I had to fill out a form that asked about religion. I wrote 'none' and they scored it out and wrote 'Protestant', because if you said 'none', you had to be a Protestant. It's outrageous isn't it?

What about John Hewitt's hierarchy of identity – Ulster, the island of Ireland, the British archipelago and Europe, as he put it. Does that hold any appeal for you?

I'm very happy with the European thing. I'm very happy to have common citizenship with the French and the Germans, despite the economic disaster. I love that. He's [Hewitt] ticked all the boxes, hasn't he? I wouldn't tick them all.

You wouldn't tick the British box?

I don't. There are points where being British and being Irish collide. When they have a big thing like the Olympics and it's all about being British, I don't feel any point of identification with that. The point at which do I feel some, and what I find very interesting, is when all these African people are running for Britain. I think that's great because now the British are having to accept their immigrants, because their immigrants are heroes. This is transforming their world and I think that's fantastic. I think it's crazy to assert your identity through a flag. It's primitive, really.

PETER ROBINSON

First Minister of Northern Ireland and leader of the Democratic Unionist Party, Peter Robinson was born in Belfast in 1948. He attended Annadale Grammar School in the city and went on to work as an estate agent, before becoming the DUP's first General Secretary in 1975. He was elected to Westminster as the MP for East Belfast in 1979 and held the seat until May 2010. He became deputy leader of the DUP in 1980 and took over as leader when Ian Paisley retired in May 2008. He became First Minister, with Sinn Fein's Martin McGuinness as Deputy First Minister, in June 2008.

We meet in his office in Parliament Buildings at Stormont.

Peter Robinson:

For me, Ulster would almost be synonymous with Northern Ireland. I used to refer to Ulster an awful lot more than I now do, because I think the recognition of Northern Ireland is much more common within the unionist community now.

Mark Carruthers:

Of course, unionist leaders in the past tended very often to use the term Ulster instead of Northern Ireland.

Yes, and I think there's been a shift in the last twenty years. I would certainly have always referred to Ulster up until about twenty years ago and Northern Ireland, I think, has probably taken over since then. I'm not quite sure why that occurred, but certainly Northern Ireland is the term that's more commonly used – but I would quite comfortably use the term Ulster.

And would you describe yourself as an Ulsterman?

Yes, I would. In identity issues I have no difficulty in calling myself an Ulsterman, someone from Northern Ireland, Northern Irish; none of those would make me feel in any way uncomfortable. I'm content with all of those.

And what about the British label? How quickly do you bring it into play?

I would very often bring it into play more whenever I'm outside Northern Ireland so that there's a better understanding that Northern Ireland is part of the United Kingdom. It allows people to determine where Northern Ireland is a lot quicker when you mention the British element of it. In terms of a number of the sports that I would be interested in, there is an Irish connection – so we're a very complex people in terms of identity. I would never try and define anybody else's identity for them. It's up to each of us to define our own identity and for the rest of us to respect that.

So what is your position on the rest of this island? How do you deal with the notion of your Irishness?

I don't really consider myself to be Irish and that is probably more because the government of the Irish Republic have attempted to define their element of the island as being Ireland. I don't recognise their authority in Northern Ireland, yet they call themselves the Irish government, so they have messed up the patch in relation to that. If they take over possession of the title 'Irish', I don't consider them to be part and parcel of Northern Ireland – so I resist that kind of description.

So you wouldn't ever feel comfortable if somebody described you as Irish?

I wouldn't be *uncomfortable* with it, with people who just don't understand the nuances of Northern Ireland and indeed the identity issues. Whenever I'm in the United States I would often be referred to as somebody who's from Ireland, or Irish, and I don't take offence at that. If it's a political gathering where I'm speaking, or if it's with friends, I might, during the course of conversation, explain some of the intricacies of Northern Ireland's position in the United Kingdom, but I wouldn't take offence and nor would I correct anybody if they were to make those kinds of comments.

You've touched on two interesting things: the notion that your identity can change through time and also that it can alter depending on where you are and who you are with.

Well, of course your *identity* doesn't change in those circumstances; your willingness to tolerate people identifying you in a way other than you would identify yourself might change. Maybe that's more to do with manners and understanding of people's knowledge of your circumstances. In terms of your identity changing over time, I don't think anything in the individual changes, because it is a multi-faceted identity. The fact that you emphasise one element of it more than another at one time or another doesn't really have much of an impact. I'm quite happy to identify myself as being an Ulsterman, as being Northern Irish, as being British. All of those I'm comfortable with, and in different sets of circumstances I would use.

How do you feel about the fact that the most recent census suggests that more people than ever before in this part of the world are happy to identify themselves as Northern Irish?

Yes, I think in people doing that there is an attempt for them to reach for something that might be a more commonly agreed identity. In some ways it's an attempt to bridge that gap and get some middle ground that everybody is comfortable with. If you say you're from Northern Ireland and you accept an identity that's Northern Irish, the two are effectively synonymous. If you refer to Northern Ireland as the North of Ireland, there isn't much of a jump to say that you accept a Northern Irish identity – so to some extent it could become the label that allows you to have a common identity.

Do you remember the point at which you became aware of your sense of identity?

I had very little interest, or indeed family background, in politics. My parents would have gone out to vote and I can recall on one occasion going with them, but they weren't involved in politics in any way. I got a very rude introduction into politics by the murder of a friend while I was in my first year out of school. A friend who I'd spent a lot of time with at Annadale was murdered by the IRA and I suppose that was the issue that caused me to question what was going on politically at that time. The first booklet that I wrote around that time was called *The North Answers Back*. Some people have since questioned my use of 'the North', but, of course, it was a take on Rudyard Kipling's poem *What Answer from the North?* This was my way of the North answering back in terms of the difficulties I faced. I assume around the late sixties when politics locally came on to the television with the civil rights movement, that would have been the period when identity became something that was inescapable.

And what specifically did that awaken in you? Was it your Protestantism, your unionism, your sense of Britishness?

Well, the underlying danger was always perceived to be Northern Ireland being removed from the United Kingdom, so it was the Britishness at that time and our ability to remain as part of the UK. Our link with the rest of the United Kingdom was in peril and therefore it was that aspect of it that was particularly to the fore.

To what extent has identity been an issue for you in over forty years of involvement in politics?

I suppose if there has been a transformation it is that in the earlier days there was a black and white issue: we are constitutionally and legally a part of the United Kingdom and whether you like it or not, you're British. Now we recognise that others may not see themselves as having a British identity, though the fact is they are part of a United Kingdom whether they like it or not. I can't individually tell anybody that they're British, but I can say we are a part of the United Kingdom and democratically it won't change.

Do you think as time has passed you have been more prepared to accept that those people have got to be accommodated in this state?

Yes. I suppose more selfishly than that I think if we are to progress as a society, not only do we need to accommodate those people but we also have to recognise that if we want to retain our position in the United Kingdom, it is vital that everybody is comfortable and content within the UK.

Do you think leadership has changed your political world view?

Anybody who is involved at a higher level in politics, from a unionist point of view, cannot be involved in any form of dialogue or debate without starting to realise that there is a wider picture that you have to take into account. I don't think leadership necessarily changes things, but it's certainly a wider exposure to the views of others.

You were seen as an uncompromising political figure in the past, but now that you are the First Minister you have had to make compromises. You are now working in government with people you might not have thought you would be able to work with twenty years ago. Is that a fair comment?

It's fair to say that I wouldn't have imagined twenty years ago that I would have been working with the people I am now working with. I think it is probably inaccurate to assume that it is being in leadership that made those changes. What made those changes was the fact that you move from a position where you are defending the Union, where you are standing up against terrorism, to a position where those issues are effectively resolved. In a peaceful climate, why would you not attempt to reach agreement on all those other social and economic issues which should be just as important for one section of our community as another? The backcloth changed very much between those two scenarios and I think that's the biggest single factor: in a peaceful climate unionists will act and behave very differently from when they have their backs against the wall.

But you have found yourself cast in the role of persuader on a lot of these issues.

The reality is that in any large group of people, some will move faster than others; some will be more ready to accept change; some will be more perceptive of the need to change than others. Society doesn't move at the one pace. It'll always be necessary to recognise if you're going to be a leader, and remain a leader, just how fast you can move a society forward. But being a leader isn't about 'follow me' politics, it's about recognising that if you're wanting to take people where they don't want to go, or don't have the natural instinct to go, then quite clearly you have to form a sufficient base to take people forward and then persuade and convince people that this is the right route. Sometimes that doesn't happen until people see that for others who've taken up that ground, it hasn't had the adverse effects they thought it might have. There are plenty of people out there who want to scaremonger and try and retain people in their present positions – usually in the silos or the trenches.

So just how important on a personal level are those symbols of the unionist tradition like the Union flag and the Twelfth of July?

All of those are important and I have been very supportive of British or Ulster-Scots culture, but I think it does have to be exercised in a way that isn't threatening. It should be part of a very rich and colourful tapestry of cultural life in Northern Ireland. What perhaps concerns me more than anything is that differences are used for the purpose of division rather than for the purpose of diversity.

And interestingly, you've never been a member of either the Orange Order or the Royal Black Preceptory. Why is that?

I was a member of the Apprentice Boys a long time ago, but I've never been in the Orange or the Black. None of my family would have been in any of the organisations. There was no conscious decision to not join, there was just no history or pattern of behaviour that took me into any of the Orders. In political life I've been so active that I don't like joining organisations I wouldn't have the time to contribute to. I have an enormous respect for many of the people who are in the Orange Order and who uphold the true aims of the institution, particularly its Christian ethos. Like any large organisation – and you shouldn't be blaming the Orange Order for it because it's hard to think of an organisation where it doesn't happen – there will be those who will be less strict in their adherence to the principles of the organisation than others.

How important is the Ulster-Scots tradition for you, and to what extent do you think it's misunderstood?

Part of the problem has been that its rise in Northern Ireland seemed to coincide with the republican campaign to increase the profile of the Gaelic tradition – Irish dancing, the Irish language and so forth – and therefore I think many people consider a sort of balancing act was underway. If you live in Northern Ireland, our education system unfortunately doesn't give those children in the controlled sector the background in Ulster history and Ulster culture that the Catholic schools would have given to Irish history and Gaelic culture. Generations of unionists have missed out on knowing more about their own background, traditions and culture. They had to take it on board through organisations outside formal education because they weren't taught it in school. I have to say, even now, I would give a higher priority to elements of the Ulster-Scots culture other than the area of language. I would be very supportive of Ulster-Scots literature, music and dance.

Do you believe that the community you represent is to some extent misunderstood as being dour, thran and uncompromising?
Well, of course, there has been an attempt to vilify and demonise the unionist community and anything that is British or Protestant or loyalist or Orange gets vilified in that way. It's part of an overall campaign by nationalists and republicans that has gone on for many generations, and obviously that has its impact because the more people name call and try to describe unionists in derogatory ways, the more it forces people to go into trenches. I think it has been bad for Northern Ireland as a whole. Irrespective of what the issue is, unionists have to be portrayed as if they're backward, thick and unable to live with their fellow countrymen. It's a description I don't recognise at all – and in terms of the good humour of people, I see it all around me within the unionist community. But for the best part of several generations it has been very hard to laugh at some of the things that have been happening in Northern Ireland. The issues that we had to deal with were the issues of murder and danger to our constitutional position. That hardly encourages you to come out with a joke or two.

Do you think unionists could have done more to help themselves, though, as far as the wider political debate is concerned?
I think we are all inclined, in those circumstances, to react to events that are occurring around us and mostly the people who would criticise past leaders are people who haven't had to lead a community through difficult days. I think you would have seen the anger expressed in much more repugnant ways, if it hadn't been for the ability of leaders to say what people were thinking and to articulate their views in the way they did. Very often, letting off steam has released some of the dangers within our community that would otherwise have occurred. I think it's interesting, first of all, that loyalist paramilitaries were never able to get the electoral support within

the unionist community that the IRA was able to get within the nationalist/republican community. That, I think, gives you some indication that, by and large, the pro-British community in Northern Ireland was a law-abiding community, even though on many occasions they would not have been supportive of some of the decisions that were being taken.

How do you respond to those within loyalist paramilitary circles, though, who say they did what they did because they were encouraged by leading political figures who, if you like, made the snowballs for them to throw?

I've heard it before and I don't really have a lot of time for that kind of apologia. The reality is that people who say that are saying they are so weak-minded and feeble, so devoid of any level of thinking for themselves, that they were going to have their strings pulled by others. I think people take their own decisions and they are responsible for their own decisions. I have to say, I come from a section of the community that perhaps has a greater understanding of the loyalist paramilitaries than many others. I grew up at a time when the violence began. I came from a background where a friend was murdered; neighbours of mine were being killed by the IRA. I was a young man and I can recall when the IRA had a campaign which was effectively to go around either shooting or leaving bombs under people's cars in unionist neighbourhoods. I remember when the vigilante process began; I lived in the Lisnasharragh area at the time – all of the men folk working out a rota where they would close off the streets around the area in the evening, and professional people were out there doing it. I was there along with others to protect our neighbourhood, to stop people from outside coming in. I noticed some of those I would have been protecting my neighbourhood with moved into the UDA, as it became. It would have been very easy for people like myself, and no doubt others, to have gone along with a more organised element of defence than had been the case before. I decided on politics. Some of those I would have been with at that time decided to move forward with paramilitary activities. Some of them are dead now and some of them spent time in prison. I think I took the right decision in believing in the primacy of politics and the democratic process, but I have some understanding of the anger that people had at what was happening in their community and the government not giving the community the level of security and defence that it needed.

Was that an easy decision for you to take?

Well, I don't know whether I would refer to it in terms of being easy or hard. I simply had to analyse where these things were likely to lead and which process was likely to lead to the kind of society that I wanted to see. I was very determined that the terrorists should not win, that democracy had to win in this process, and I didn't see that becoming a terrorist or counter-terrorist was going to achieve the aim of defeating terrorism. The only way to defeat terrorism was through the democratic process and support for the rule of law and those who upheld it, in terms of our security forces. But I can understand why in many areas where people had lost loved ones, that anger might have driven them to a different conclusion. I can understand that for those where there was perhaps less of an academic analysis, they might have been led to another conclusion as well. So I, perhaps better than many, understand how people ended up in paramilitary organisations. All I know at the present time is that we have a massive opportunity to make things different. However we all arrived here, we have an opportunity which, unless we grasp it, could drift back into the bad old days of the past and I find that particularly frightening when I look at young people who weren't about when there was a full-blown IRA campaign in Northern Ireland.

So, in order to make sure that doesn't happen you are having to work very closely with your one-time nemesis, Martin McGuinness. How big a challenge is it for you to be sitting in government with an individual who is a self-confessed former IRA commander?

Certainly initially it was very difficult, not just in terms of Martin McGuinness, but I mentioned earlier that I came into politics because a friend was murdered by the IRA. I remember reading a book which went over the period when my friend was killed and the book pointed out that one Gerard Adams had been controlling the IRA in the Belfast area during that period of time. So I was in circumstances where I was having to look across a chamber, when we came into the Assembly, at someone who this book had identified as being responsible for the murder of my friend – and that's not easy. Even in the context of the IRA moving to the position where they were accepting a democratic way forward, there's a lot of baggage there. I have to say that knowing a number of the people I now know in Sinn Féin, I think it would have been difficult for us to be able to move forward if it had been someone other than Martin McGuinness, because I think he has been very ready to move on. I would never get the impression from anything I hear or see that there's any part of him that would ever want to go back to violence and to previous patterns of behaviour. I think he genuinely does want to find a way forward and I have no doubt that he wants to do that in the context that is consistent with his republicanism, but also in terms of the general good of the people that we both represent. I recognise that he does want to move forward and I'm very happy to engage on that basis. I couldn't otherwise, if I didn't believe that of him.

But you don't believe you've compromised your Britishness or your Northern Irishness in doing that?
I think that what we now do is perfectly consistent and it has led to a much wider acceptance of the Union than had hitherto been the case. [A recent poll] was an indicator that in a settled and peaceful and stable society, Catholics are much more content to remain part of the United Kingdom. But if you show Northern Ireland as an entity that hasn't got stability, people want to move to something where they think it might be more likely that you will have a stable future. The very fact that we now have a majority of Protestants and Roman Catholics who are content to remain within the United Kingdom with various levels of enthusiasm, I think shows that there is nothing inconsistent with what we are doing and a future in the Union.

Do you think working closely with Martin McGuinness has in any sense altered your understanding of Irishness?
I've met many people in different political parties and in none who would describe themselves as Irish and who would have a pro-Irish outlook. I respect that; they are perfectly entitled to it. What they're not entitled to do, though, is to force it down my throat and as long as somebody respects my Britishness, I'm quite content to respect their Irishness.

PETER TAYLOR

A seasoned documentary maker, Peter Taylor has been making programmes about Northern Ireland for over four decades and knows the place and its people as well as anybody. Born and brought up in Yorkshire, he read Classics at Cambridge University before joining ITV's *This Week* programme. In 1980 he joined the BBC as a reporter on *Panorama*. In the 1990s he made a series of documentaries, including films on Bloody Sunday and the Maze Prison, before concentrating on his trilogy of landmark books and television documentaries: *Provos, Loyalists* and *Brits*. Peter's distinguished career has earned him many prizes, including five Royal Television Society awards and two BAFTA nominations.

We meet in a café in the centre of Belfast.

Peter Taylor:

I very seldom refer to this place as Ulster because one of the first lessons I learned as a young journalist back in the early '70s, when I was ignorant about Northern Ireland, was about the use of words. I learned very early on that if I referred to 'Ulster' that would be fine with one section of the community because that's what they called Northern Ireland. If you're talking to a nationalist or a republican, however, and you refer to Ulster, it means something entirely different – it's nine counties rather than six, which takes you back to the origins of the conflict and I very rapidly learned how to navigate my way through the semantic minefield. I learned very early on that the same applied to whether Derry was Derry or whether Derry was Londonderry, so from a very early stage I knew what Ulster was and I knew what it meant to unionists, Protestants and loyalists, but I also knew how unnaturally that word would be used by the other community. I have always referred to Northern Ireland as Northern Ireland, occasionally as the 'province' – because politically, geographically and constitutionally, that's what it is – or I've referred to it as the North. I very seldom used the word Ulster, unless I was trying to explain the origins of the conflict.

Mark Carruthers:

Do you think that's partly because one section of the community here almost took possession of the word Ulster?

I think so, and again if you look at it historically – 'Ulster will fight and Ulster will be right'. Ian Paisley, in his earlier days, would talk about Ulster; 'Ulster says no'. The way in which Dr. Paisley intonated the word Ulster, to me said everything about the Protestant, loyalist, unionist perception of Ulster in which it was a self-contained entity, with walls around it – it was 'ours'. Ulster was also about possession and in the end it was about possession of territory, because that's what the conflict is about. Ulster, to Protestants, is about identity and it's about territory – the six counties of Northern Ireland are part of the United Kingdom. It's a hugely emotive word which I learned to use with caution. I also found that people judged you by the terminology you used, so in the early days I used to have to put my brain in gear before I opened my mouth when I was referring to Derry, Londonderry, Ulster, Northern Ireland and those emotive terms. Ulster to me is ultimately about identity, it's about territory, it's about belonging, it's about the Union – that's what Ulster means to me. That's what I understand Ulster to be, but, of course, to the other side of the community, to nationalists, to Catholics and republicans, Ulster is a word they would not use except in the context of the historical province of Ulster. I discovered all this when, as a young journalist, I first went to Derry, or Londonderry, on Bloody Sunday and I was ignorant about the conflict and thought I'd better try and find out what was going on and why.

Perhaps more than any other journalist from outside Northern Ireland, you have tried to understand the nature of the conflict here down the years. You've met and interviewed a lot of the paramilitaries. Is there something in their character that unites them, in your view?

I found talking to the paramilitaries on both sides there were similarities, the similarity essentially being the determination of each group of paramilitaries to use violence to achieve what their end was. The IRA, obviously, wanted to ultimately achieve a United Ireland and on the loyalist side it was to maintain and fight for the union with Britain – but in terms of individuals, because I got to know some of them very well over the years, they are very different. What strikes me about both loyalist and republican paramilitaries is how normal both sides are. I think that's the unifying factor when you actually get to meet these people who've done dreadful things, and a good number of them on both sides were prepared to talk about it. What strikes you is that the people I talk to who've been involved in political violence are ordinary people. That's the thing about so-called 'terrorism': the things they do are dreadful and reprehensible, but they do them for reasons in which most of them firmly believe. I always felt more cautious and slightly more uncomfortable dealing with loyalist paramilitaries who were much harder. They were more distrustful of the media and if ever I felt uneasy dealing with the paramilitaries, it was with the loyalist paramilitaries rather than the republican paramilitaries. If you were doing something with republican paramilitaries, I never thought that I was going to be kidnapped or hurt in any way. With the loyalists, one was never quite sure. The only time I was ever really threatened was by loyalists back in the 1970s. What they have in common is the justification for using violence and the determination to use it. The extent to which those involved in using violence had actually thought it through and had considered its morality, though, I'm not sure.

As far as loyalist paramilitaries were concerned, two things are often said about them – they were splintered and they were sectarian.
I think the problem for loyalists is that what they were fighting for was essentially negative – it was about maintaining the status quo. Republicans were about destroying the status quo and I think, in political terms, loyalism never got its act together in the way that republicans did. There were loyalist paramilitary politicians whom I knew and respected – people like the late David Ervine, who did have a vision of what loyalism was and were able to discern what loyalism or unionism had to do to accommodate the other tradition if there was ever to be a peaceful settlement in Northern Ireland. But I was never convinced that that message seeped through deep within the paramilitary organisation. Also, by the same token, you have to give the loyalist paramilitaries credit for declaring a ceasefire and for accepting decommissioning. That was difficult for them, but I also thought that

loyalists and unionists never quite grasped what they achieved in the Good Friday Agreement. What they achieved was the maintenance of the Union, which is what they had been fighting for, and I always felt they never quite grasped that they had won. If you look at the peace process, everybody won because it produced peace and stability that Northern Ireland hasn't known for many, many years – but I think that the unionists, loyalists and Protestants won in the short to medium term, because the Union is guaranteed and that's what the loyalist paramilitaries were fighting for.

So does that lead you to the uncomfortable conclusion that, in that instance if in no other, violence paid?

I think the uncomfortable lesson of the conflict in Northern Ireland over the past thirty years plus, is that violence has paid, in particular on the republican side. It's uncomfortable to accept that violence has paid dividends, but I think on both sides it helped achieve what both sides were fighting for. What violence did not achieve for the republicans, though, was a United Ireland. There are those dissident voices within republicanism who say that a United Ireland is as far away today as it ever was thirty or forty years ago – so violence did not achieve a United Ireland and I don't think violence will ever achieve a United Ireland. If a United Ireland is ever to be achieved at some stage in the distant future, I think it will be as a result of the process that we're seeing at the moment.

I don't want to oversimplify this, but basically your view is that you have to look at the recent history of republicanism in two stages: pre-hunger strike and post-hunger strike?

Pre-hunger strike [in 1981], Sinn Féin barely existed. It was the IRA that was running everything. There were members of the IRA who were members of Sinn Féin, but it was the IRA that was the dominant element in the republican armed struggle. If you trace the rise of Sinn Féin in the 1980s, it all stems from the hunger strike. The Sinn Féin/IRA strategy was really thought out initially by Gerry Adams when he was interned in Long Kesh along with Brendan Hughes [a former leading republican and IRA commander]. In the 1980s Sinn Féin were able to build the base that resulted in their having an electoral mandate that the British could accept as being their democratic credentials. The origins of the peace process really stem from the hunger strike, but it was nearly twenty years before it became a reality.

You never found that on the loyalist side. The unionists had their politicians and the loyalists had their politicians, but the loyalist paramilitaries never had any political agenda in the same way as Sinn Féin had a political agenda, because their political agenda was this: we will fight, we will bomb and we will kill Catholics in the name of maintaining Ulster and the connection with the United Kingdom. It was simplistic, it was brutal – but also, it was quite effective in that it sent a message to the IRA that the loyalists weren't a pushover and at some stage an accommodation would have to be reached.

Do you accept the argument that many of those who were caught up in the violence did what they did because of their upbringing and circumstances?

Perhaps I was one of the first to use the cliché describing individuals on both sides as being prisoners of their respective histories. I've talked to many IRA men and women over the years and I've sometimes thought, if they hadn't been born here, some might have become doctors, lawyers or academics; and the same might have applied to the loyalist side too, although perhaps not to the same extent. If you look at the evolution of Sinn Féin, they were attracting into their ranks university and college students in a way that the loyalist paramilitaries never did. But if paramilitaries from both sides had been brought up elsewhere, some of them might have gone into violence or drugs or criminality but, by and large, they wouldn't have been paramilitaries using violence to achieve their political ends. In that sense we're all prisoners of history. I'm a Brit. When I say I'm a Brit there's nothing personal about it, but I am conscious that I am an outsider commentating on a conflict which is essentially inter-communal. It's a conflict which is three-sided, which people forget – hence the books: *Provos*, *Loyalists* and *Brits*. I never set out to write a trilogy of books or make a trilogy of television programmes but we, the Brits, are the root cause of the conflict, historically. The partition of Ireland is the heart of the current conflict and how we reconcile the tripartite relationship between Northern Ireland, Great Britain and the Irish Republic is the key to medium and long-term peace in Ireland.

Yet the course of history was very often influenced by the actions of very ordinary individuals on the ground who were caught up in both the politics and the violence.

I think that's true, but they made their decisions based on what they saw and what they feared and what they wanted to achieve. I think the difference between loyalist violence and republican violence was that loyalist violence was primarily reactive to IRA violence.

Though not exclusively so.

No, but the *raison d'être* of loyalist paramilitary violence again lies in that critical period in the early 1970s when loyalists feared that the IRA were in the ascendancy. They knew that the British had talked to the IRA and they felt they had to hit back to let the IRA know that loyalism was not going to give in. Although Ian Paisley was never a paramilitary – and I don't think he approved of what some of the paramilitaries were doing – nevertheless he articulated the poorly-articulated politics of the loyalist paramilitaries.

Have you taken away from your many visits here any sense of an over-arching Ulster character trait? Does that description of the dour, straight-talking, no-nonsense personality make sense?

I think it's broadly accurate, but as ever in these generalisations, once you get beneath the surface you find there's something very different. It takes two sides, or three sides, to make peace and I think the unionist contribution to the process cannot be underestimated. I think unionists in their heart of hearts knew they had certainly maintained what they set out to maintain, both politically and militarily, which is the Union with Great Britain. Talking to former IRA volunteers whom I met and interviewed about twenty years ago who are no longer militarily active, who haven't joined the dissidents, one of them said to me just the other day, 'We lost the war'. Well, the IRA didn't win the war because they didn't get rid of the Brits and they haven't got a United Ireland. But he was realistic when he said we can't hope to get at the negotiating table what we failed to achieve on the battlefield. He also said, and I agree with him, the peace that we now have as a result of the Belfast Agreement, with Sinn Féin sharing power at Stormont, is probably better than we ever had reason to hope for. It's difficult but it works and, by and large, I think most people accept it. The war is over as several former IRA volunteers have told me recently. We're not going to go back to the war.

Just how big a challenge was it for you to come here as a journalist to talk to people who were responsible for the murder and mayhem on the streets?

It was a very testing experience. It was something that I knew I had to do, but also that I wanted to do. What I've always tried to find out and explain, is the reason why people do what they do and it's just wrong for people in the rest of the United Kingdom to dismiss Northern Ireland because they're all Irish. That's just racist and untrue. So, what I tried to do was to get to know some of the people who were actually fighting the so-called war on both sides and make my own assessment of them both as individuals and to ask, why are they prepared to do these horrific things? I wanted to try to explain to viewers, readers and listeners why they were involved, because it's only when people begin to understand why there is conflict that people can begin to see how, if at all, the conflict can be resolved. The critical thing was meeting these people face-to-face. I remember interviewing a loyalist former prisoner who'd served life for murder for assassinating a Catholic. He didn't know who he was, but he knew that the person was a Catholic, and he walked up to him, put the gun to the person's head and pulled the trigger because he was a Catholic. I asked him, 'Why did you do it?' He said, 'Because he was a Catholic'. That was a chilling moment, the recognition that he did it purely as a sectarian act. His defence, such as it was, was that he and his colleagues were murdering Catholics to put pressure on the Catholic community, on the nationalist community, to get the IRA to stop. When I say that this individual was a perfectly normal human being, of course he wasn't in order to do that, but it was getting inside the mindset of the so-called men of violence on both sides that was really difficult. There were times when I felt really uncomfortable, in particular, interviewing some of the loyalist paramilitaries from the UDA, UFF and UVF when I had to put questions to them that they didn't like. In all the interviews I did, although in some cases it came pretty close to it, no-one ever walked out, because they decided to engage and that meant they wanted the reasons for their actions to be explained and conveyed to a much wider audience – most of whom would not agree with what they said, but at least would have some understanding of it.

Did you ever have to wrestle with your own conscience that in explaining what these people were doing you were, in some sense, helping to legitimise it? Were you arguably setting yourself up as an apologist for them?

I was never an apologist for any of the organisations.

But did you ever feel you came close to being that?

I knew there was a danger of being seen as an apologist for them and giving them Mrs. Thatcher's 'oxygen of publicity'. I was always conscious of that and that's why, when I was interviewing IRA men and women or their loyalist equivalents, I was always conscious that I had to ask the questions that viewers would be wanting me to ask. Those interviews were difficult, sometimes very difficult. I had to confront them with the hard reality of what they were doing. It was a very narrow tightrope that I walked, but I had to make clear to the audience that I appeared not to approve of what they were doing, although I understood why they were doing it. There's a difference between understanding what they were doing and approving of it. If you're studying conflict – and I've studied conflict in other parts of the world like the Middle East and South Africa – people have to understand why political violence takes place. And that applies to Al Qaeda and Islamist extremism too.

Do you see Northern Ireland as a model solution for other conflicts in the world, or is that an idea which has been dangerously overplayed?

I think there's a danger in overplaying it, but I certainly think that the process is a template. I did an interview with the former Director General of MI5, Eliza Manningham-Buller, who would have had intimate knowledge of the back channel talks between MI6 and MI5 over the years with Martin McGuinness and the IRA's Army Council. She said, in the end, if you can't defeat your enemy you've got to talk to them; you've got to know who your enemy is and you've got to engage them. I said, 'Should we be talking to Al Qaeda?' To my surprise she said, 'Yes, because that's the only way you resolve conflict'. Looking back on what I've done over forty years, I like to think that what I've been able to do is to present each side to the other – what the problem is, who the people are who are involved, why they are involved and what has to be done to reach some kind of accommodation. That is why I think the Northern Irish peace process is a template. You cannot do that without engaging your enemy in some kind of dialogue – initially covertly but then overtly – and it's very difficult for governments to do this. The prerequisite of the British government engaging with the IRA was that the IRA first had to declare an end to violence and that's in fact what ultimately happened.

The challenge, of course, was to encourage people to talk to each other rather than at each other, which is what they were always very good at.
I think that's a false preconception – although an understandable one – because if you look at the evolution of the peace process, Sinn Féin were listening. We mustn't forget the role of John Hume and Seamus Mallon in the SDLP in the mid-1980s; in that process in which nationalism and republicanism were hearing what loyalists were saying and recognising that there would have to be an accommodation of some kind. By the same token some elements of loyalists – I'm thinking of the Jackie McDonalds, David Ervines and Billy Hutchinsons of this world – were also listening to what Sinn Féin and the IRA were saying. If nobody listens to the other side, if they're too busy shouting at each other and killing each other, you never get anywhere. I think the lesson of the peace process is that you can bring a kind of peace from violence. You can do it, but the prerequisite is both sides being prepared to talk to each other, the government of the day being prepared to engage and an acceptance on all sides that the only way out of conflict is compromise. Those compromises are really difficult. The compromise that Sinn Féin and the IRA have made to be where they are is massive – which is why there are dissidents. They believe that Martin McGuinness and others have betrayed what they fought for for so long – and when Martin McGuinness calls the dissidents traitors, the dissidents believe that the real traitor is Martin McGuinness.